BIG-NOTE PIANO

CONTEMPORARY CHRISTIAN CLASSICS

ISBN 0-634-03378-6

7777 W. BLUEMOUND RD. P.O. BOX 13819 MILWAUKEE, WI 53213

ABBA
(Father)

Words and Music by REBECCA ST. JAMES,
TEDD TJORNHOM and OTTO PRICE

Moderately fast

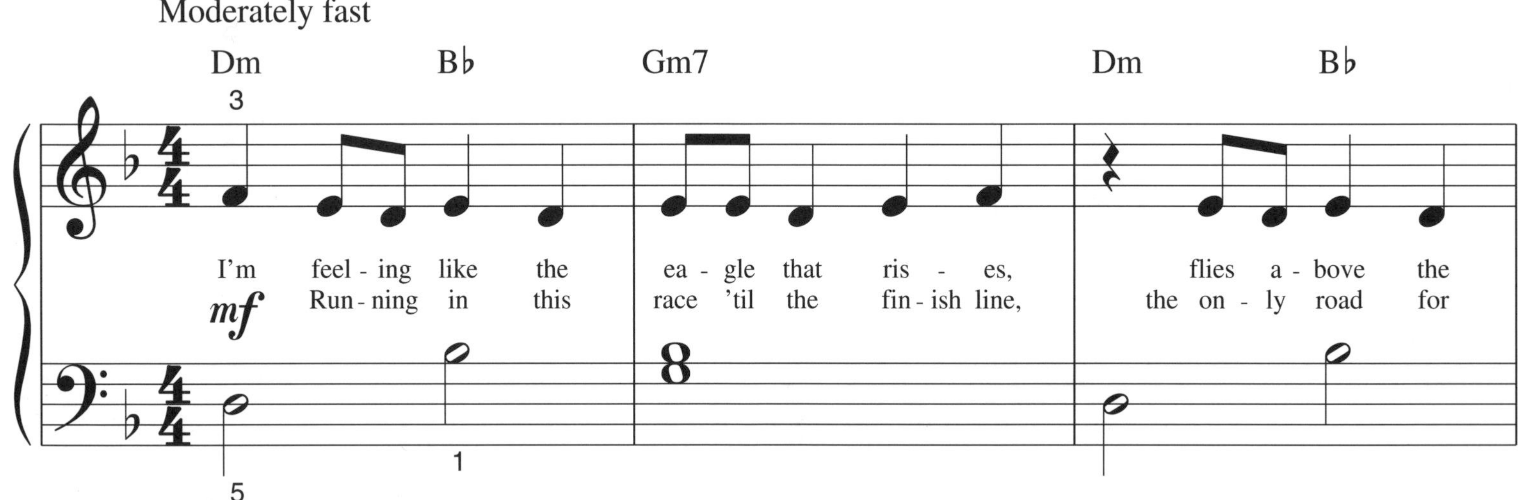

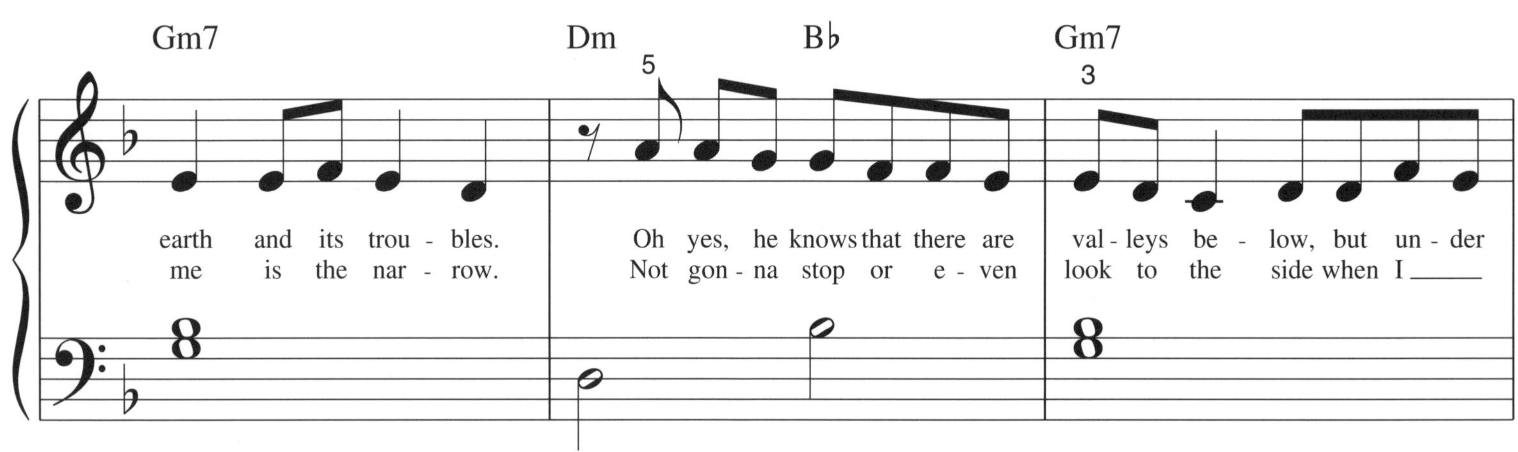

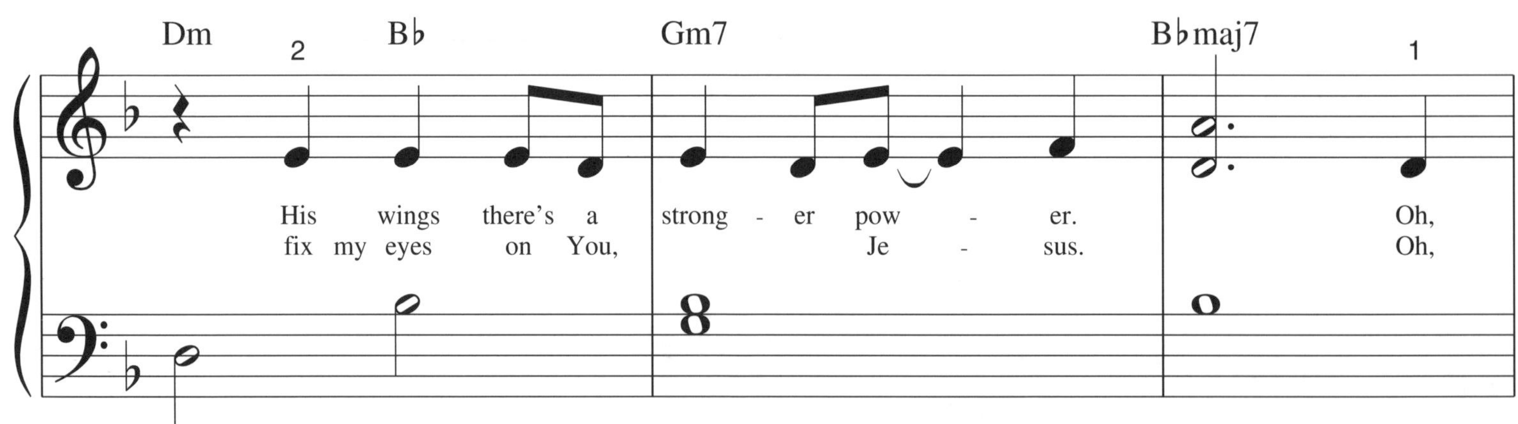

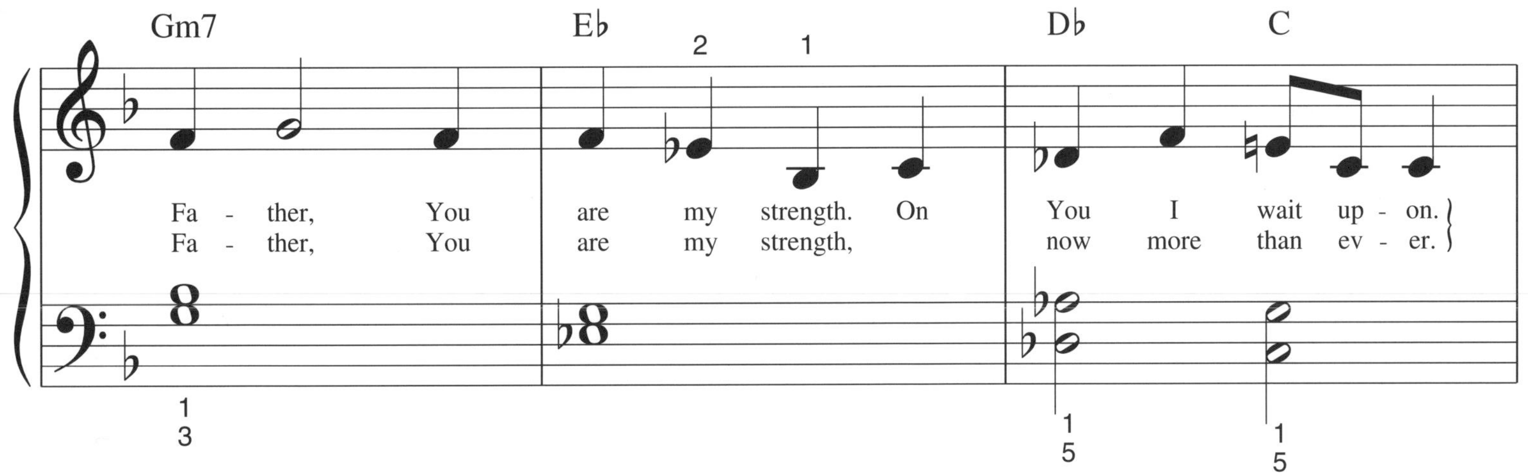

Gm7
E♭
D♭
C
Fa - ther, You are my strength. On You I wait up - on.
Fa - ther, You are my strength, now more than ev - er.

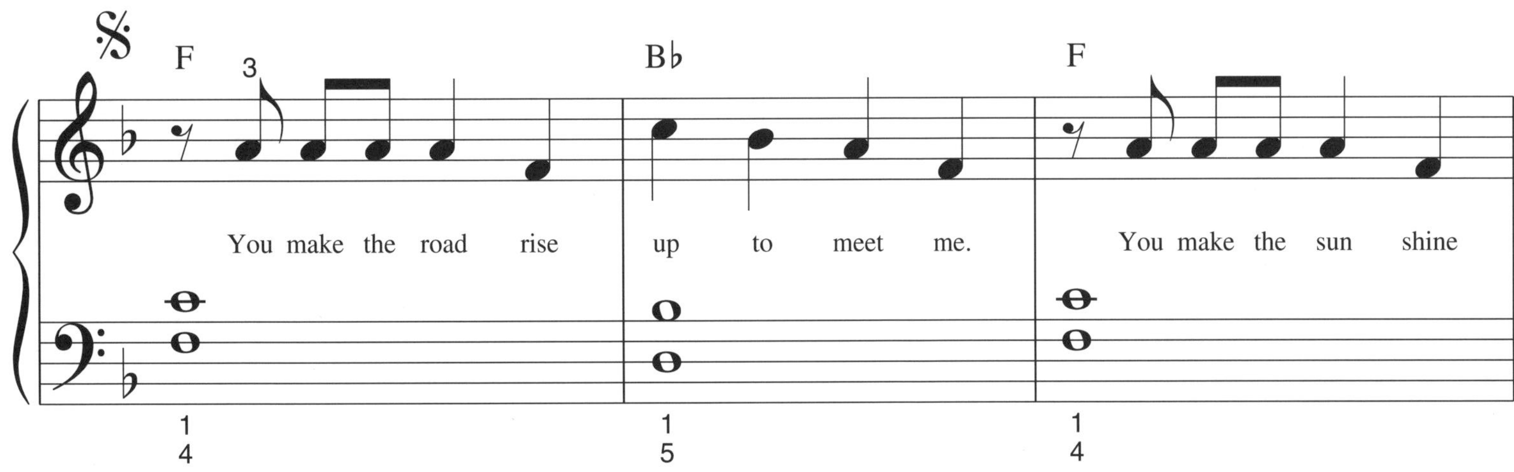

F
B♭
F
You make the road rise up to meet me. You make the sun shine

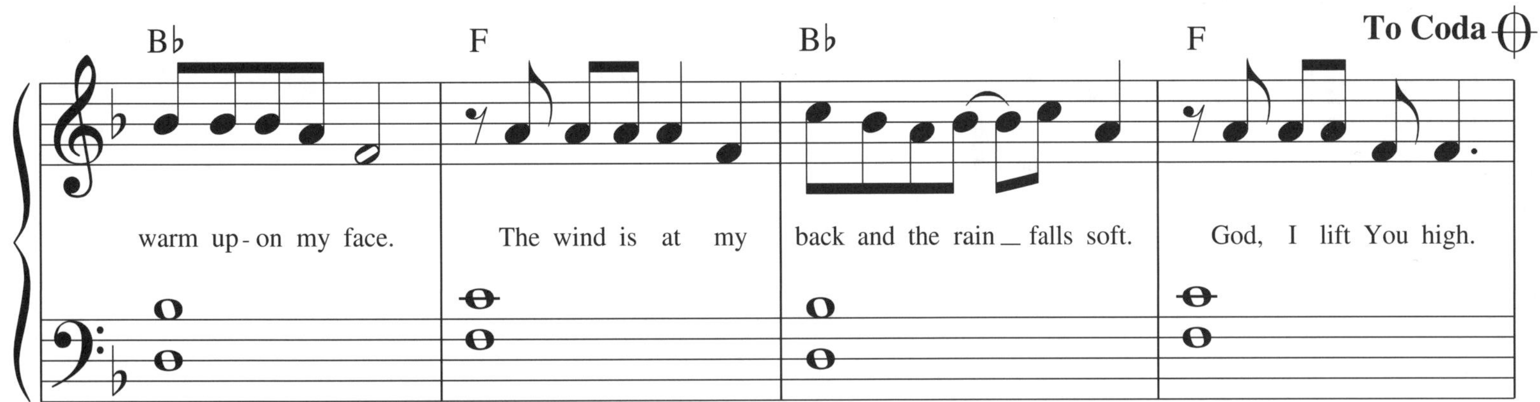

B♭
F
B♭
F
To Coda
warm up-on my face. The wind is at my back and the rain _ falls soft. God, I lift You high.

B♭
2nd time D.S. al Coda
You are my Ab - ba.

CODA
B♭
F
You are my Ab - ba. _____

AWESOME GOD

Words and Music by
RICH MULLINS

Heavy Rock beat, not too fast

Gm Cm7 Dm

mf

Cm7 Dm Gm

Gm

When he rolls up His sleeves, He ain't just put - tin' on the ritz. Our
sky was___ star - less in the void___ of the night, our

Cm7
Dm
Gm
light - ning in His fists. Our
cre - at - ed the light. Our
God is an awe - some
God is an awe - some
God. The
God.
Cm7
Dm
Lord was - n't jok - ing when He
Judge - ment and wrath He
kicked them out of E - den. It
poured out on Sod - om,
was - n't for no rea - son that He
mer - cy and grace He gave
E♭
shed His blood. His re -
us at the cross. I
turn is ver - y close, so you'd
hope that we have not too
bet - ter be be - liev - in' that our
quick - ly for - got - ten that our
Cm7
Dm
Gm
E♭
God is an awe - some
God is an awe - some
God.
God.
Our
God is an

B♭/D
F
Gm
awe - some God. He
reigns from
heav - en a - bove with
1
3
1
2

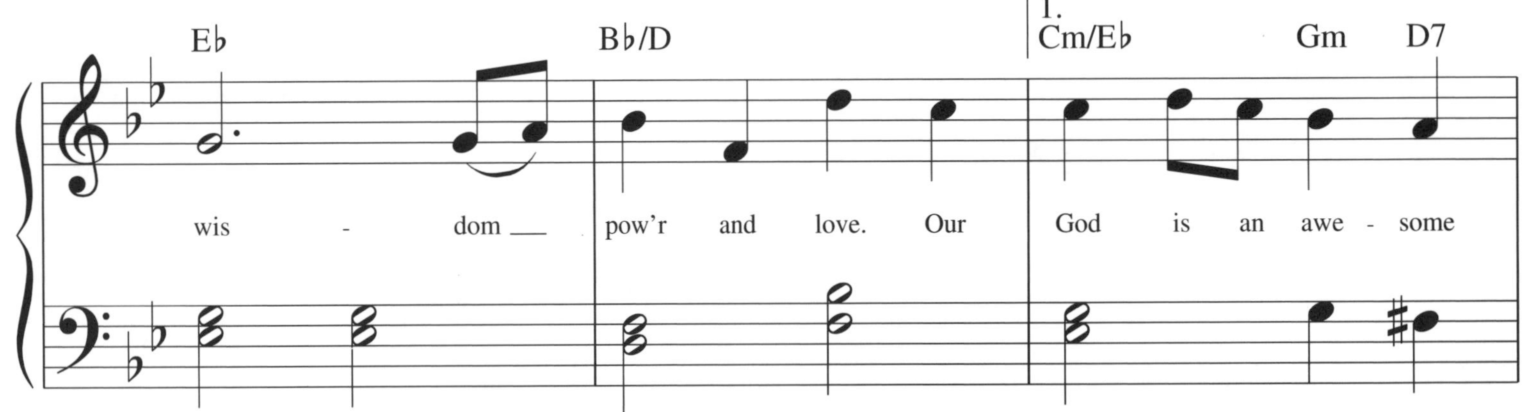
E♭
B♭/D
1.
Cm/E♭
Gm
D7
wis - dom
pow'r and love. Our
God is an awe - some

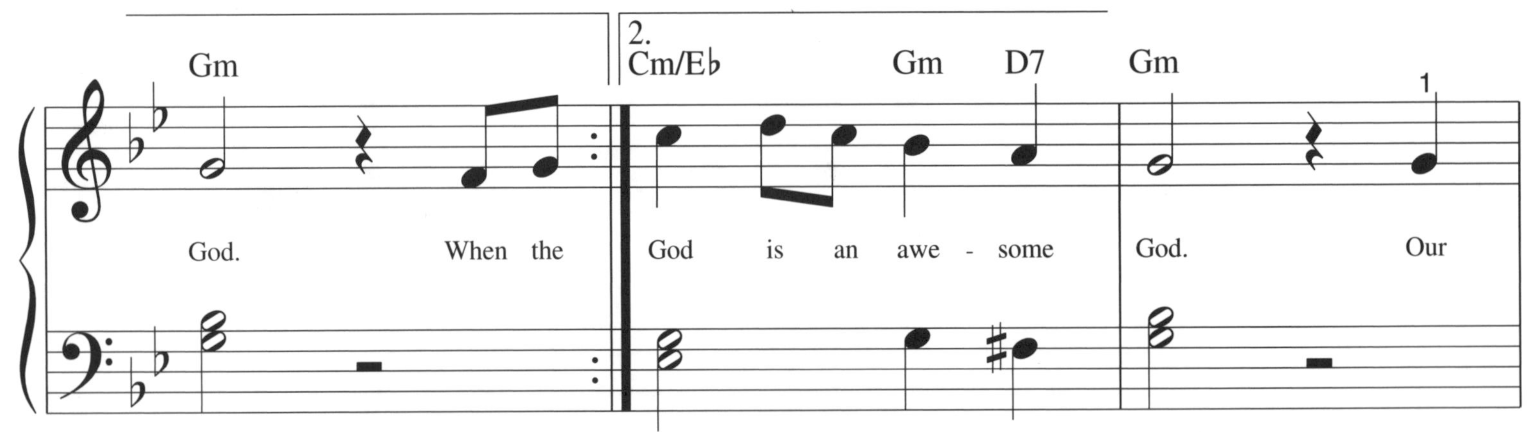
Gm
2.
Cm/E♭
Gm
D7
Gm
1
God. When the
God is an awe - some
God. Our

E♭
B♭/D
F
God is an
awe - some God. He
reigns from
2
4
1
3

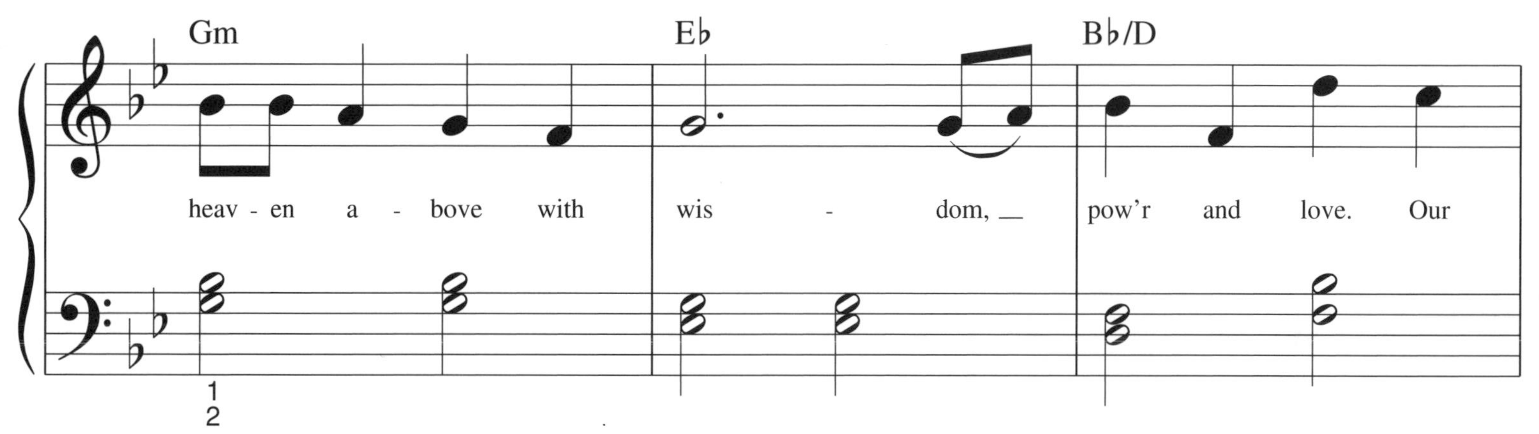
Gm
Eb
Bb/D
heav - en a - bove with wis - dom, pow'r and love. Our
1
2

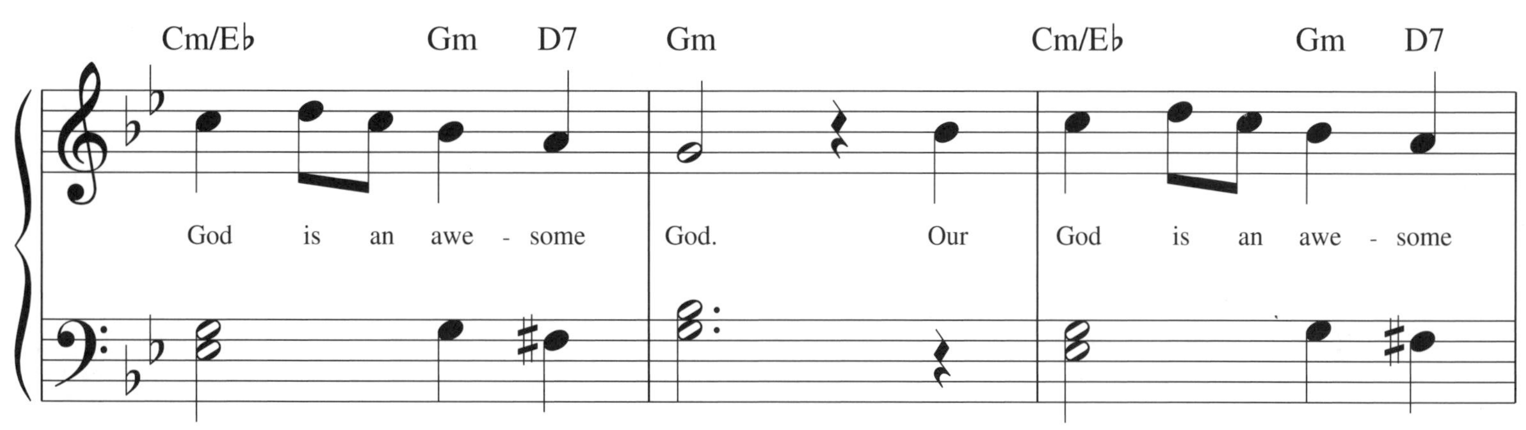
Cm/Eb
Gm
D7
Gm
Cm/Eb
Gm
D7
God is an awe - some God. Our God is an awe - some

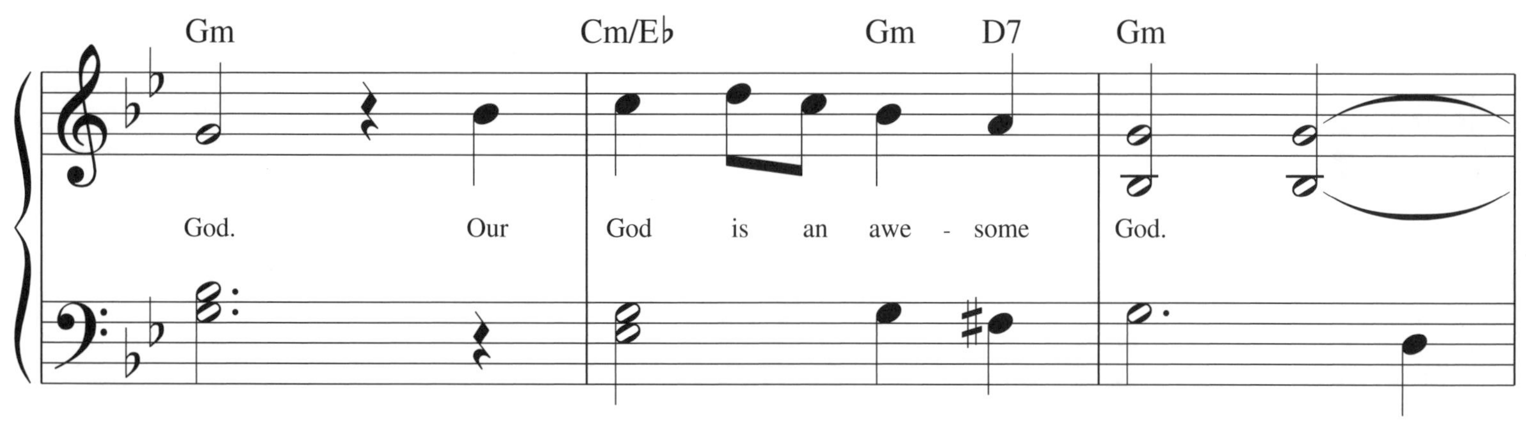
Gm
Cm/Eb
Gm
D7
Gm
God. Our God is an awe - some God.

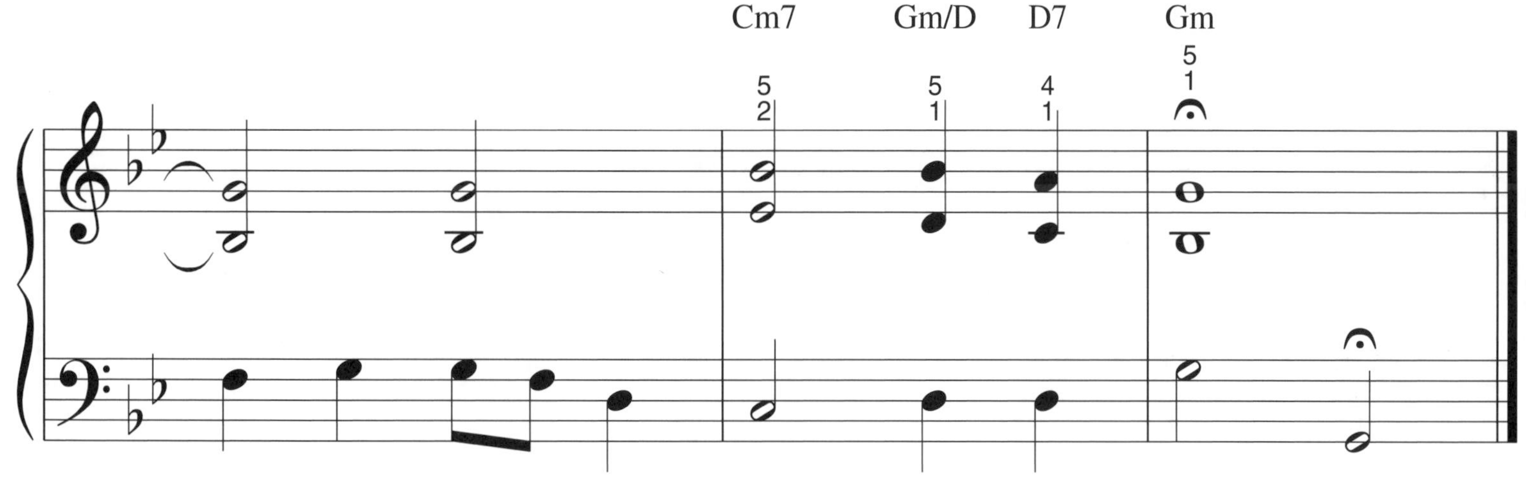
Cm7
Gm/D
D7
Gm
5
2
5
1
4
1
5
1

CALVARY'S LOVE

Words and Music by PHILL McHUGH and GREG NELSON

To Coda
A/D
D
A
D
G
D
Asus
A
B♭dim7
safe - ty on the sea of hu - man
prom - ise fills with joy once emp - ty
pas - sage, sins a - toned and heav - en
need. Through the hours of all the
eyes. So de - sire to tell the
a - ges, those tired of sail - ing on their
sto - ry of a love that loved e - nough to
own; fin - n'lly rest in - side the
die; burns a - way all oth - er

Bm G D/A A7
shad - ow cast by Cal - v'ry's love across their
pas - sions and fed by Cal - v'ry's love be - comes a
Dsus D Bm
souls.
fire.
Cal - v'r'ys love Cal - v'ry's
F♯m/A G A D
love, price - less gift Christ makes us wor - thy of The deep - est
Bm Esus E C
sin can't rise a - bove Cal - v'ry's love.

Asus
1.
A
Cal - v'ry's

2.
A
D
D.S. al Coda
Cal - v'ry's
5

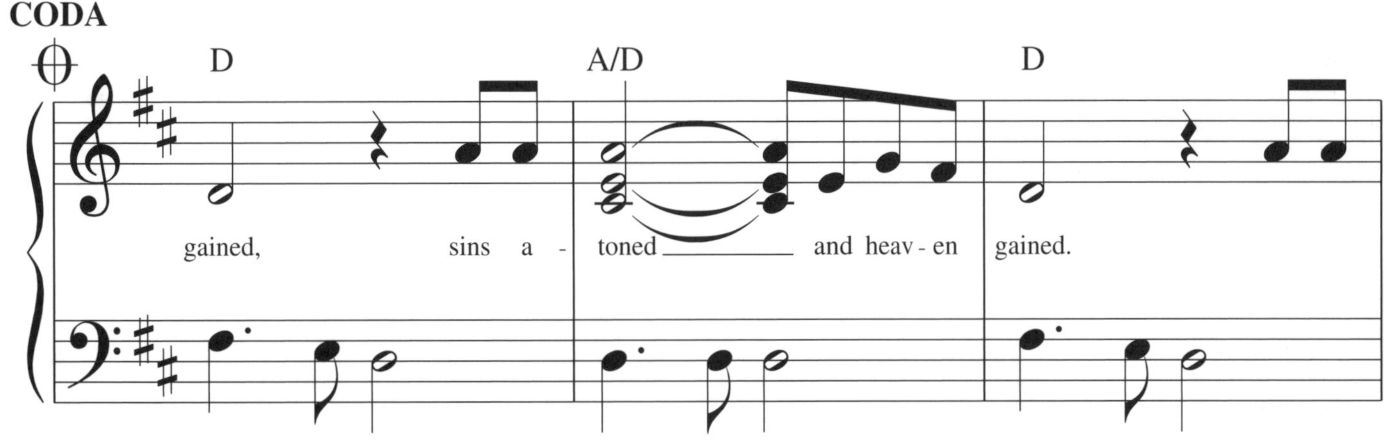
CODA
D
A/D
D
gained, sins a - toned and heav - en gained.

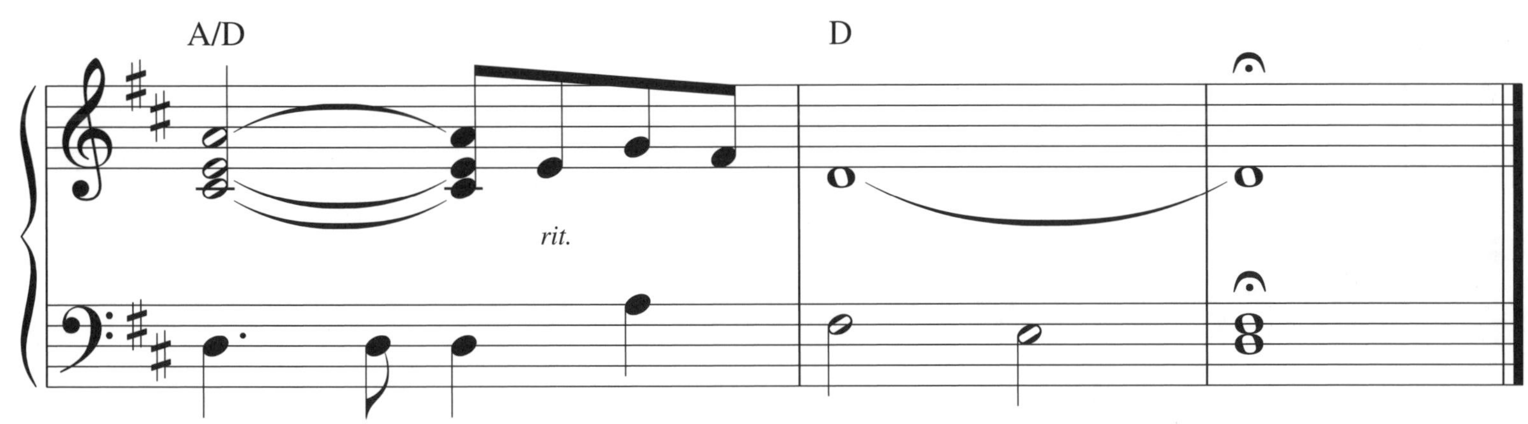
A/D
D
rit.

EL SHADDAI

Words and Music by MICHAEL CARD
and JOHN THOMPSON

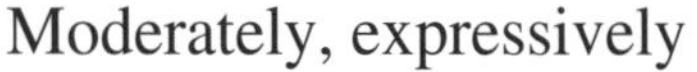

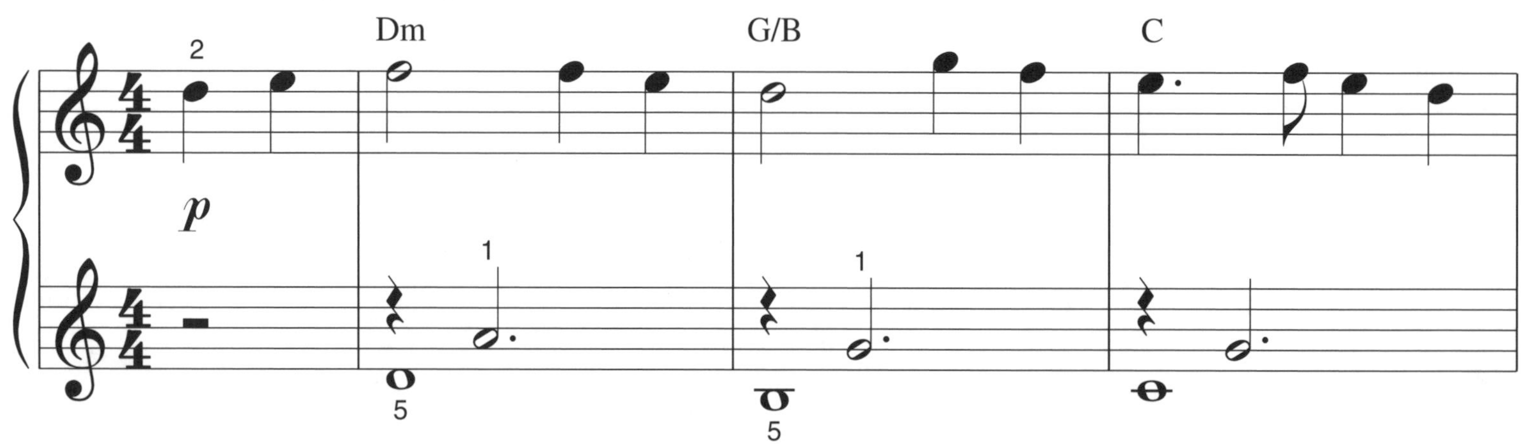

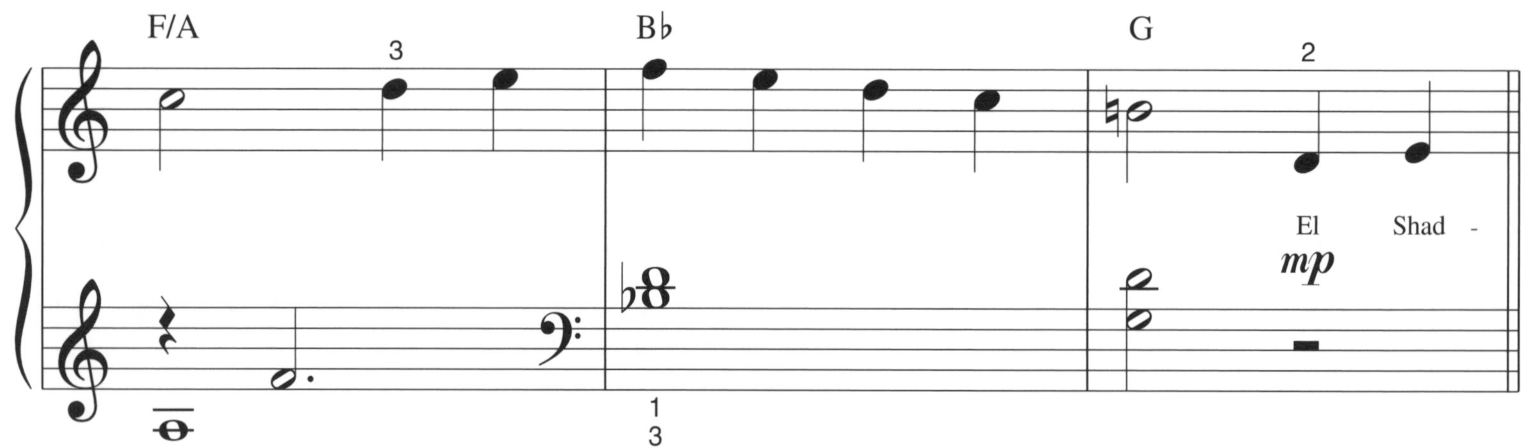

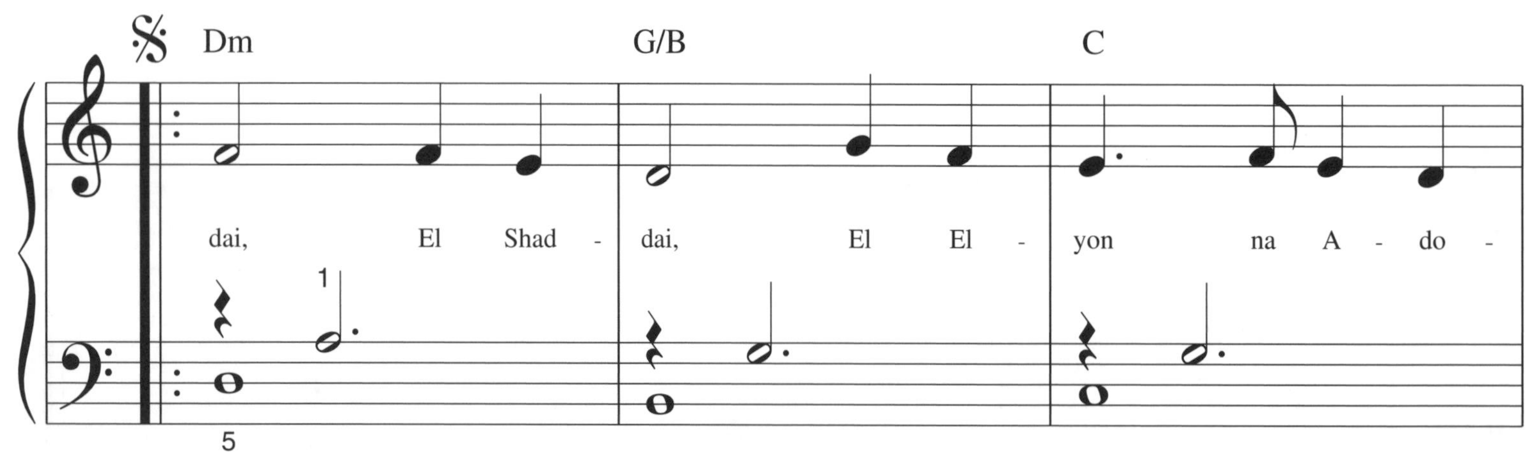

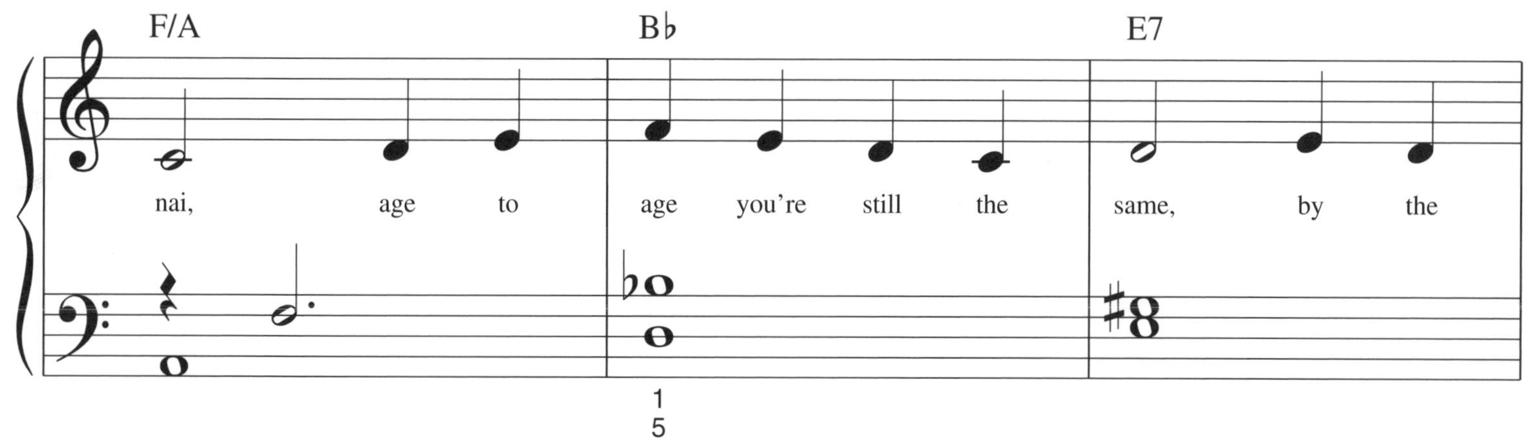
F/A
B♭
E7
nai, age to
age you're still the
same, by the
1
5

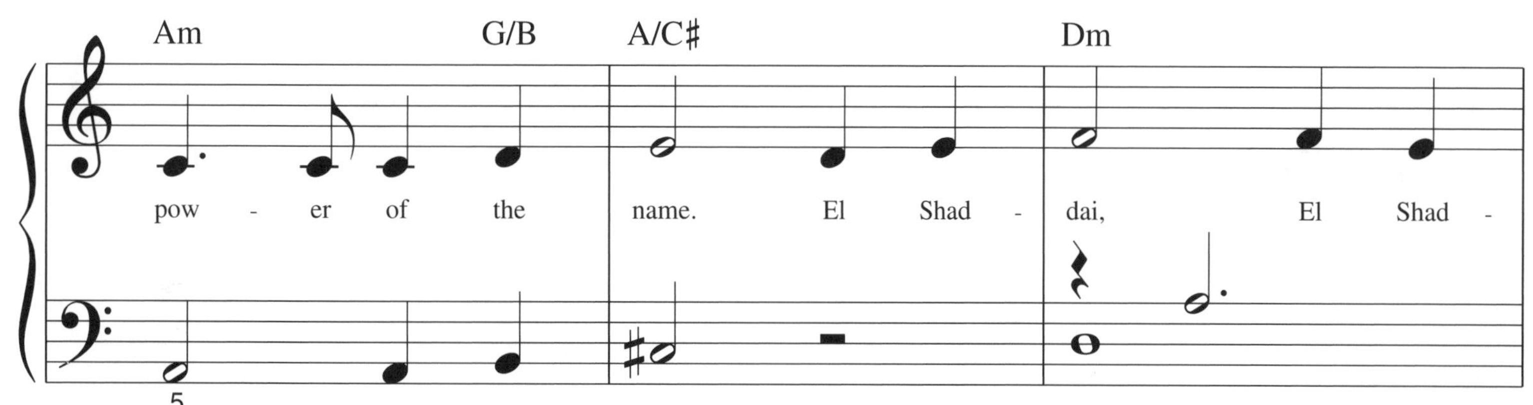
Am
G/B
A/C♯
Dm
pow - er of the
name. El Shad -
dai, El Shad -
5

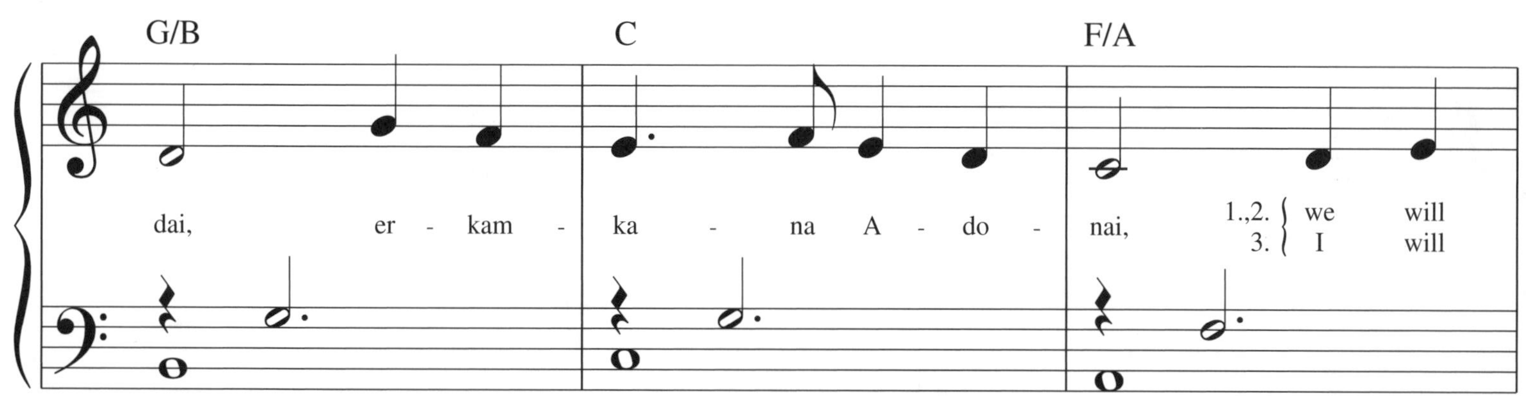
G/B
C
F/A
dai, er - kam -
ka - na A - do -
nai, 1.,2. { we will
3. { I will

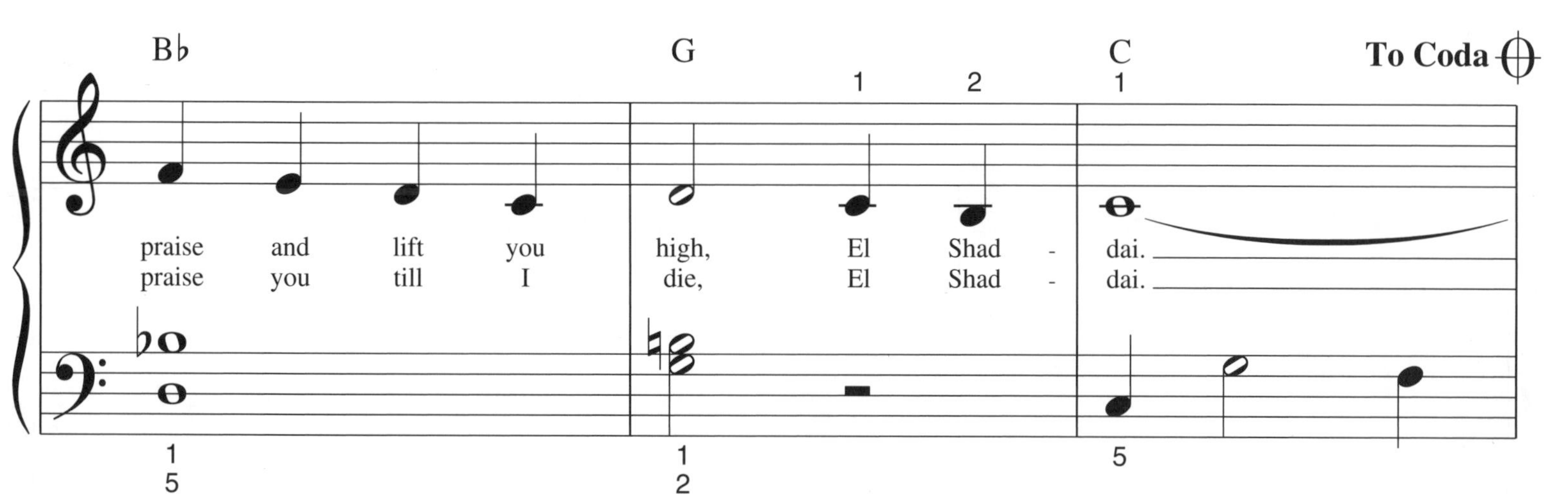
B♭
G
C
To Coda
1 2
1
praise and lift you
high, El Shad -
dai.
praise you till I
die, El Shad -
dai.
1
5
1
2
5

Dm G/B
2
Through your love and through the ram, you saved the
Through the years you made it clear that the
p

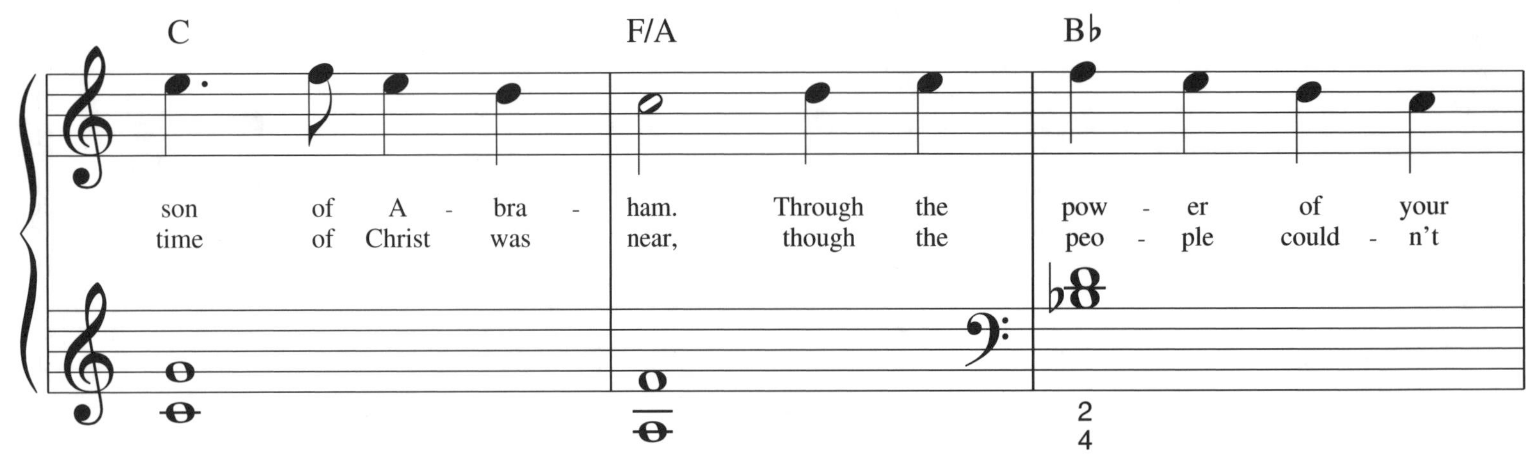
C F/A B♭
son of A - bra - ham. Through the pow - er of your
time of Christ was near, though the peo - ple could - n't
2
4

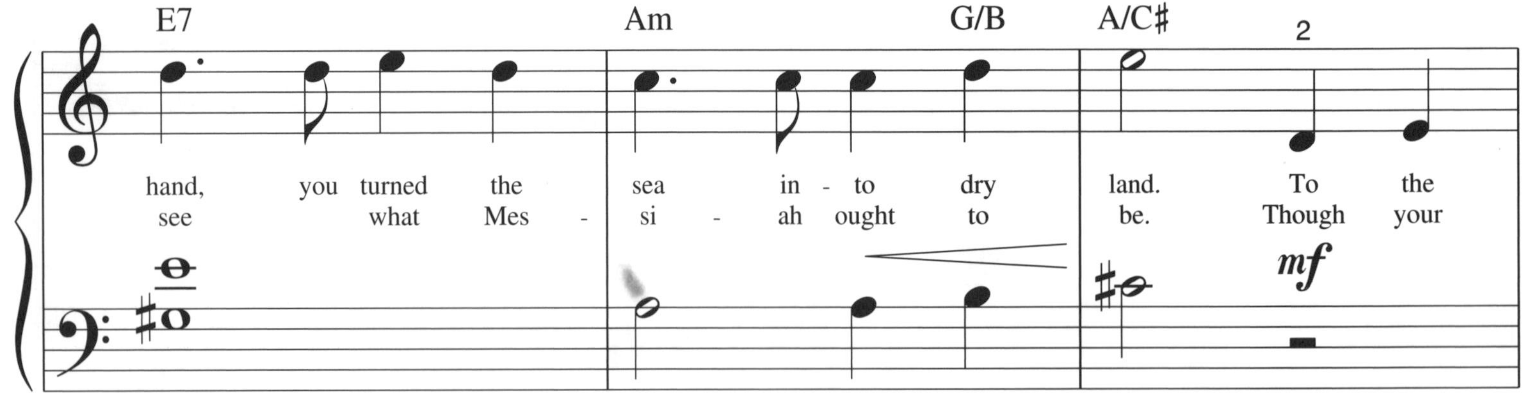
E7 Am G/B A/C♯
2
hand, you turned the sea in - to dry land. To the
see what Mes - si - ah ought to be. Though your
mf

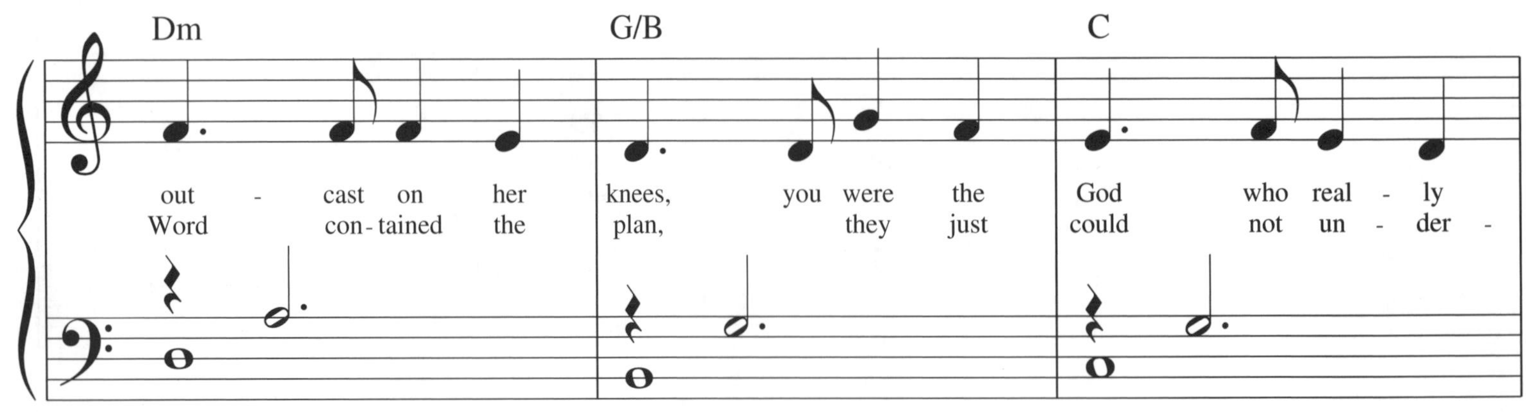
Dm G/B C
out - cast on her knees, you were the God who real - ly
Word con-tained the plan, they just could not un - der -

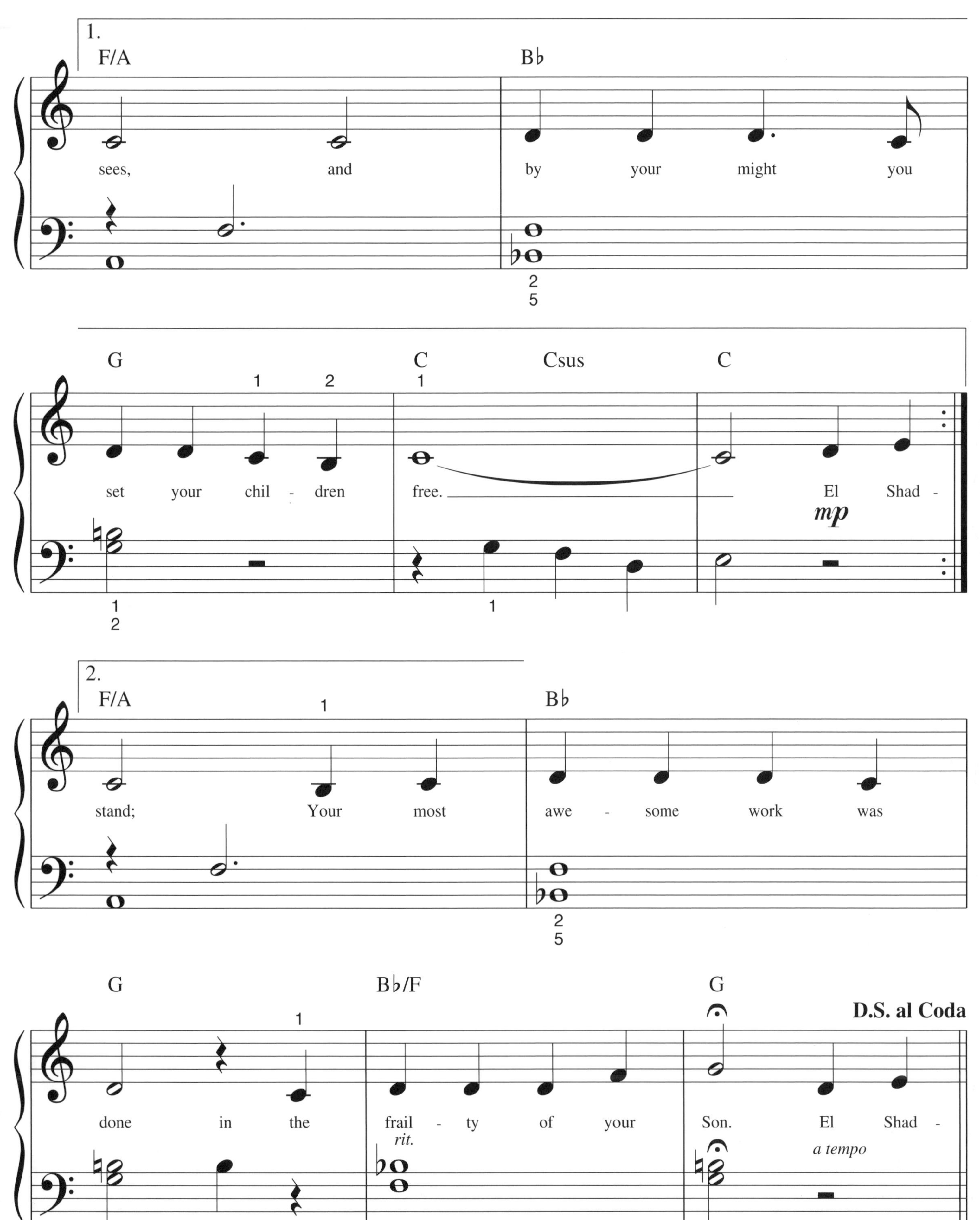
1.
F/A
B♭
sees, and by your might you
2
5
G
C
Csus
C
1 2
1
set your chil - dren free. El Shad -
mp
1
2
1
2.
F/A
1
B♭
stand; Your most awe - some work was
2
5
G
B♭/F
G
D.S. al Coda
1
done in the frail - ty of your Son. El Shad -
rit.
a tempo
1
2
1

CODA
C
2
p
Dm
G/B
C
F/A
3
B♭
2
4
E7
3
rit.
Dm
Am
1
2
1
3

GOD IS IN CONTROL

Words and Music by
TWILA PARIS

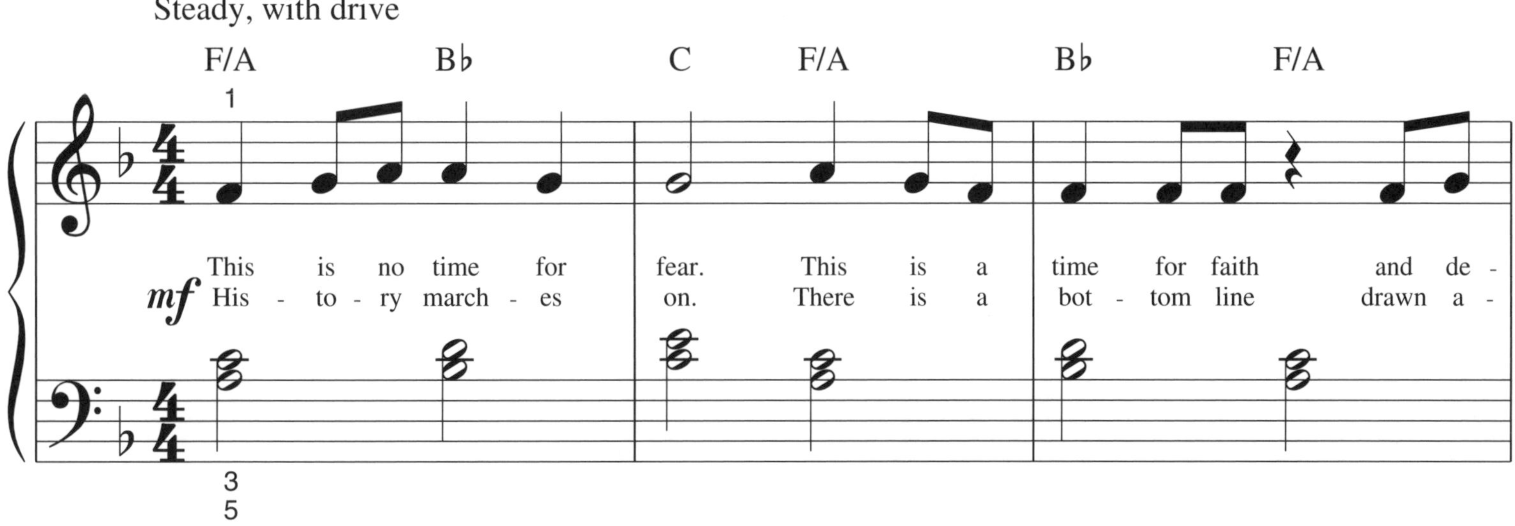

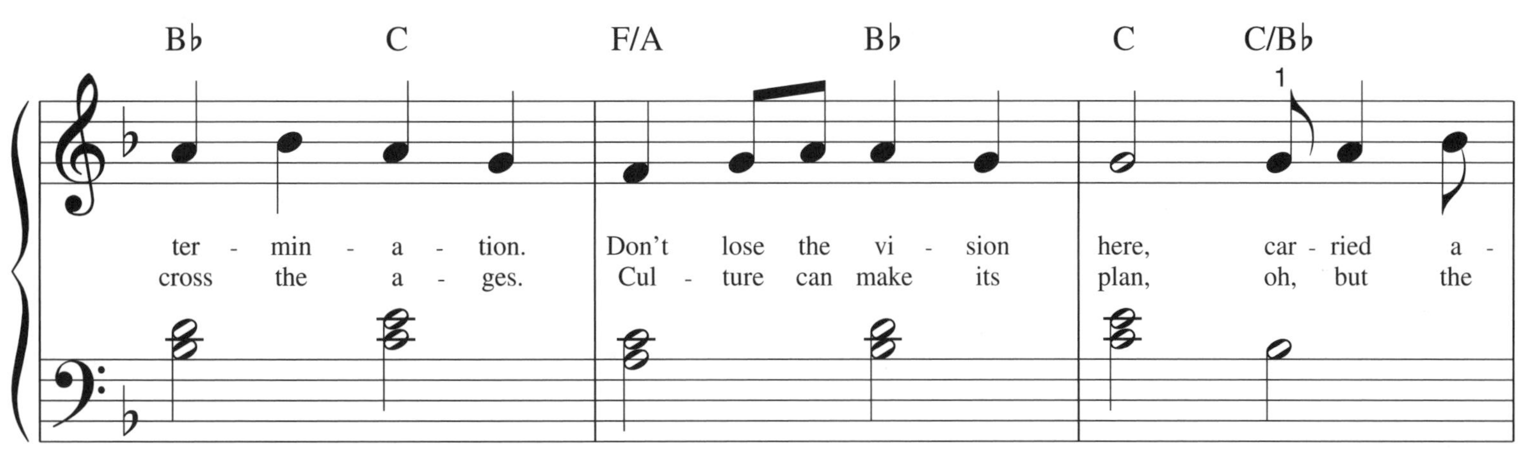

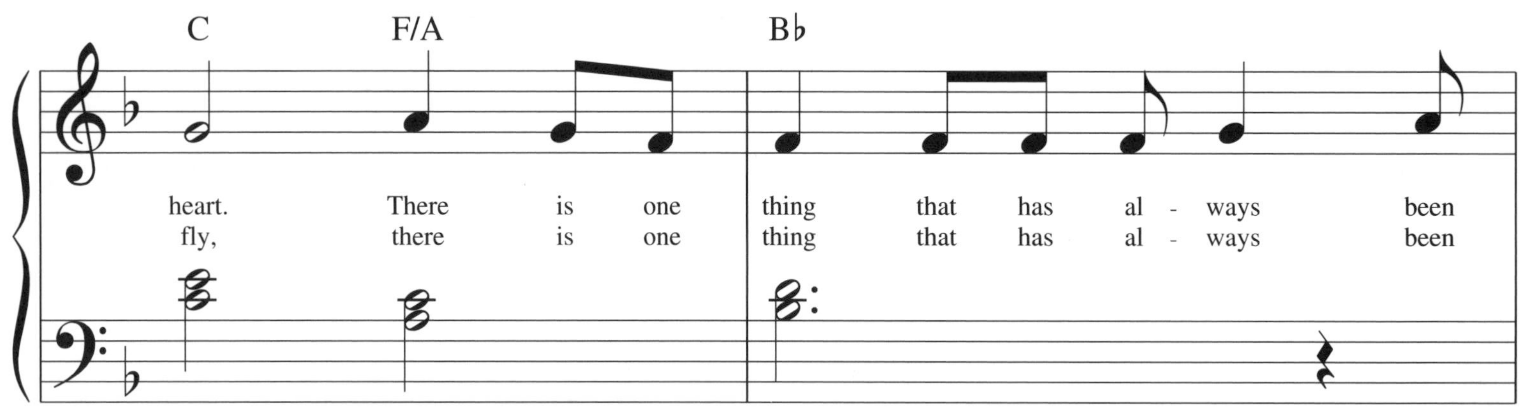

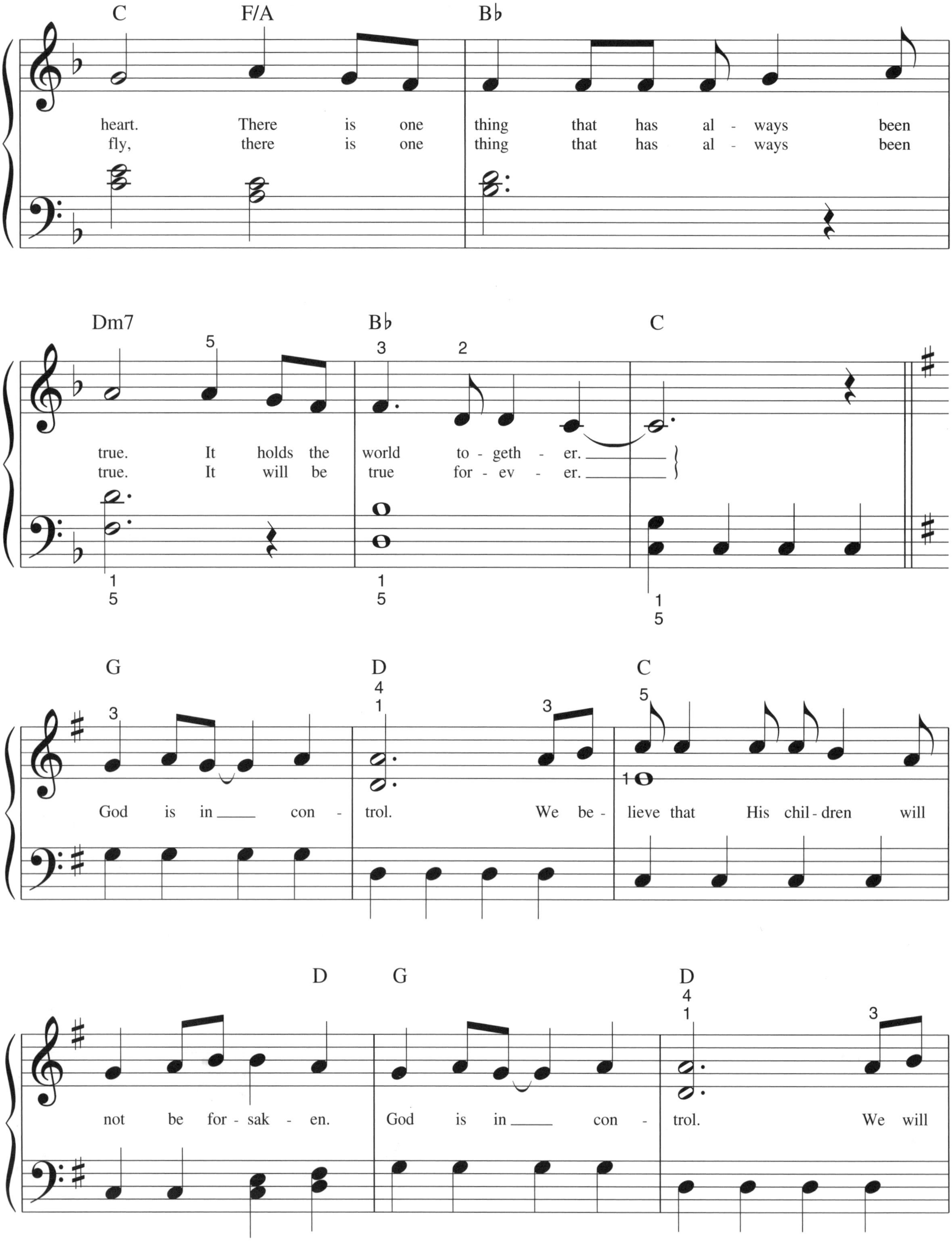

Dm7 B♭ C
true. It holds the world to - geth - er.
true. It will be true for - ev - er.

G D C
God is in con - trol. We be - lieve that His chil - dren will

D G D
not be for - sak - en. God is in con - trol. We will

C
D
G/B
choose to re - mem - ber and
nev - er be shak - en.
There is no pow - er a -
C/E
D/F♯
C/E
Dsus
D
bove or be - side Him. We
know, oh,
God is in con -
C
Dsus
D
1.
G
trol. Oh,
God is in con - trol.
Csus2
2.
G
trol.

FRIENDS

Words and Music by MICHAEL W. SMITH
and DEBORAH D. SMITH

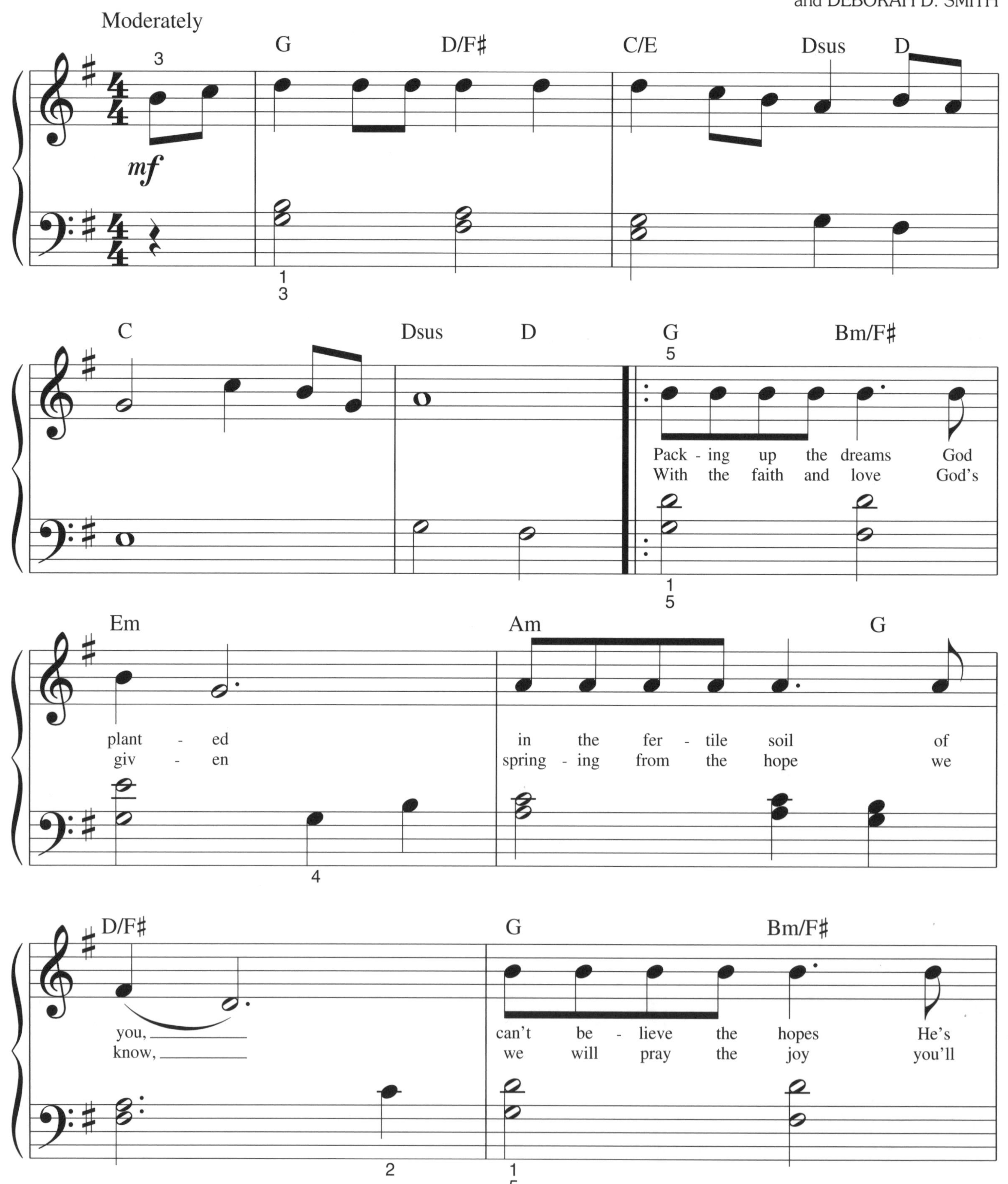

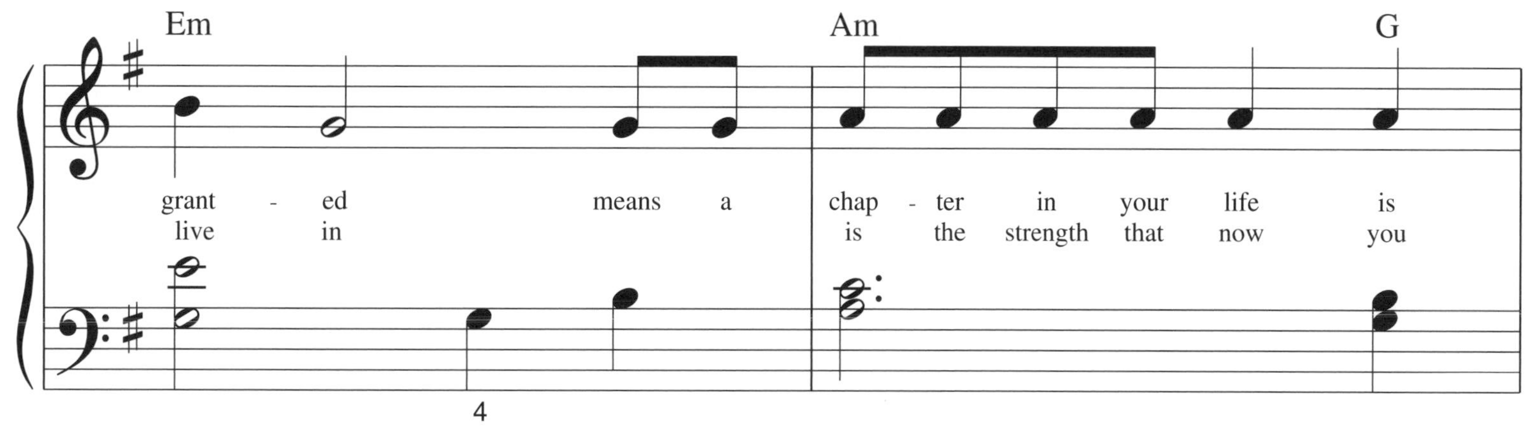
Em
Am
G
grant - ed means a chap - ter in your life is
live in is the strength that now you
4

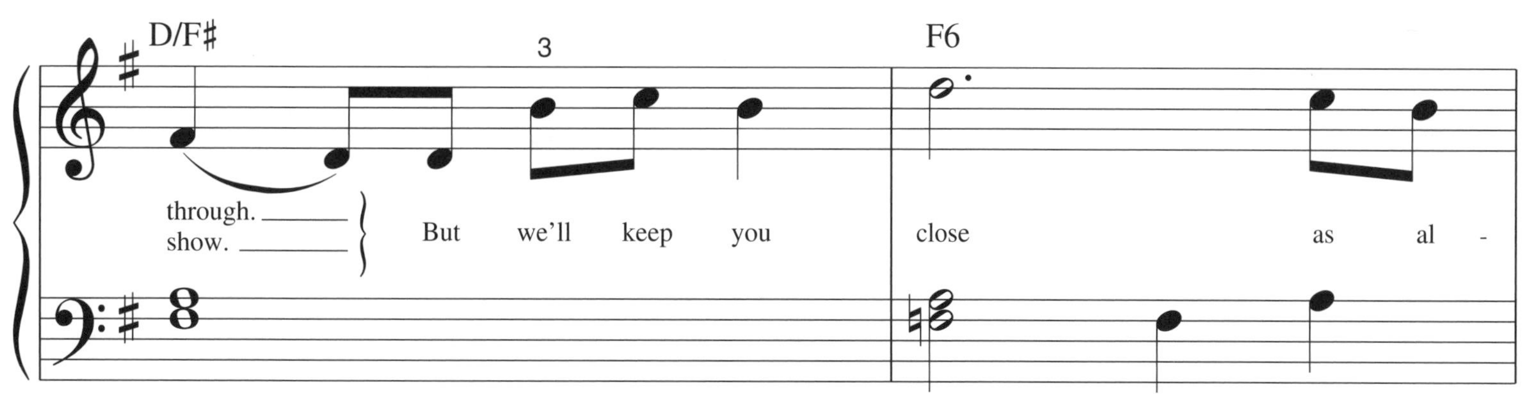
D/F♯
3
F6
through.
show.
But we'll keep you close as al -

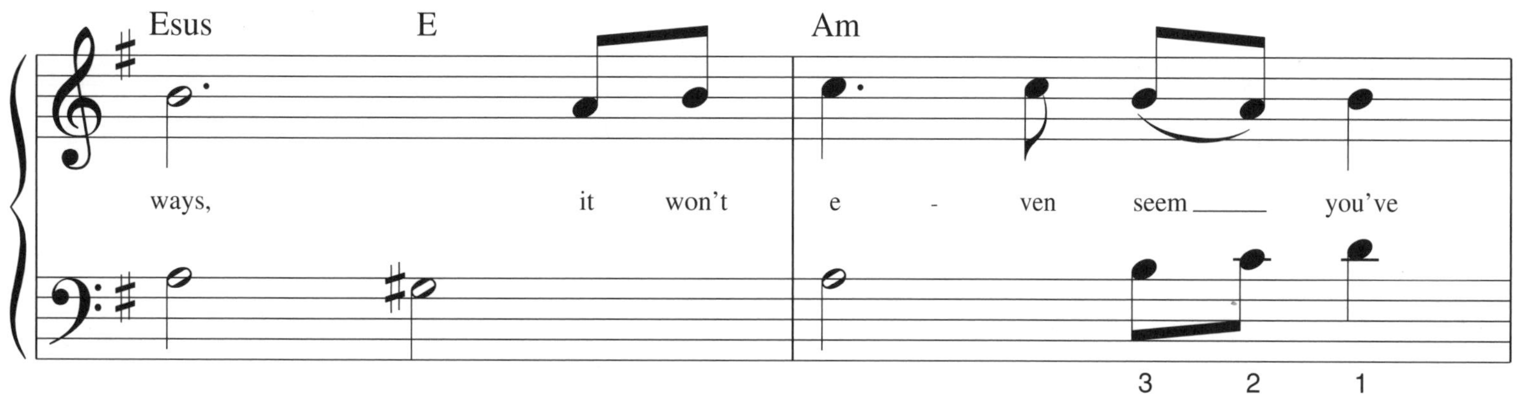
Esus
E
Am
ways, it won't e - ven seem you've
3 2 1

Cm
G
Bm/F♯
gone 'cause our hearts in big and
2

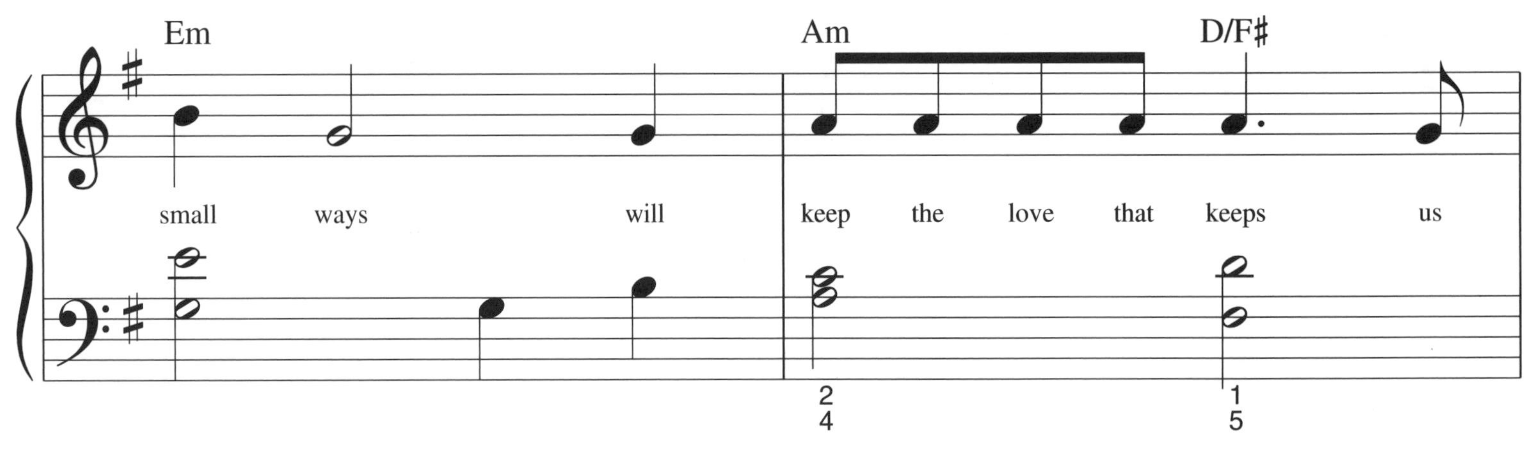
Em
Am
D/F♯
small ways will keep the love that keeps us
2
4
1
5

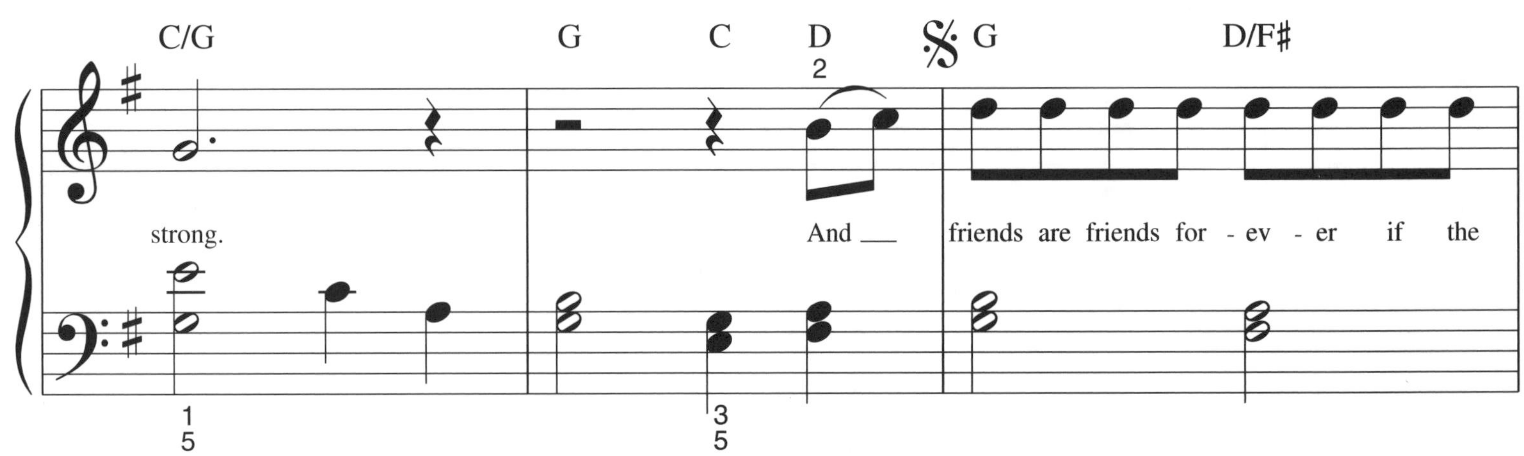
C/G
G
C
D
2
G
D/F♯
strong.
And
friends are friends for - ev - er if the
1
5
3
5

C/E
Dsus
D
G
D/F♯
Lord's the Lord of them. And a friend will not say "nev - er" 'cause the

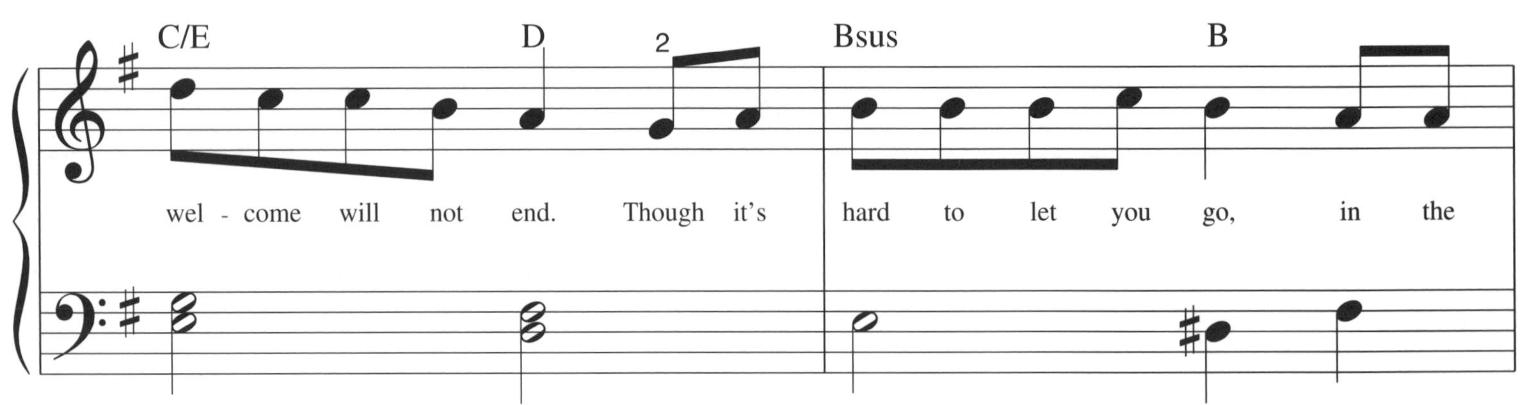
C/E
D
2
Bsus
B
wel - come will not end. Though it's hard to let you go, in the

Em D C
Am
D7sus
To Coda
Fa - ther's hands we know that a
life - time's not too long
to live as
1.
2.
D.S. al Coda
G D/F♯ C/E D7
G C D
friends.
friends.
And
CODA
Em
Am
D7sus
friends.
No a
life - time's not too long
to live as
rit.
G D/F♯ C/E Dsus D G
friends.
a tempo
rit.

THE GREAT DIVIDE

Words and Music by MATT HUESMANN
and GRANT CUNNINGHAM

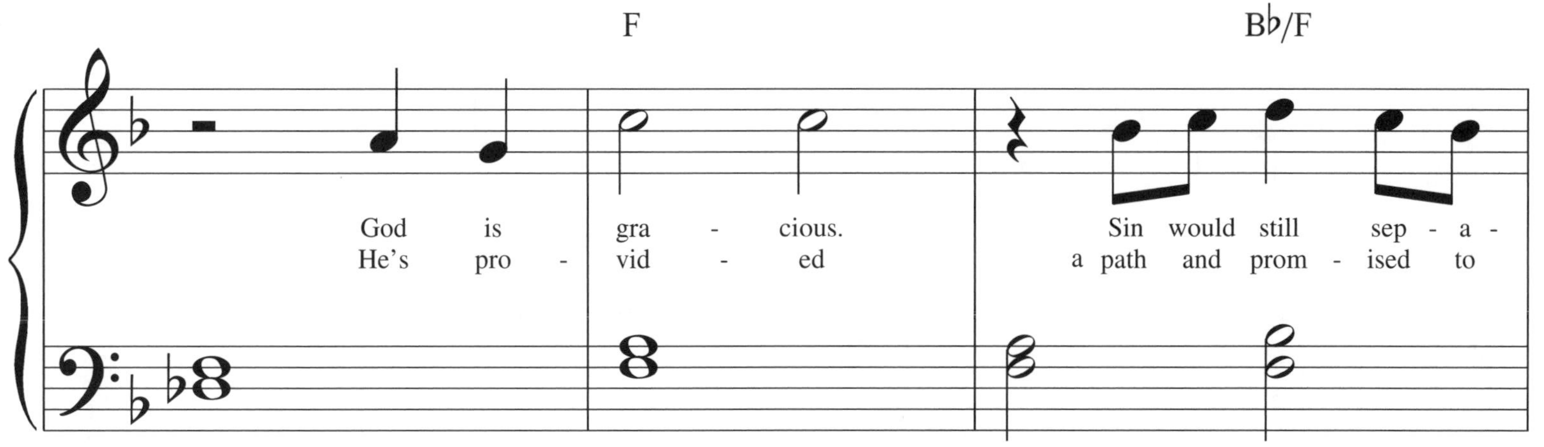
F
Bb/F
God is gra - cious. Sin would still sep - a -
He's pro - vid - ed a path and prom - ised to

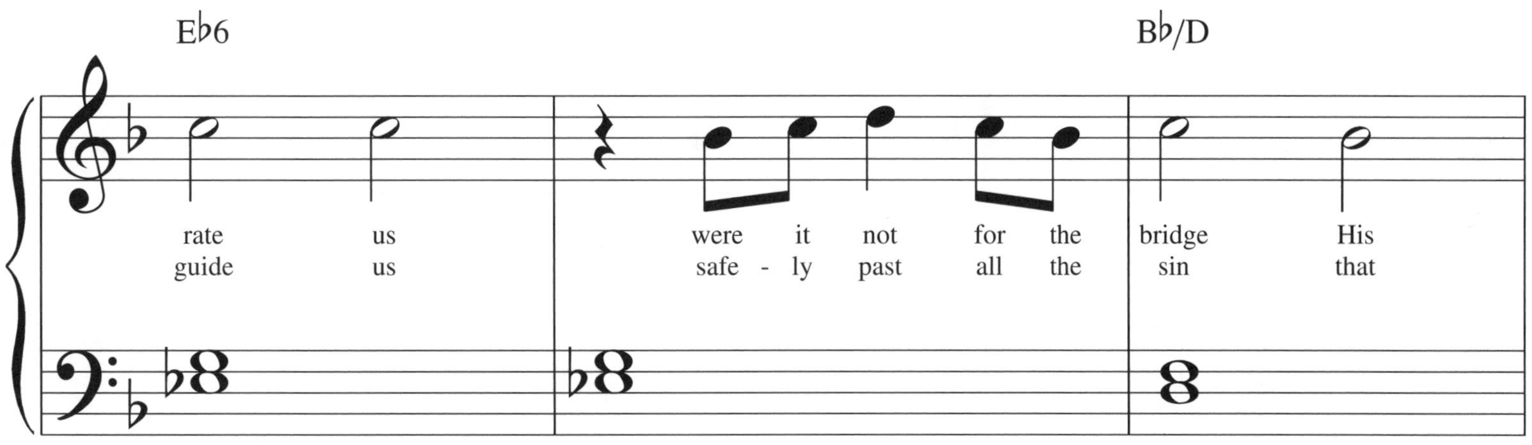
Eb6
Bb/D
rate us were it not for the bridge His
guide us safe - ly past all the sin that

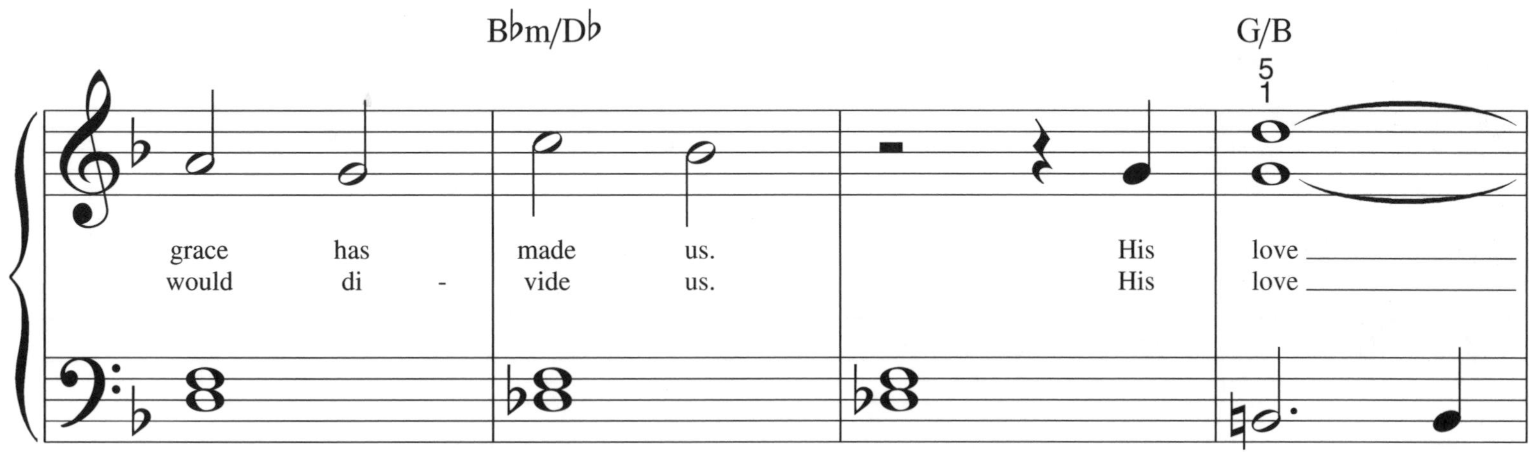
Bbm/Db
G/B
grace has made us. His love
would di - vide us. His love

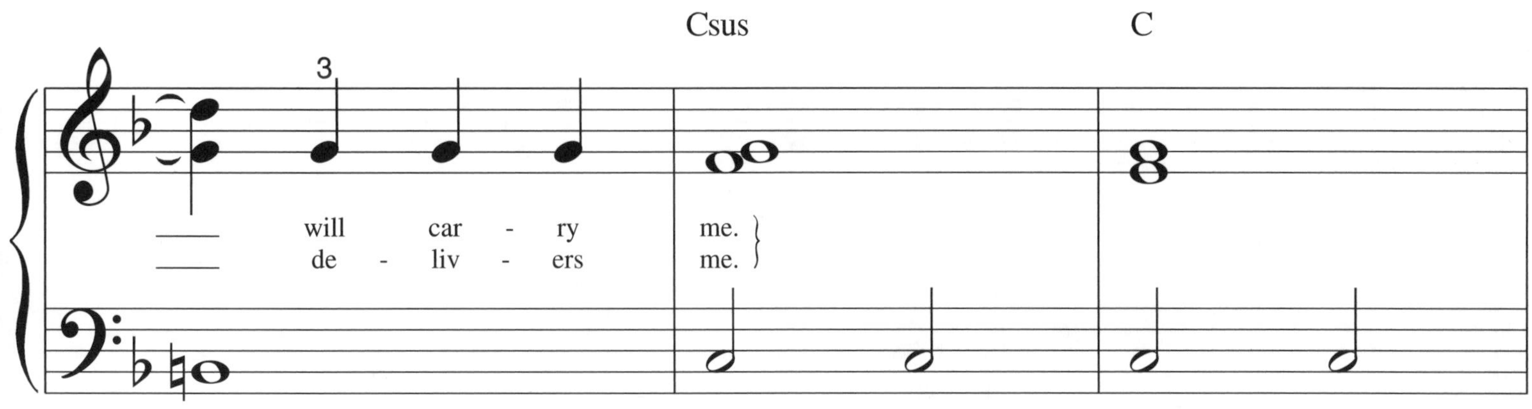
Csus
C
will car - ry me.
de - liv - ers me.

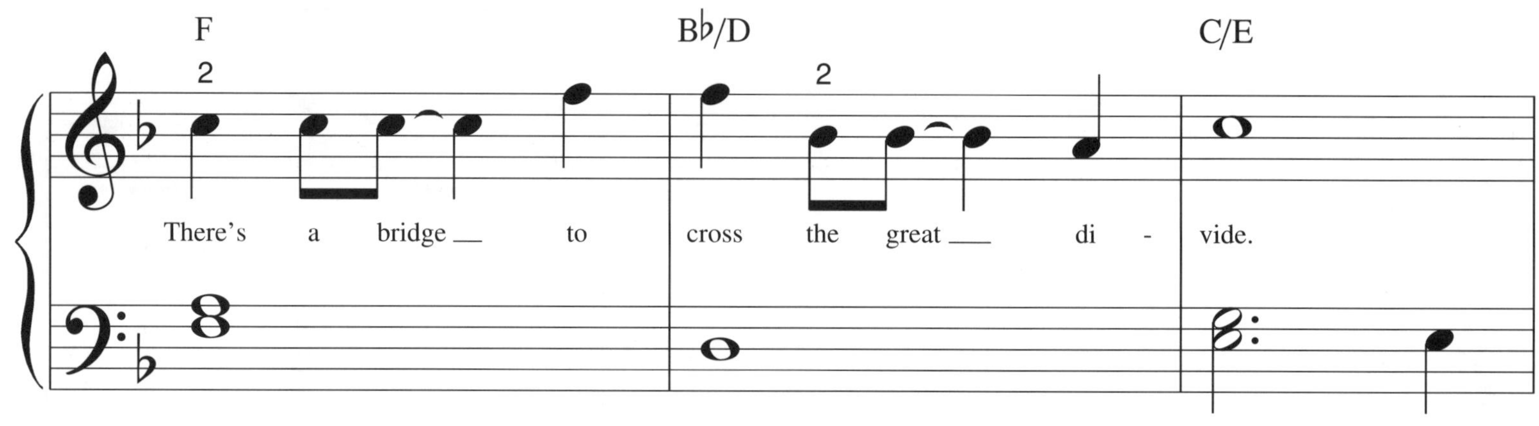
F
B♭/D
C/E
2
2
There's a bridge to cross the great di - vide.

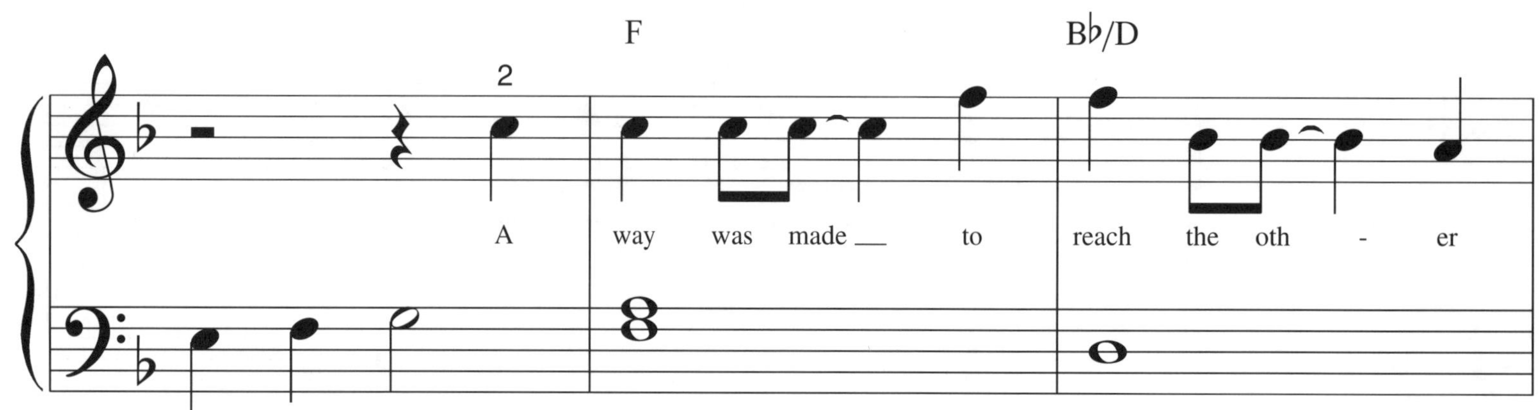
F
B♭/D
2
A way was made to reach the oth - er

C/E
F
2
side.
The mer - cy of the

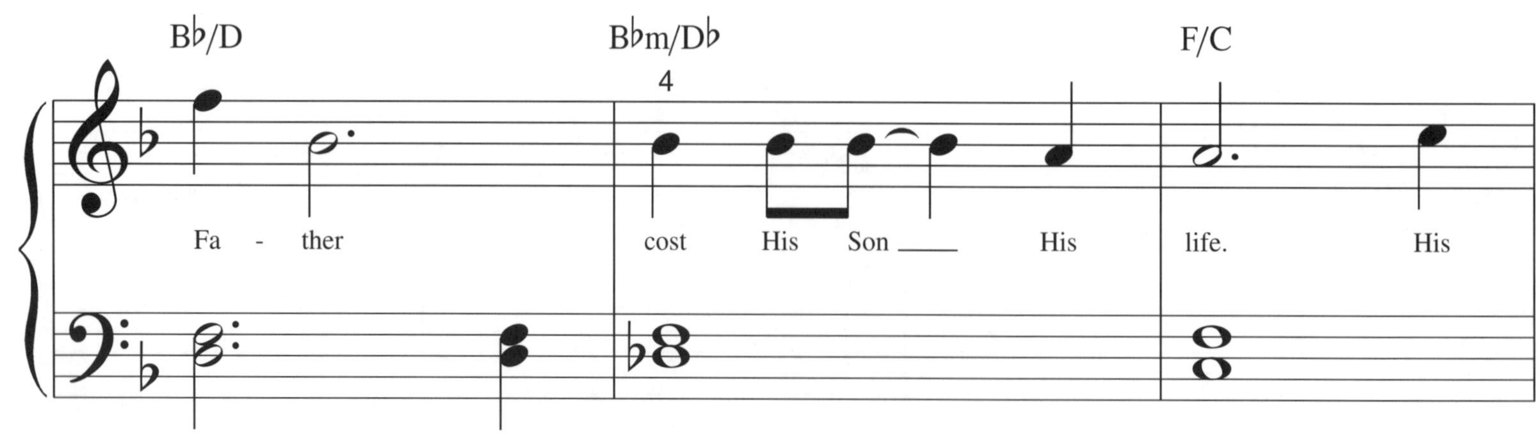
B♭/D
B♭m/D♭
F/C
4
Fa - ther cost His Son His life. His

Gm7
F/A
E♭
Dm
love is deep, His love is wide.
Gm7
B♭/C
There's a cross to bridge the great di -
1.
Dm
B♭
F/A
B♭
vide.
God is
2.
Dm
C
B♭
vide. The cross that cost my Lord His

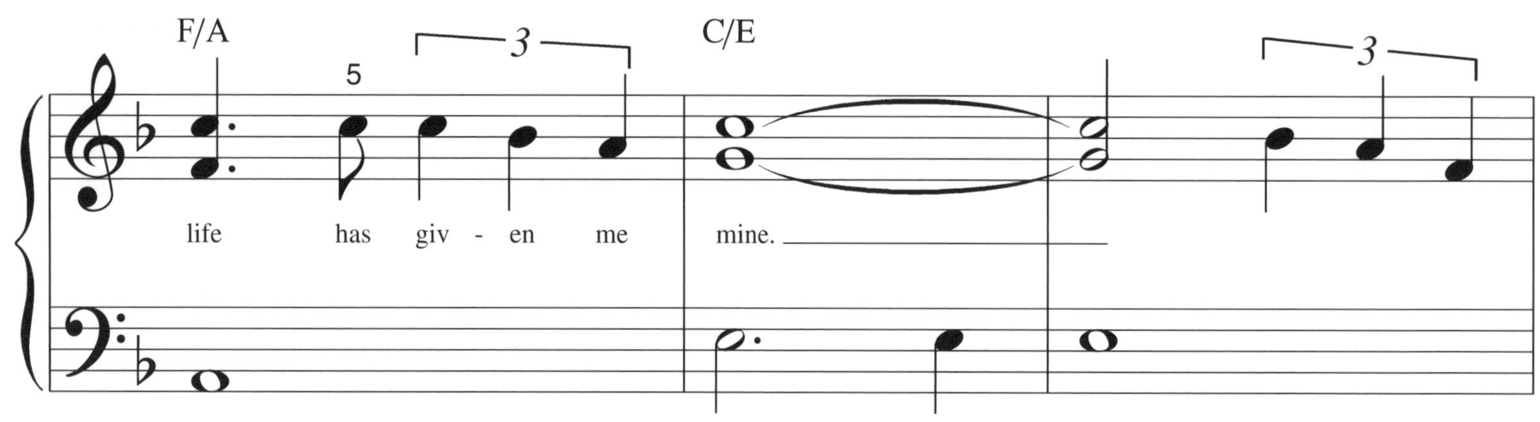
F/A
C/E
life has giv - en me mine.

Dm
C
F
There's a bridge to

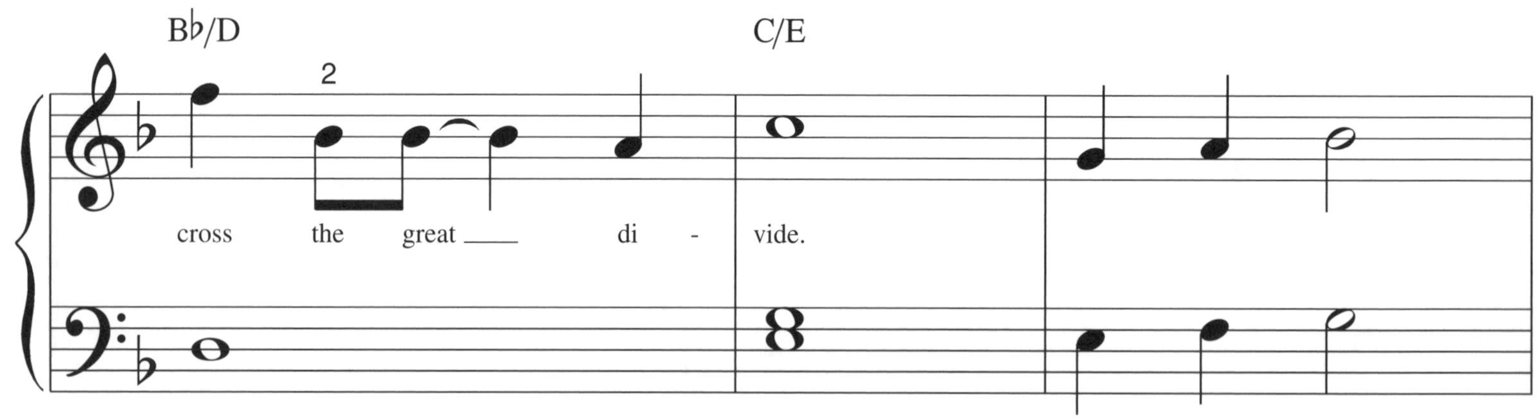
B♭/D
C/E
cross the great di - vide.

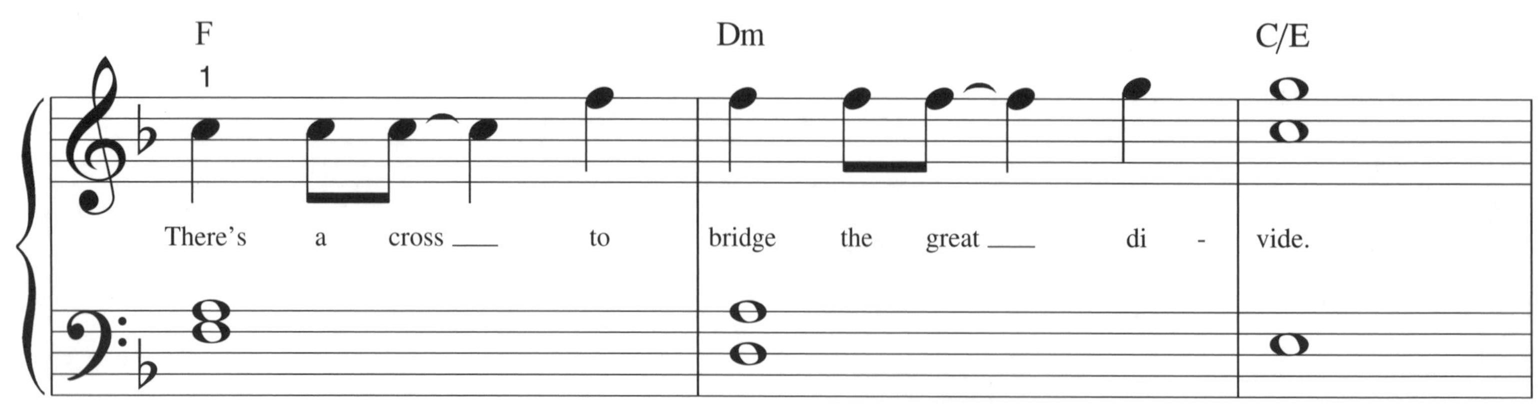
F
Dm
C/E
There's a cross to bridge the great di - vide.

G
C/E
2
There's a bridge to cross the great di -

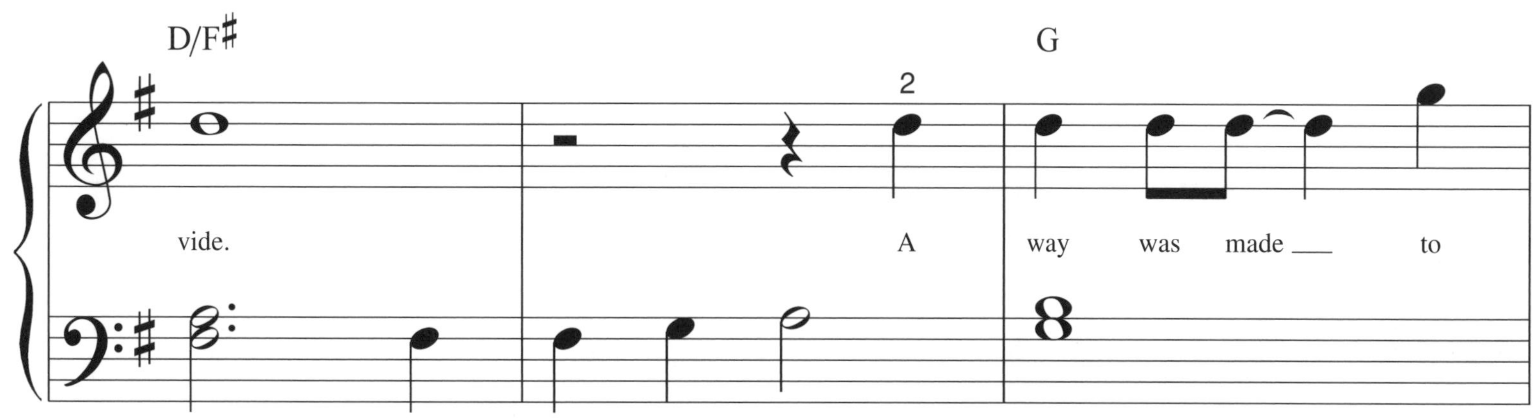
D/F♯
G
2
vide. A way was made to

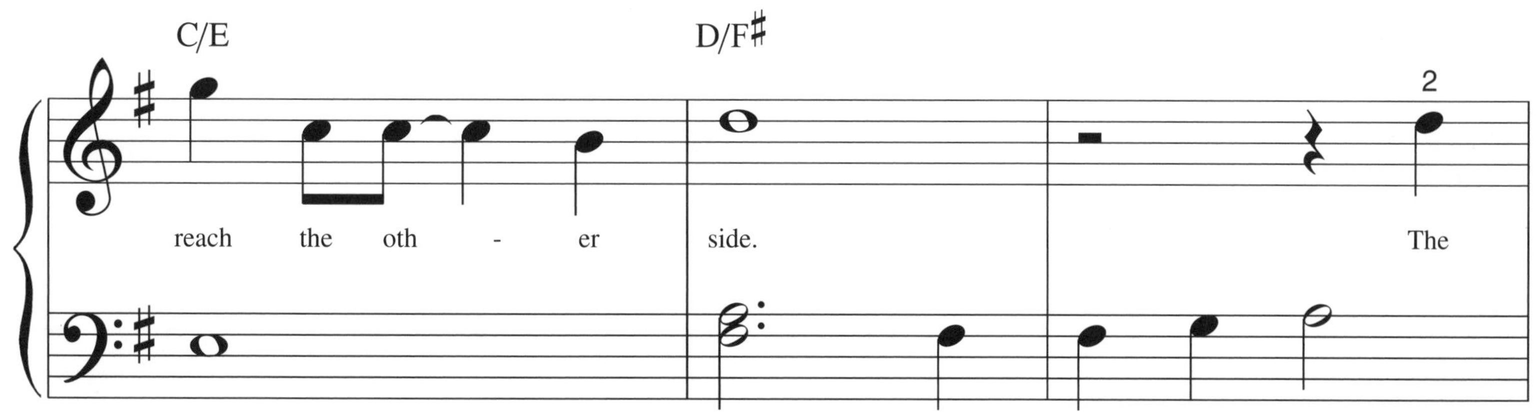
C/E
D/F♯
2
reach the oth - er side. The

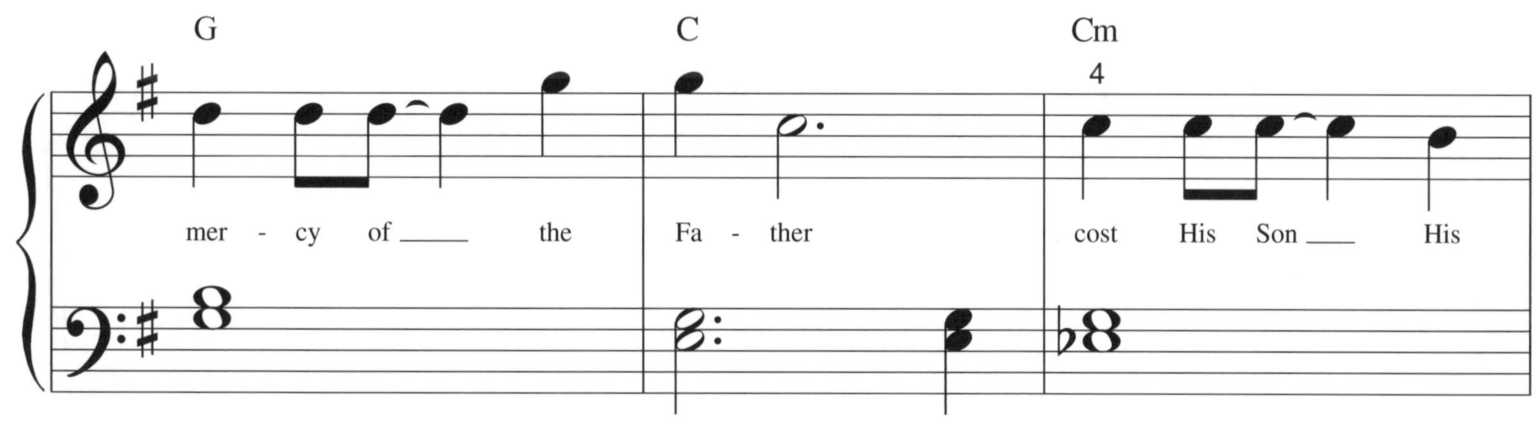
G
C
Cm
4
mer - cy of the Fa - ther cost His Son His

G/D
Am7
G/B
life. His love is deep, His

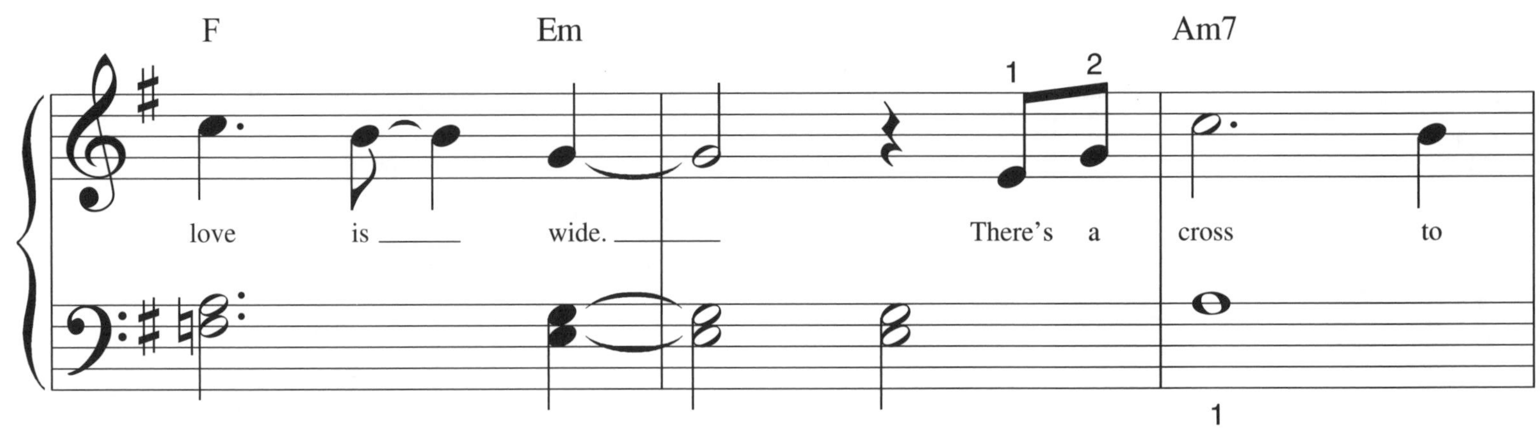
F
Em
Am7
1 2
love is wide. There's a cross to
1

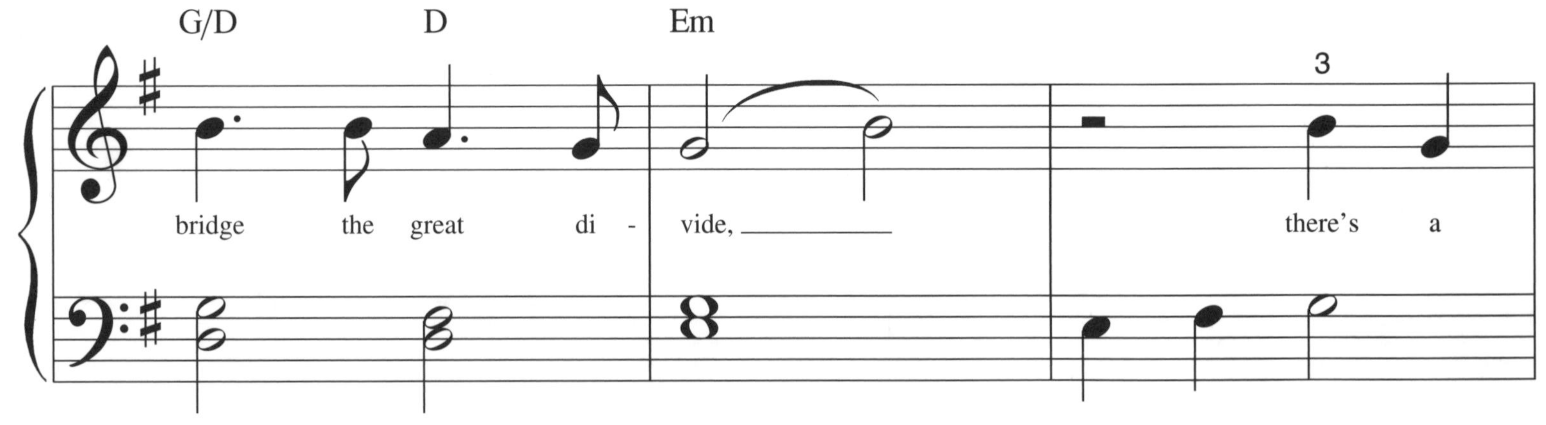
G/D
D
Em
3
bridge the great di - vide, there's a

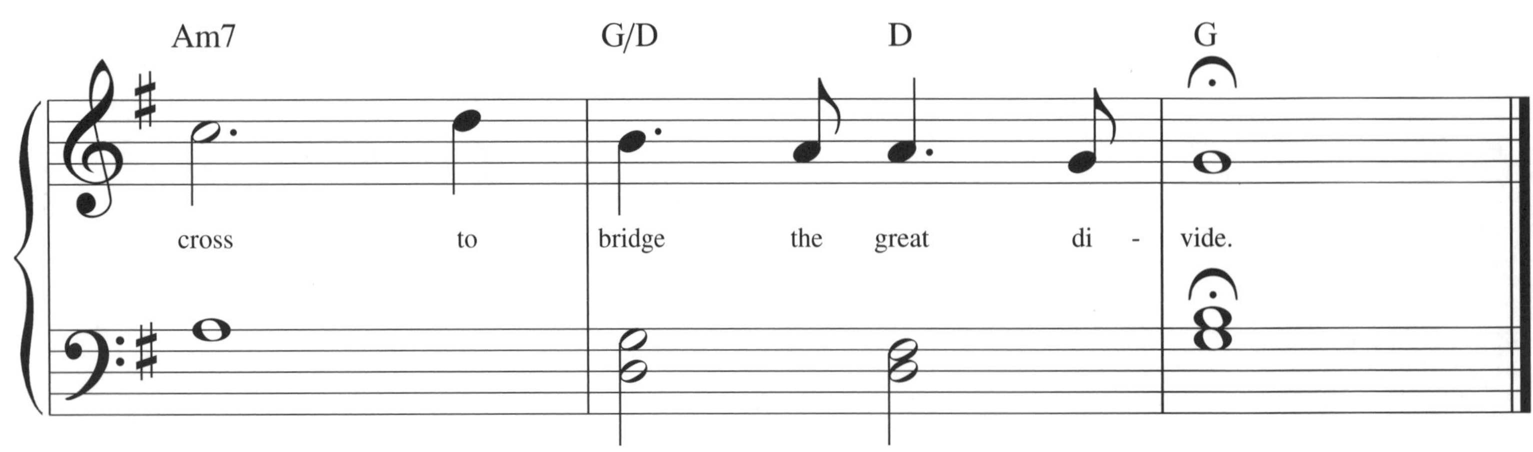
Am7
G/D
D
G
cross to bridge the great di - vide.

HIS STRENGTH IS PERFECT

Words and Music by STEVEN CURTIS CHAPMAN
and JERRY SALLEY

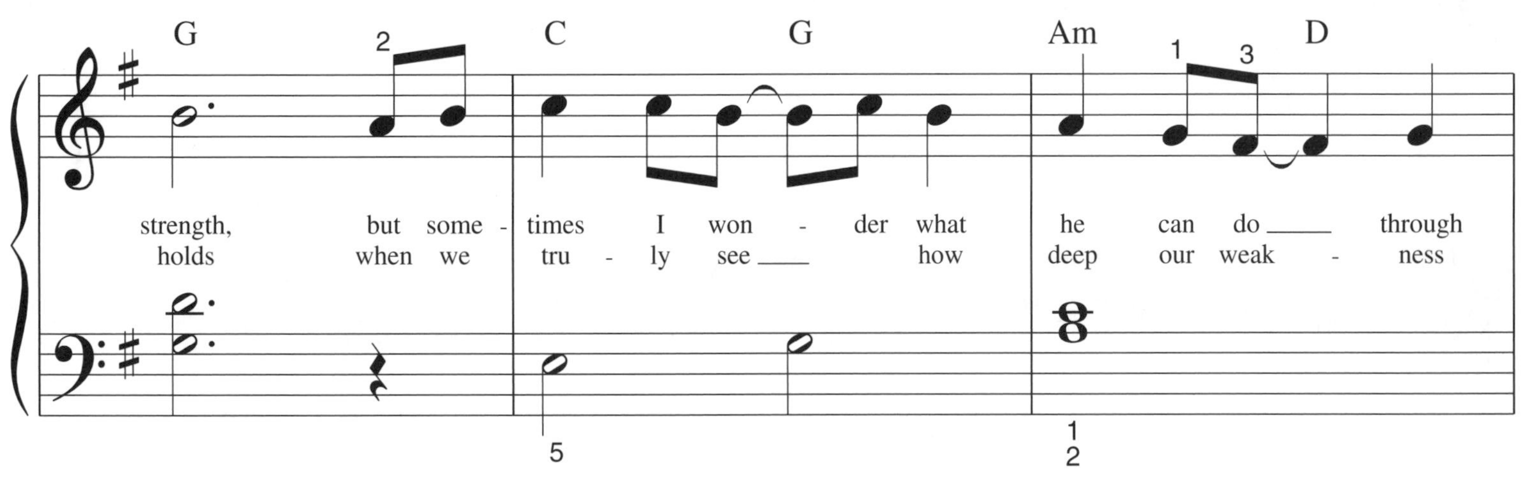

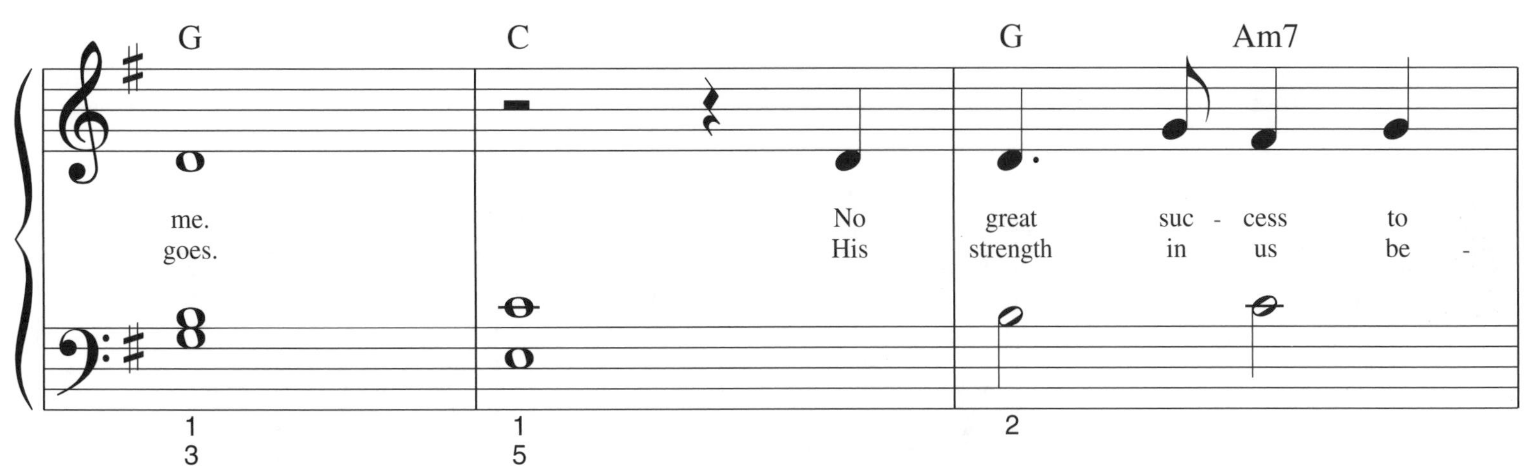

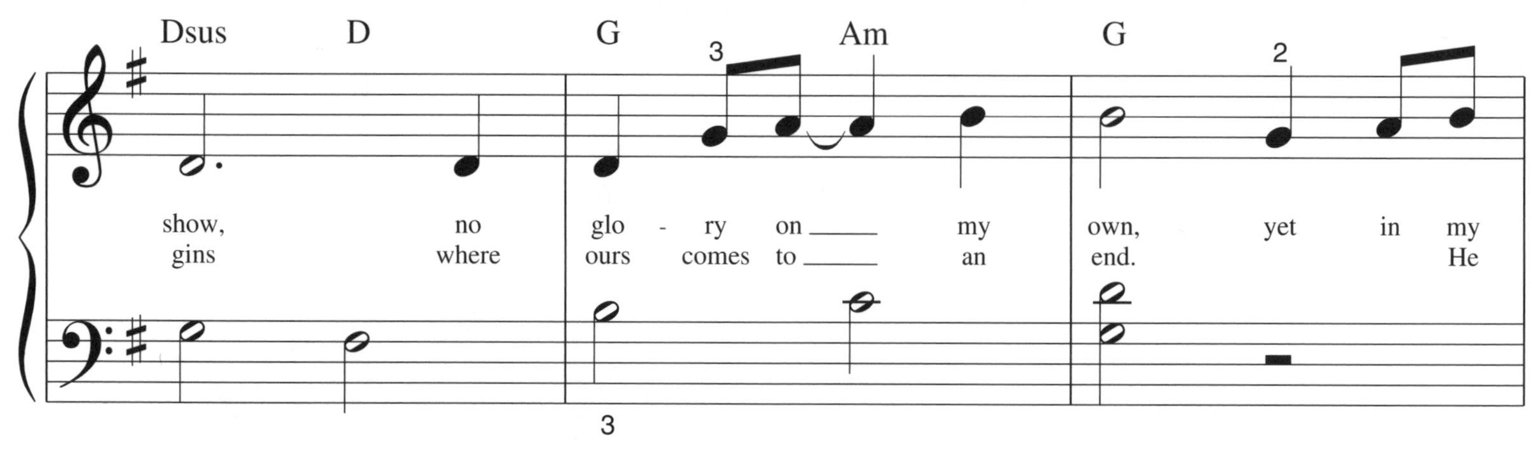
Dsus
D
G
Am
G
3
2
show, no glo - ry on ___ my own, yet in my
gins where ours comes to ___ an end. He
3

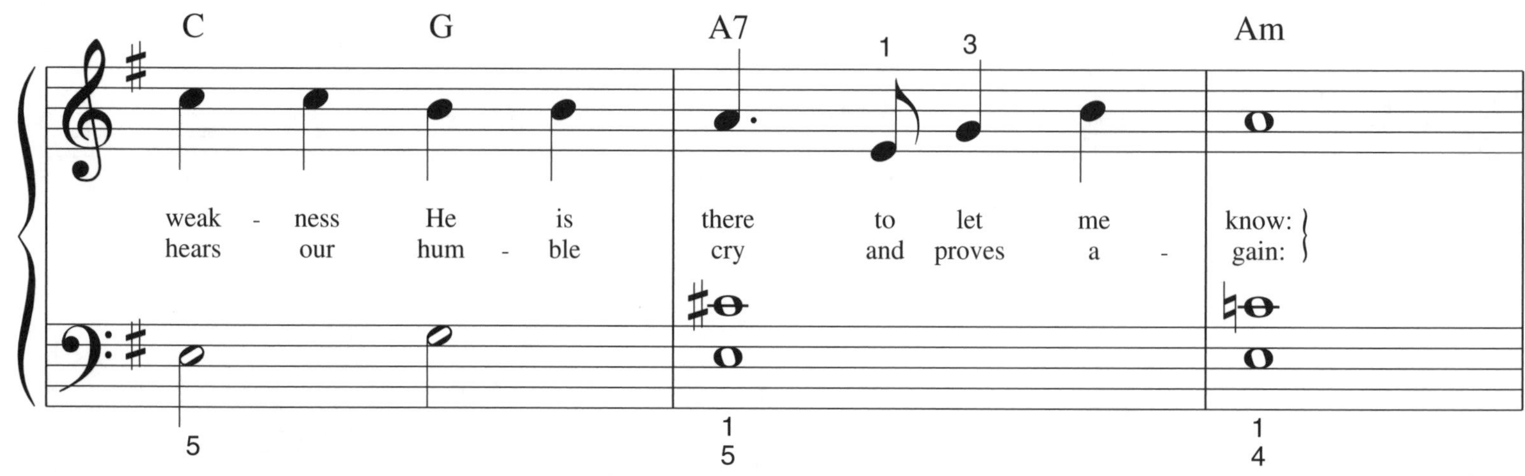
C
G
A7
Am
1 3
weak - ness He is there to let me know:
hears our hum - ble cry and proves a - gain:
5
1
5
1
4

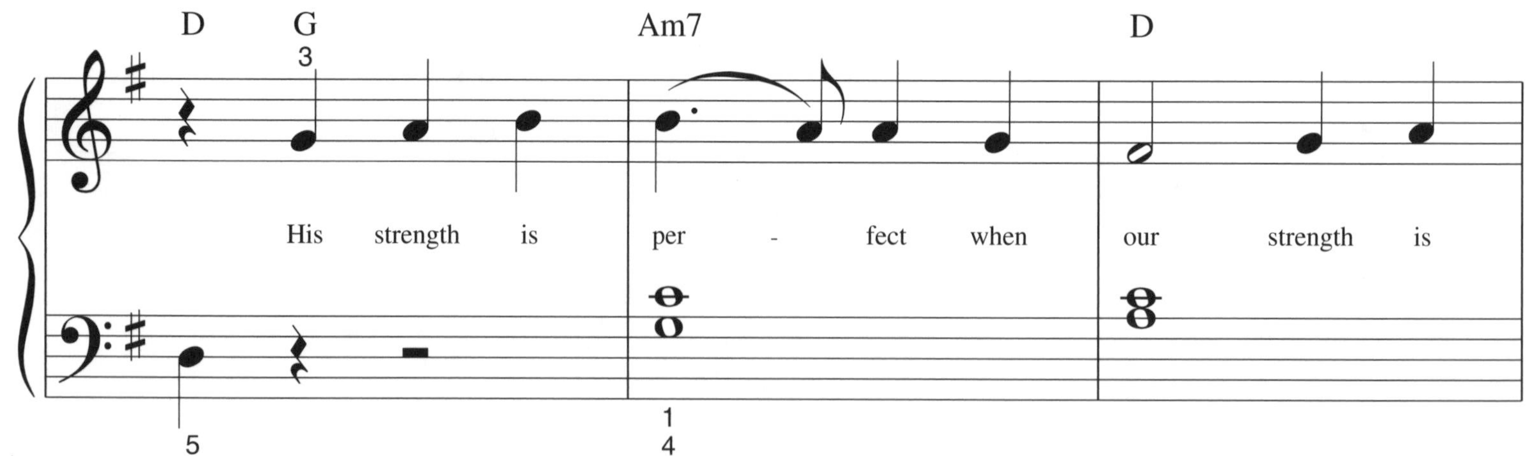
D
G
Am7
D
3
His strength is per - fect when our strength is
5
1
4

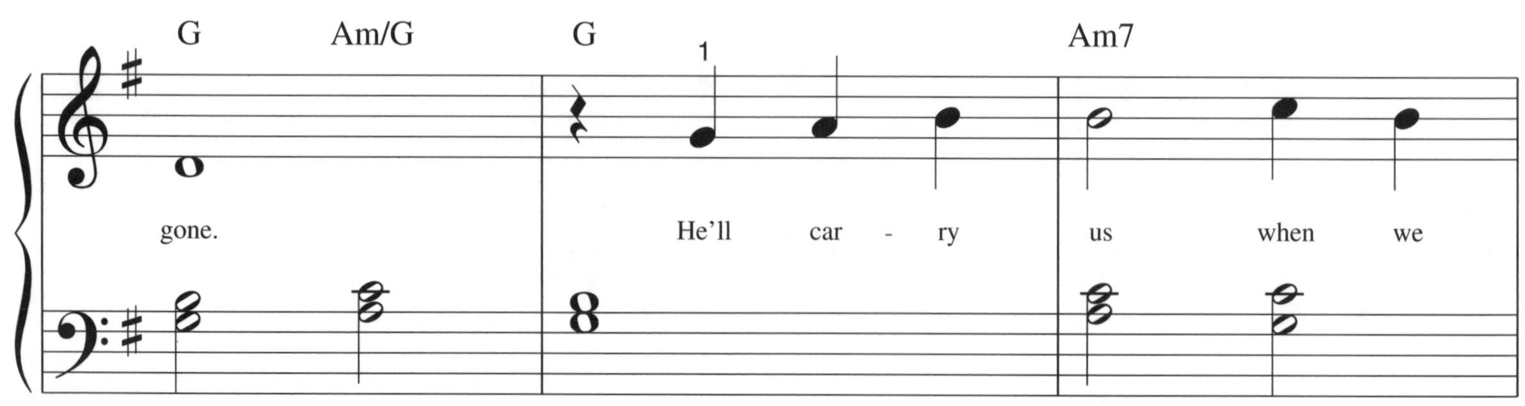
G
Am/G
G
Am7
1
gone. He'll car - ry us when we

D/F♯
Dm/F
E7
can't car - ry on. Raised in His
Am
Am/G
D/F♯
B/D♯
Em
Em/D
pow - er, the weak be - come strong.
C♯m7♭5
Am7
D
His strength is per - fect, His strength is
1.
C/G
G
per - fect.
2.
C
G
per - fect.
rit.

GREAT IS THE LORD

Words and Music by MICHAEL W. SMITH
and DEBORAH D. SMITH

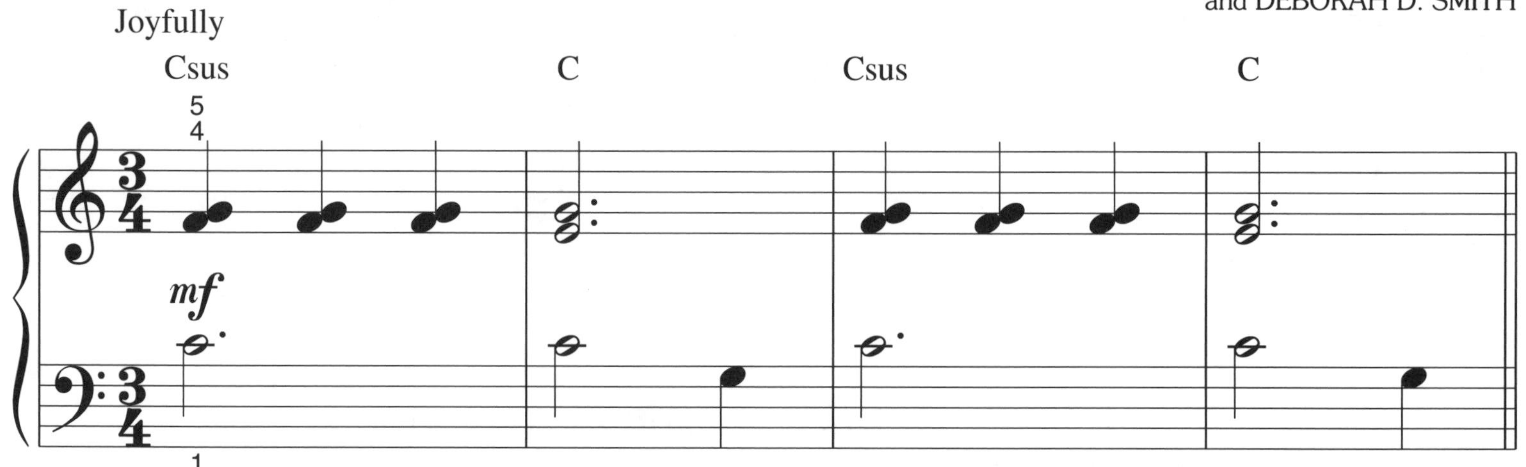

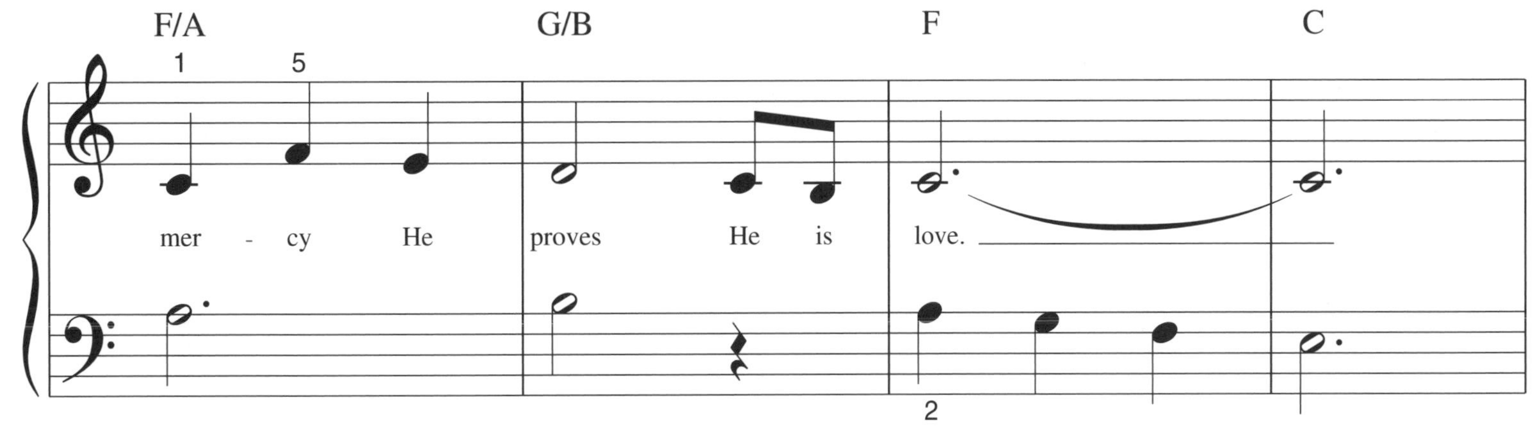
F/A
G/B
F
C
1
5
mer - cy He
proves He is
love.
2

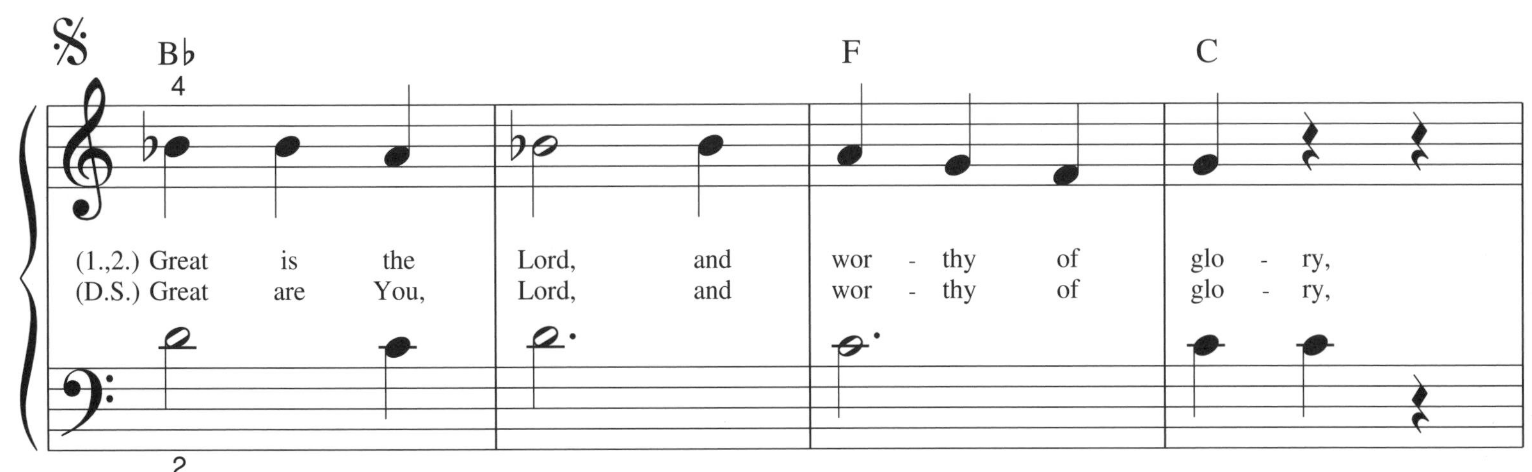
B♭
F
C
4
(1.,2.) Great is the
Lord, and
wor - thy of
glo - ry,
(D.S.) Great are You,
Lord, and
wor - thy of
glo - ry,
2

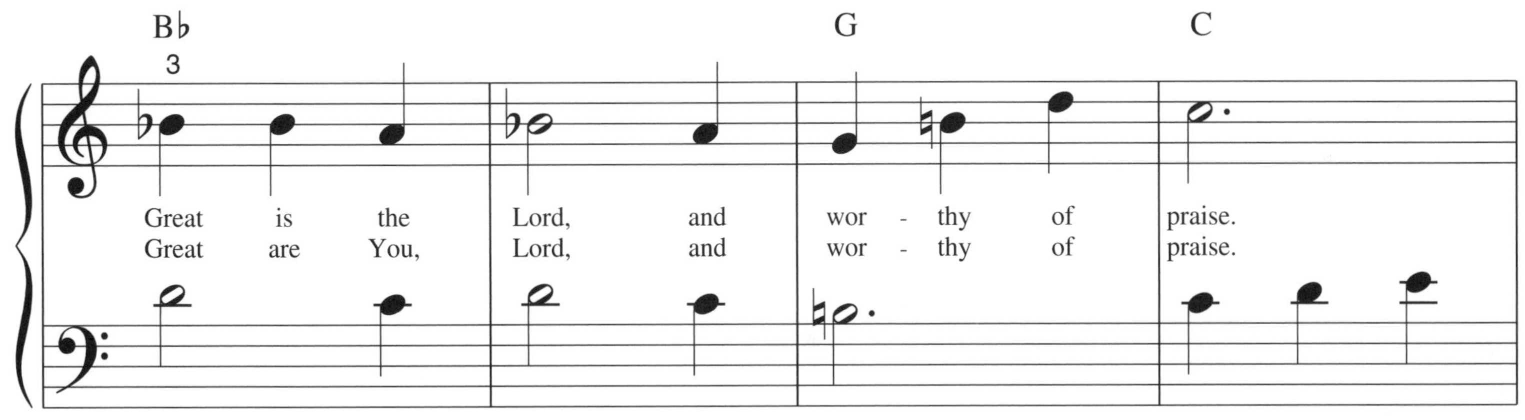
B♭
G
C
3
Great is the
Lord, and
wor - thy of
praise.
Great are You,
Lord, and
wor - thy of
praise.

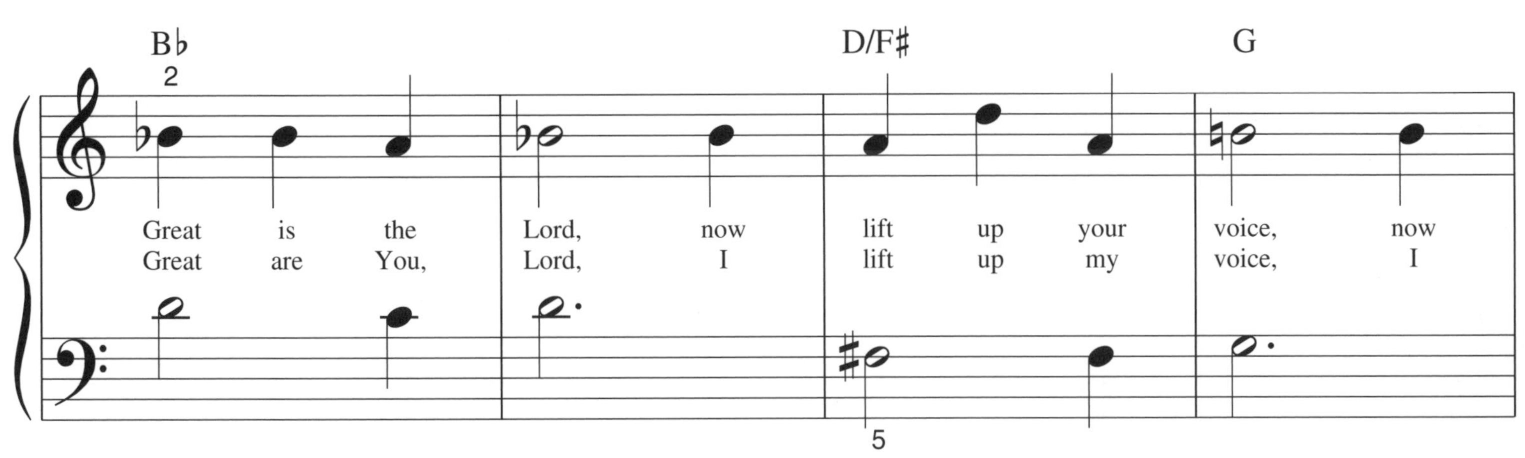
B♭
D/F♯
G
2
Great is the
Lord, now
lift up your
voice, now
Great are You,
Lord, I
lift up my
voice, I
5

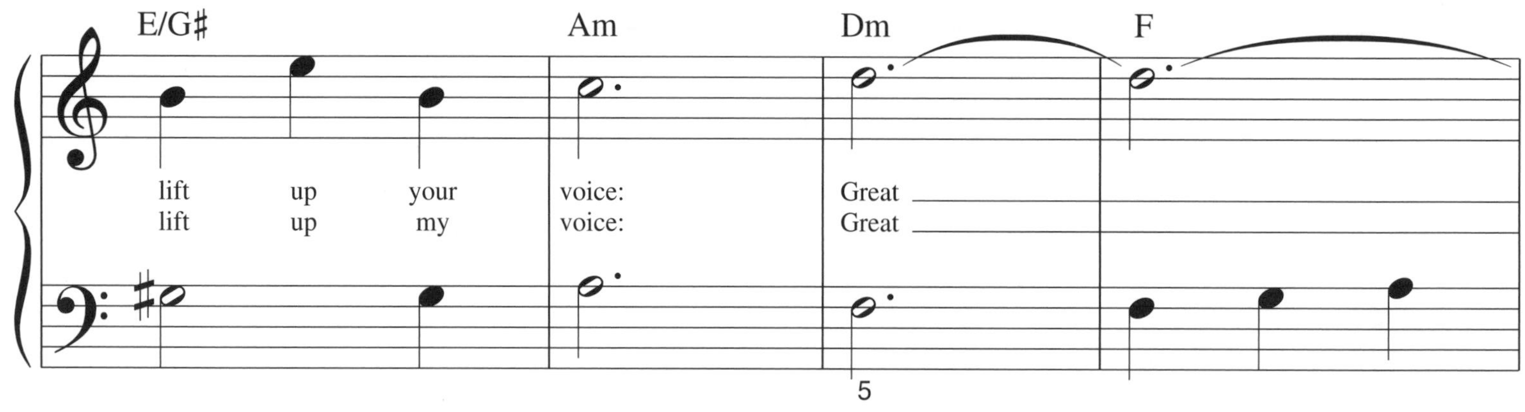
E/G♯
Am
Dm
F
lift up your voice: Great
lift up my voice: Great
5

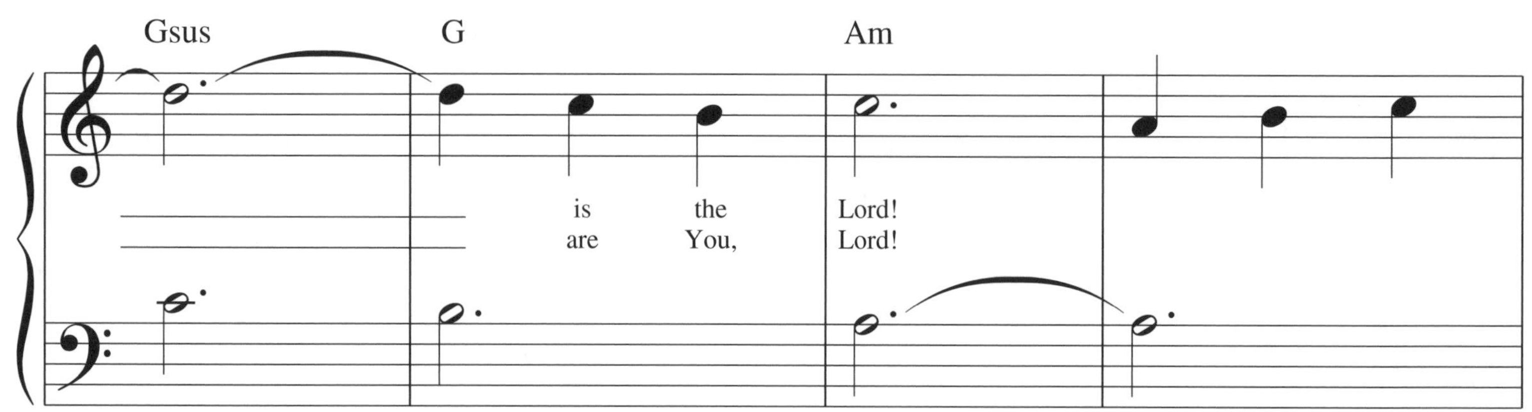
Gsus
G
Am
is the Lord!
are You, Lord!

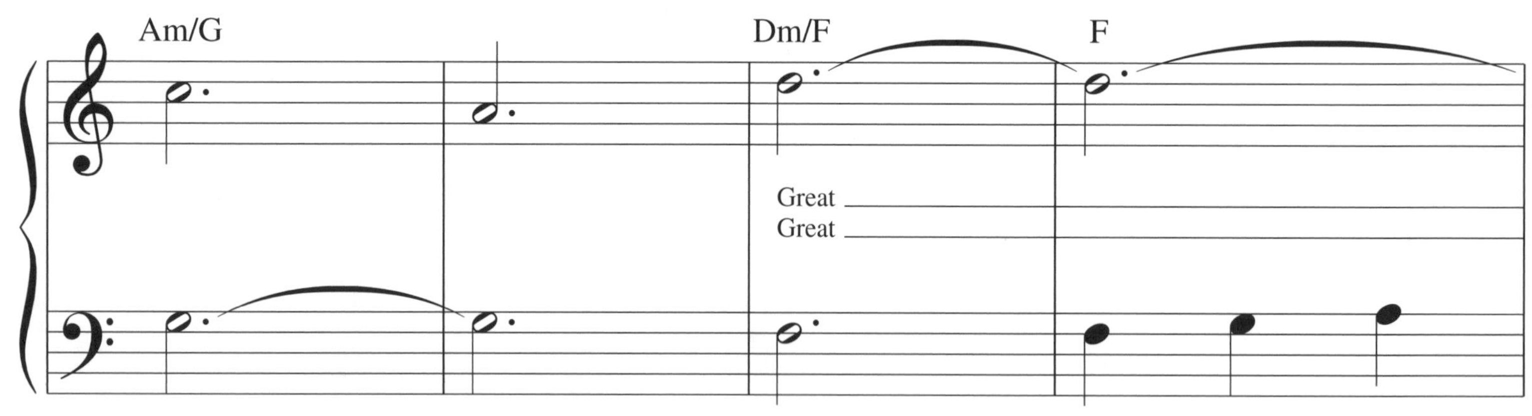
Am/G
Dm/F
F
Great
Great

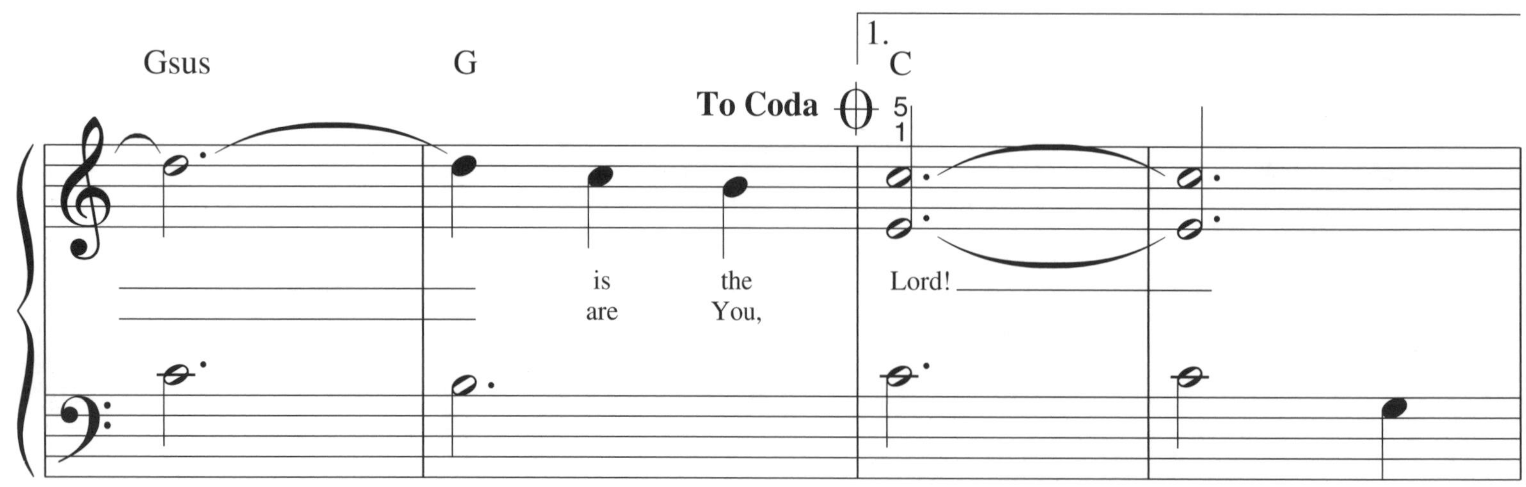
Gsus
G
1.
C
To Coda
5
1
is the Lord!
are You,

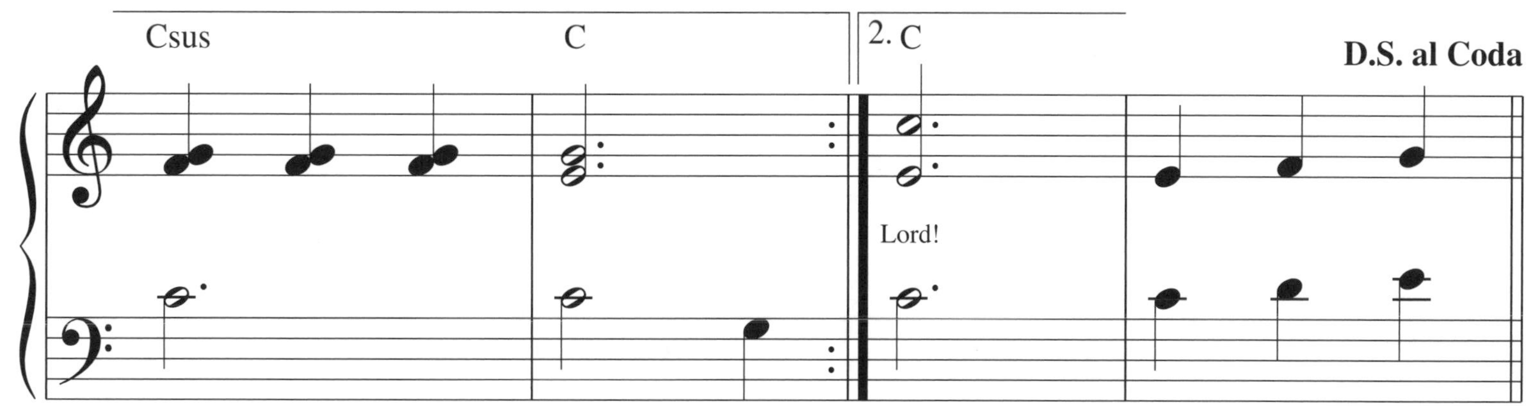
Csus
C
2. C
D.S. al Coda
Lord!

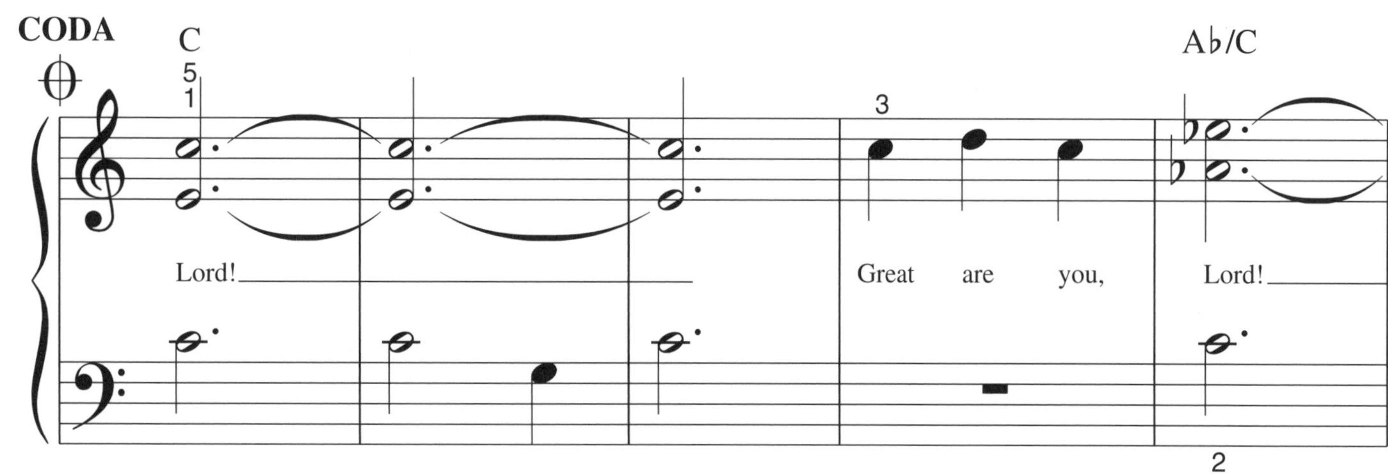
CODA
C
A♭/C
Lord!
Great are you,
Lord!

B♭/D
Great are you,
Lord!

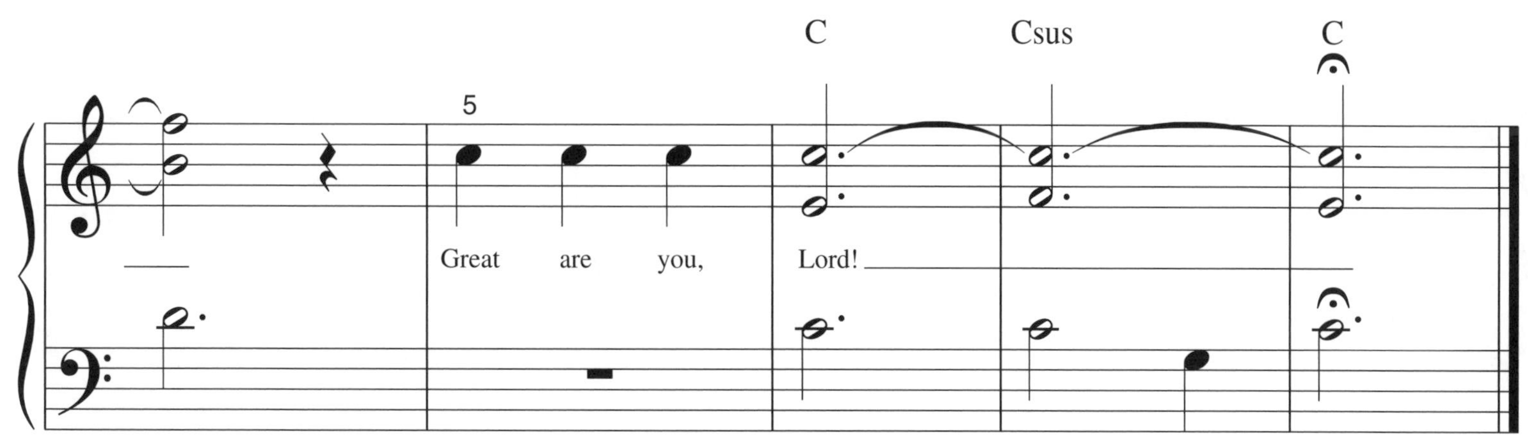
C
Csus
C
Great are you,
Lord!

HOW BEAUTIFUL

Words and Music by
TWILA PARIS

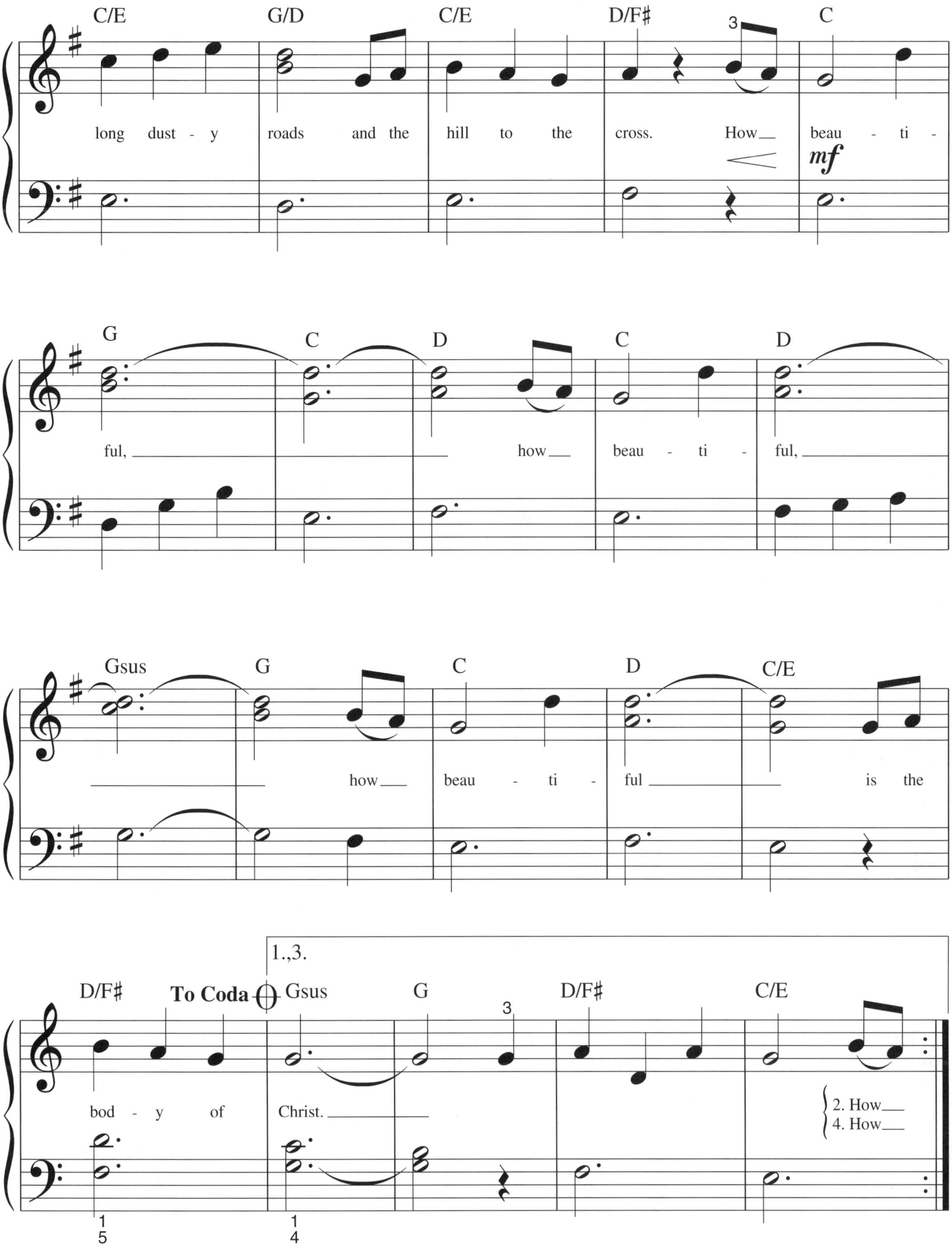

C/E G/D C/E D/F♯ 3 C

long dust - y roads and the hill to the cross. How beau - ti -

mf

G C D C D

ful, how beau - ti - ful,

Gsus G C D C/E

how beau - ti - ful is the

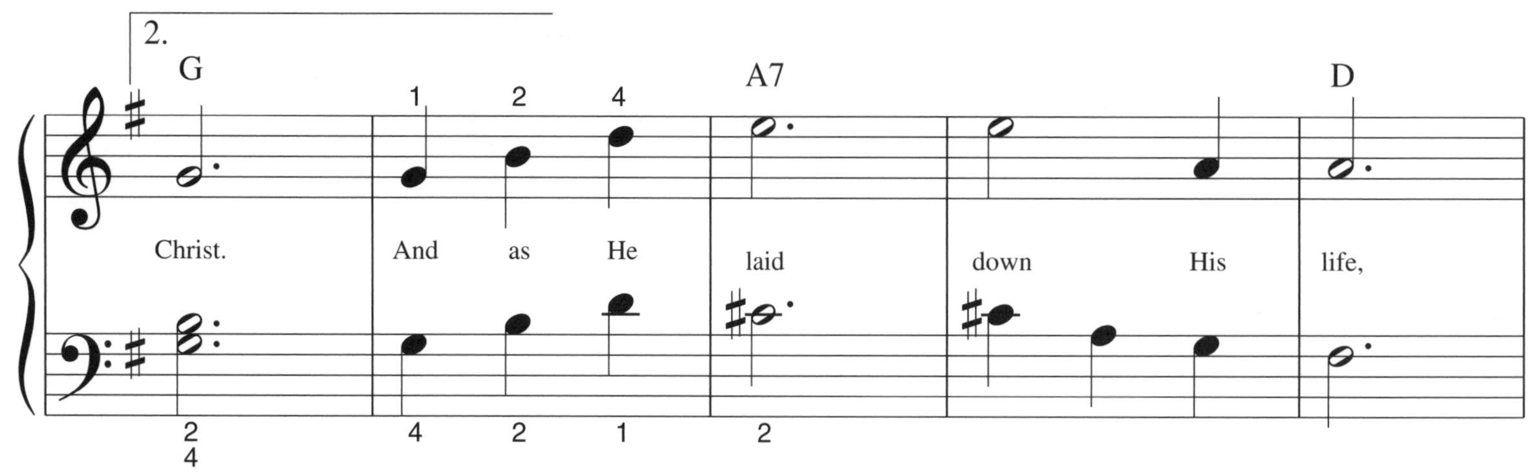
2.
G
A7
D
1
2
4
Christ. And as He laid down His life,
2
4
4
2
1
2

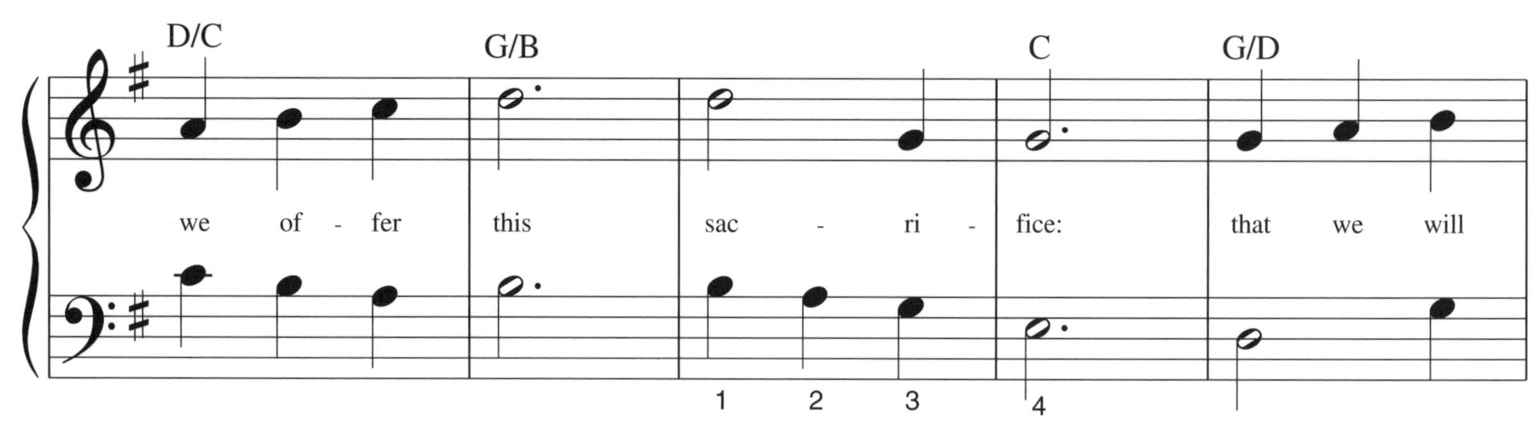
D/C
G/B
C
G/D
we of - fer this sac - ri - fice: that we will
1
2
3
4

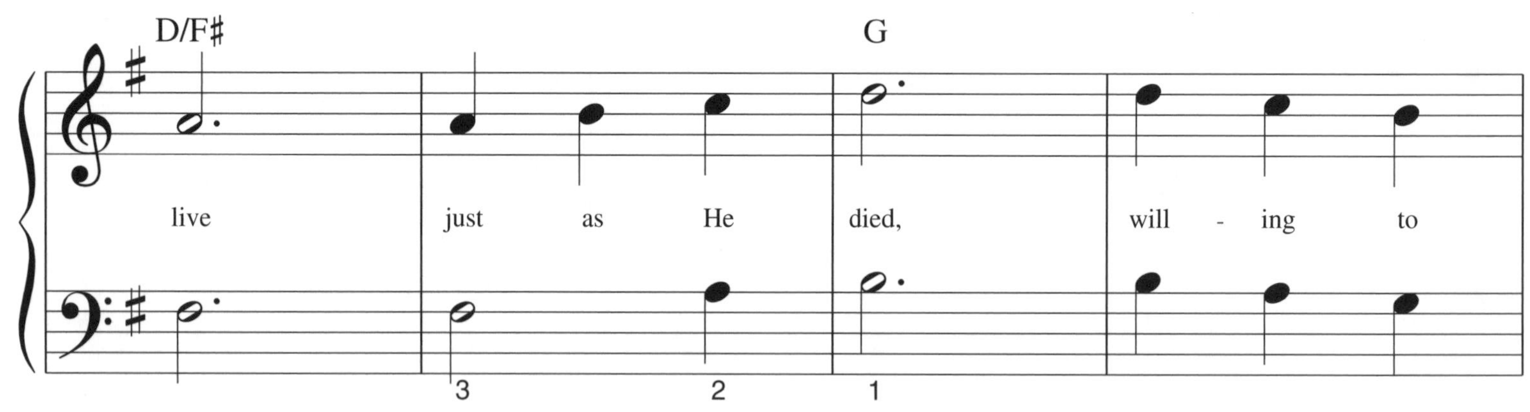
D/F#
G
live just as He died, will - ing to
3
2
1

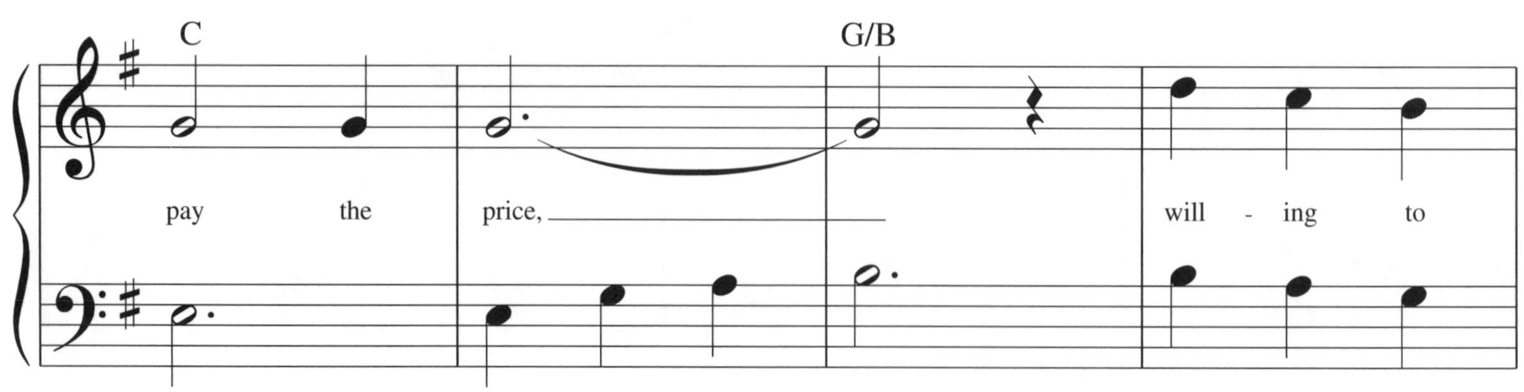
C
G/B
pay the price,
will - ing to

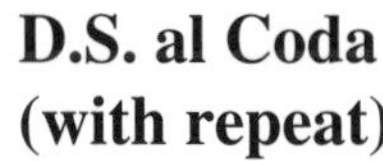

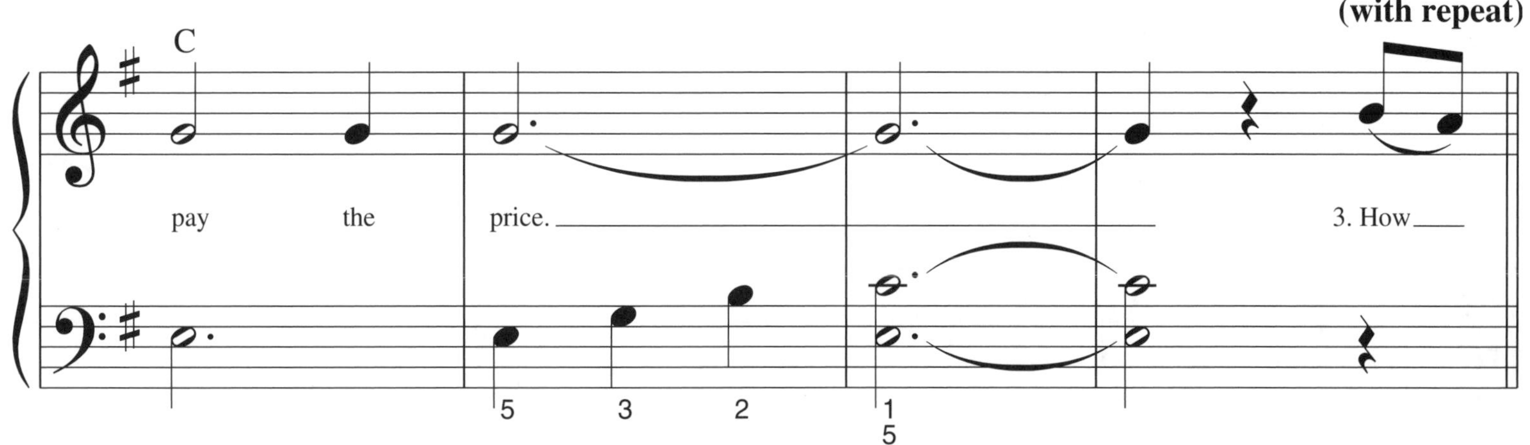

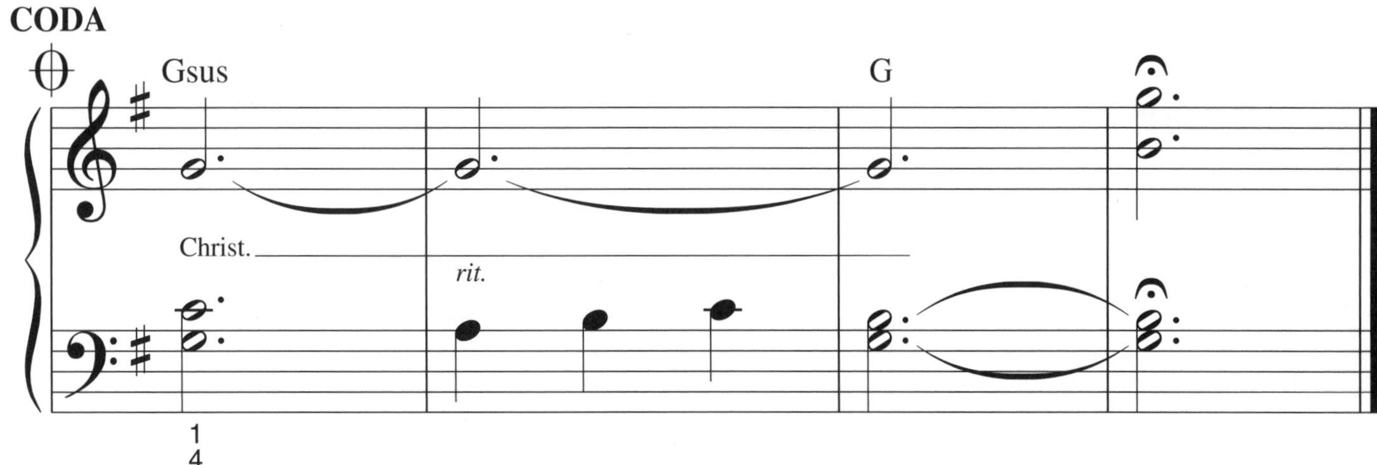

Additional Lyrics

2. How beautiful the heart that bled,
   That took all my sin and bore it instead.
   How beautiful the tender eyes,
   That choose to forgive and never despise.
   How beautiful, how beautiful,
   How beautiful is the body of Christ.

3. How beautiful the radiant bride,
   Who waits for her Groom with His light in her eyes.
   How beautiful when humble hearts give
   The fruit of pure lives so that others may live.
   How beautiful, how beautiful,
   How beautiful is the body of Christ.

4. How beautiful the feet that bring
   The sound of good news and the love of the King.
   How beautiful the hands that serve
   The wine and the bread and the sons of the earth.
   How beautiful, how beautiful,
   How beautiful is the body of Christ.

I WILL BE HERE

Words and Music by
STEVEN CURTIS CHAPMAN

Moderately, gently

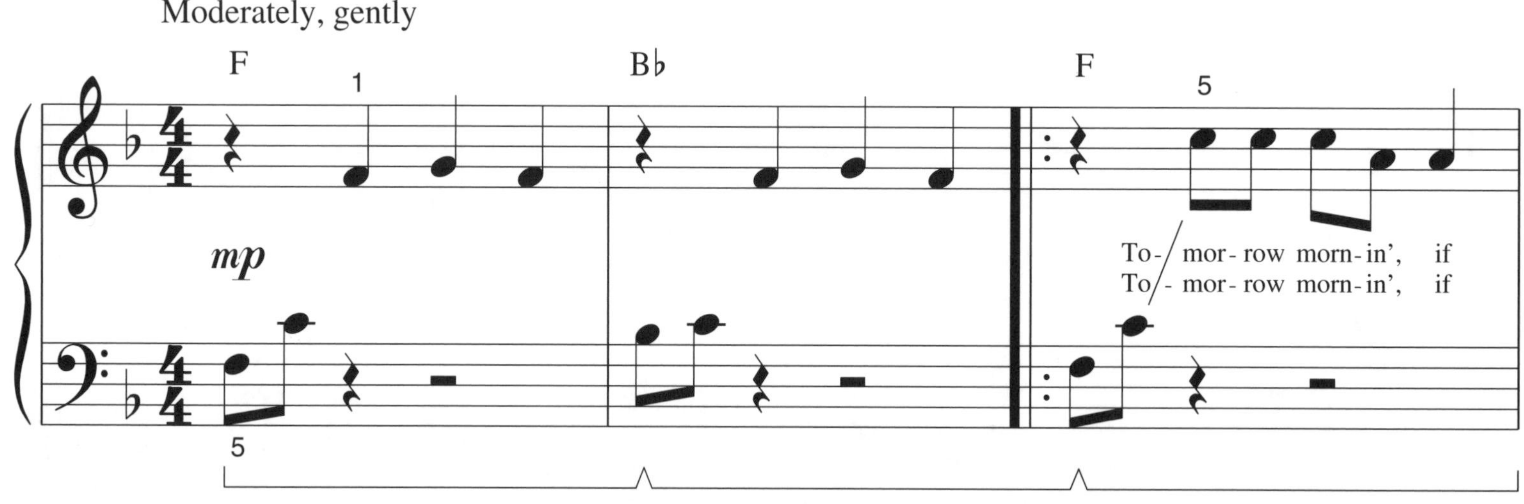

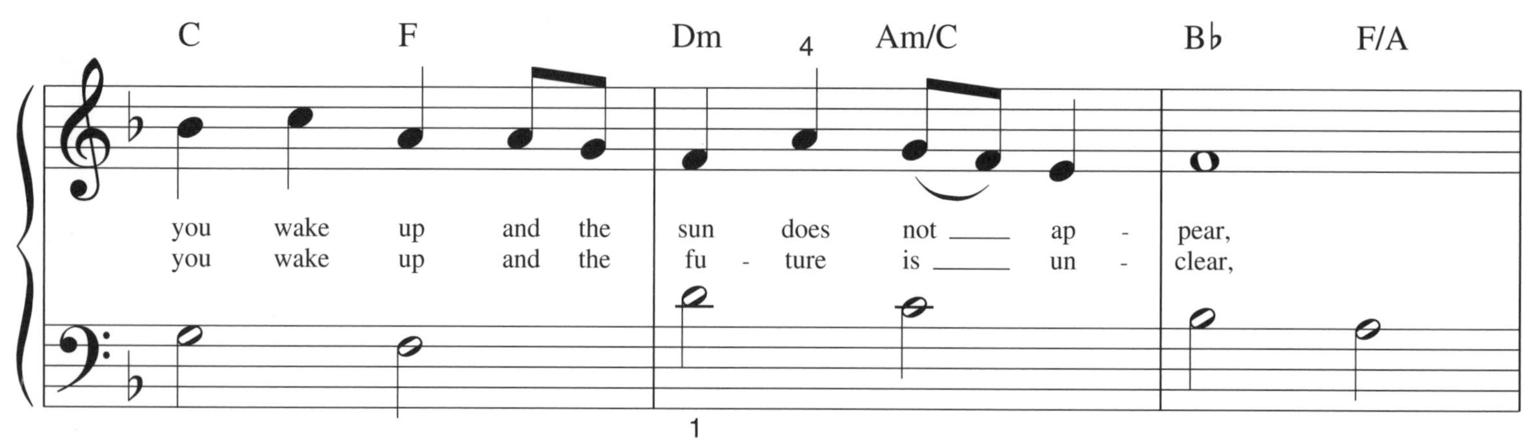

B♭
F
C
F
(mp)
If in the dark we lose sight of love, hold my
(D.S.) As sure as sea - sons are made for change, our

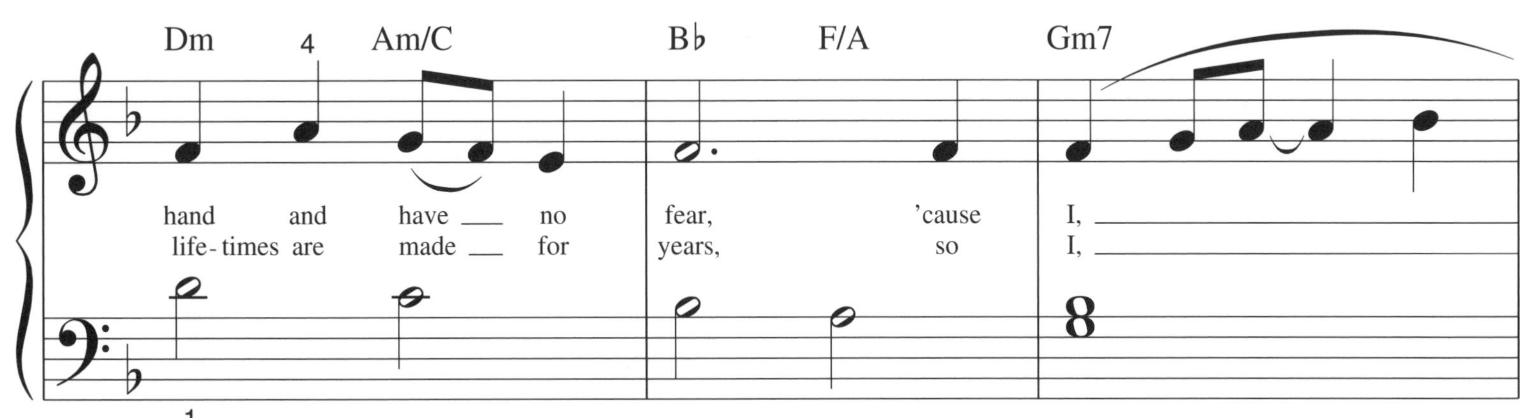
Dm
Am/C
B♭
F/A
Gm7
hand and have no fear, 'cause I,
life - times are made for years, so I,

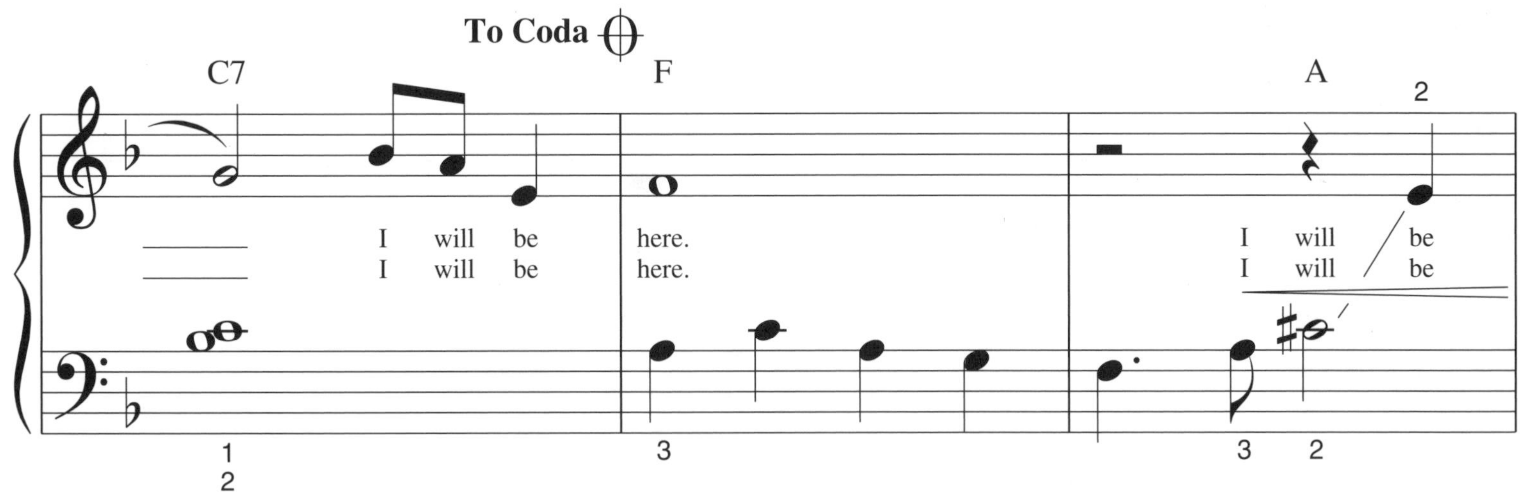
To Coda
C7
F
A
I will be here. I will be
I will be here. I will be

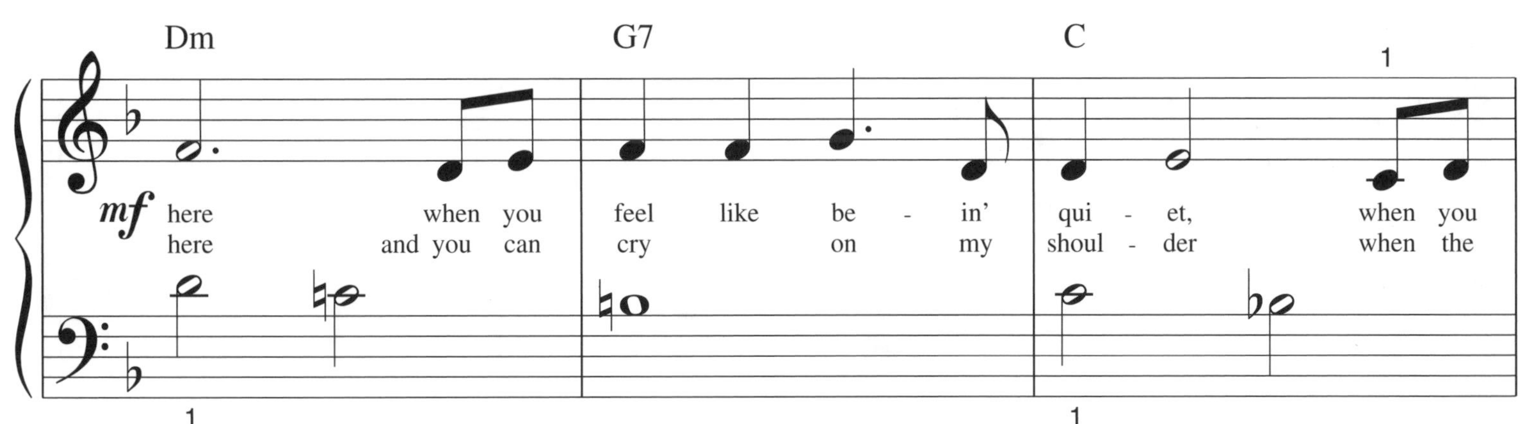
Dm
G7
C
mf
here when you feel like be - in' qui - et, when you
here and you can cry on my shoul - der when the

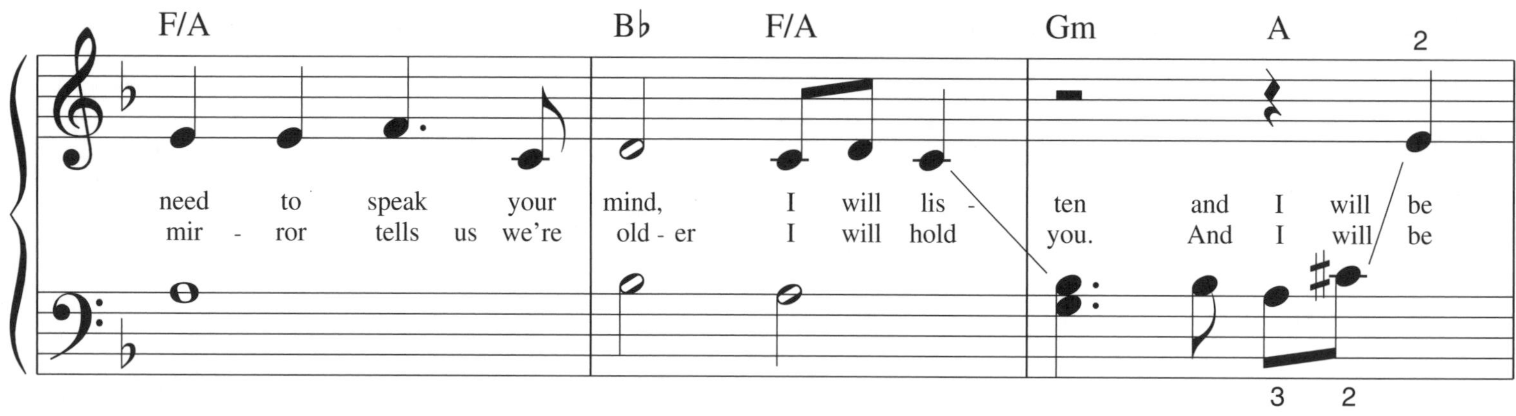
F/A
B♭
F/A
Gm
A
2
need to speak your mind, I will lis - ten and I will be
mir - ror tells us we're old - er I will hold you. And I will be
3 2

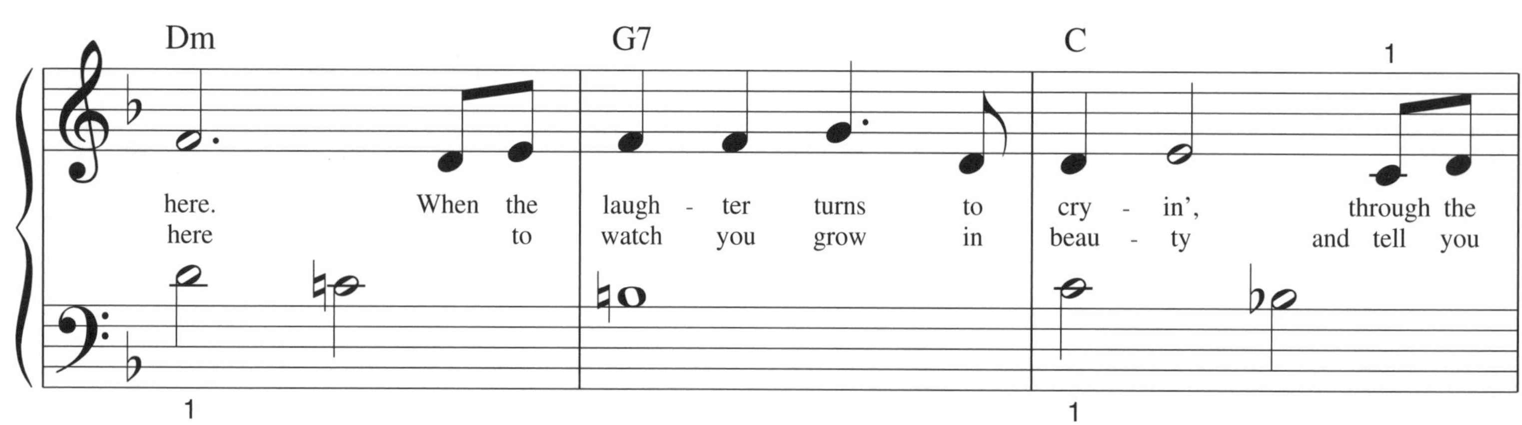
Dm
G7
C
1
here. When the laugh - ter turns to cry - in', through the
here to watch you grow in beau - ty and tell you
1
1

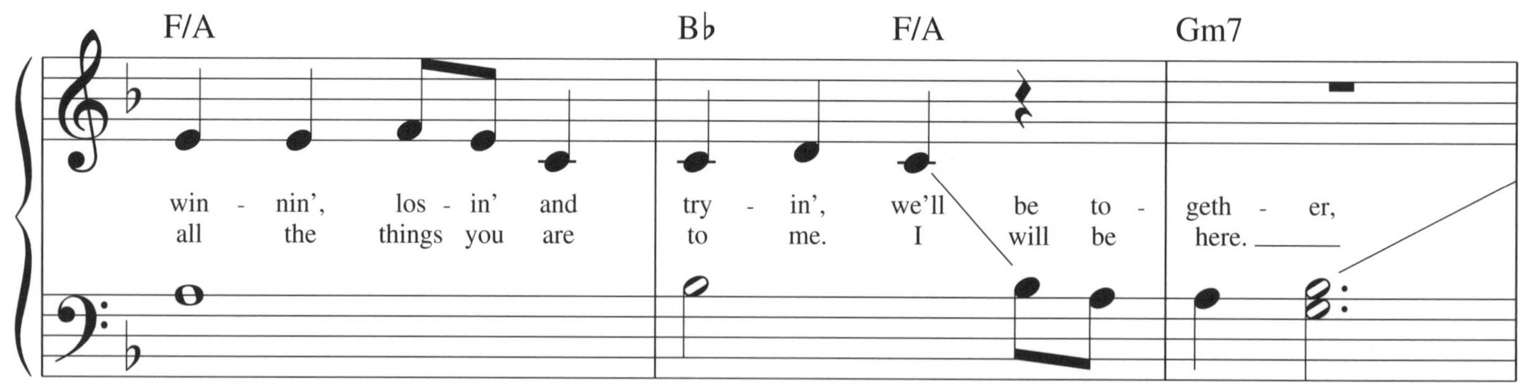
F/A
B♭
F/A
Gm7
win - nin', los - in' and try - in', we'll be to - geth - er,
all the things you are to me. I will be here.

1.
B♭/C
1
5
F
1
B♭
mp
'cause I will be here.
1
5
5

2.
B♭/C
A7/C♯
Dm
G7
C
Hmm
I will be true to the prom - ise I have
F
B♭
F/A
Gm7
B♭/C
made to you and to the One who gave you to
C7
D.S. al Coda
me.
CODA
F
Gm7
here.
I,
C7
F
I will be here.
p

IN CHRIST ALONE

Words and Music by DON KOCH
and SHAWN CRAIG

Slowly

F C/E Dm7

mp

G7

In Christ a -

C

lone will I glo - ry, though
lone will I glo - ry, for

Am Dm7 Am G

I could pride my - self in bat - tles won, for I've been
on - ly by His grace I am re - deemed. And on - ly

C Am Dm7

blessed be - yond meas - ure and by His strength a - lone I o - ver -
His ten - der mer - cy could reach be - yond my weak - ness to my

Gsus
G
F
G
come.
need.
Oh, I could stop and count suc -
Now I could seek no great - er

C
F/A
G
F
cess - es like dia - monds in my
hon - or than just to know Him
hand. But those
more and to

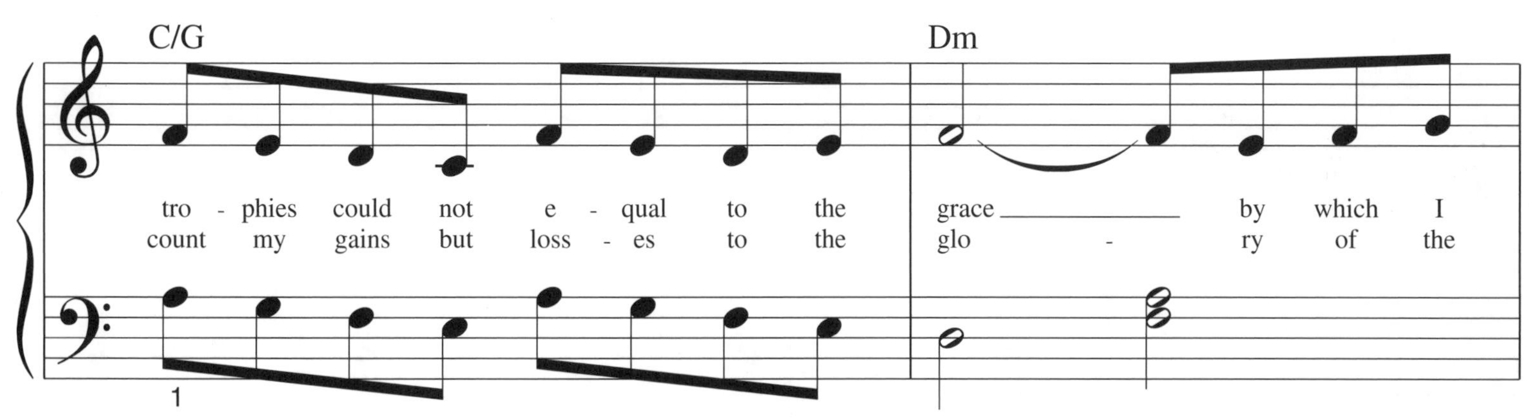
C/G
Dm
tro - phies could not e - qual to the
count my gains but loss - es to the
grace by which I
glo - ry of the
1

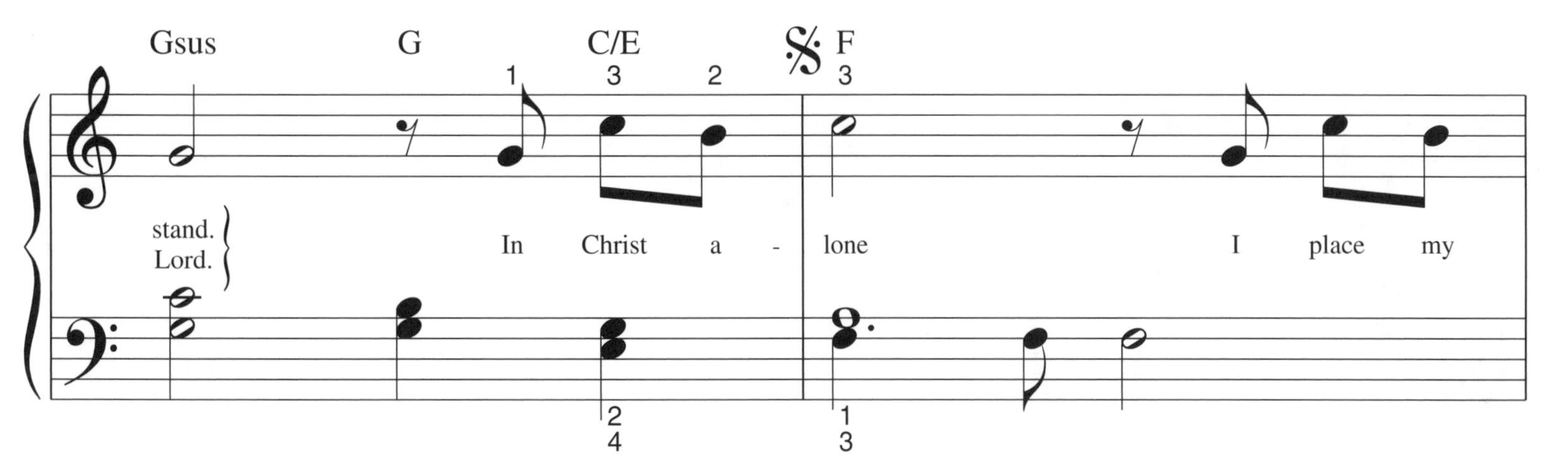
Gsus
G
C/E
F
1 3 2
3
stand.
Lord.
In Christ a -
lone I place my
2
4
1
3

C/E
Dm7
Gsus
G
trust and find my glo - ry in the pow - er of the
C
Am
Fmaj7
Gsus
G
cross. In ev - 'ry vic - to - ry, let it be
C
Am7
Dm7
To Coda
said of me, my source of strength, my
1.
Gsus
G
F
C/E
source of hope is Christ a - lone.

Dm7
G7
In Christ a -
2.
D.S. al Coda
CODA
Gsus
G
C/E
source of hope. In Christ a -
Gsus
G
source of hope is Christ a -
Am
Am/G
F
lone. My source of strength, my
Gsus
G
C
source of hope is Christ a - lone.
rit.

IN HIS PRESENCE

Words and Music by DICK TUNNEY
and MELODIE TUNNEY

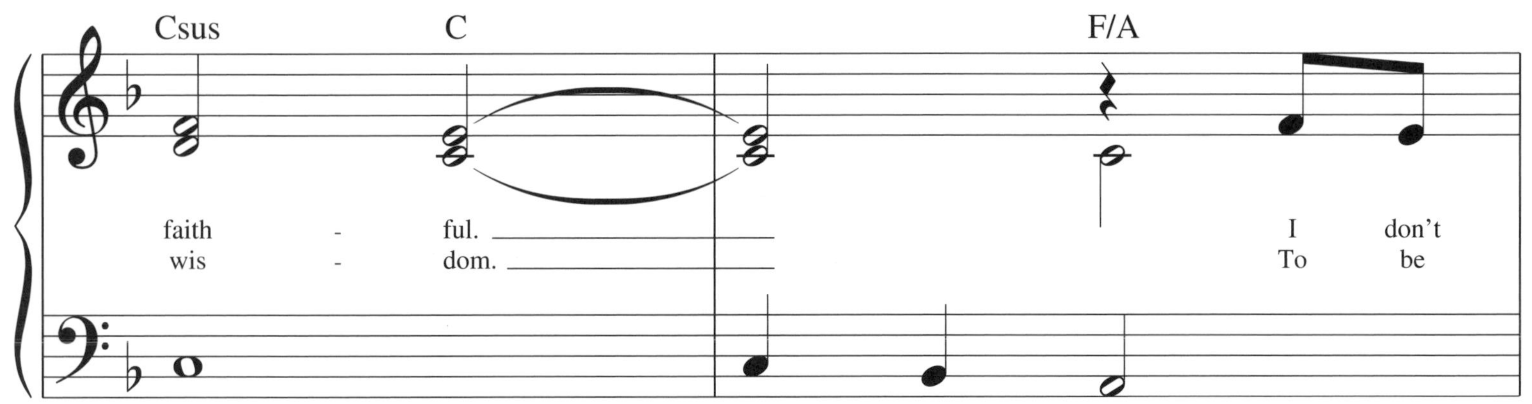
Csus
C
F/A
faith - ful.
wis - dom.
I don't
To be

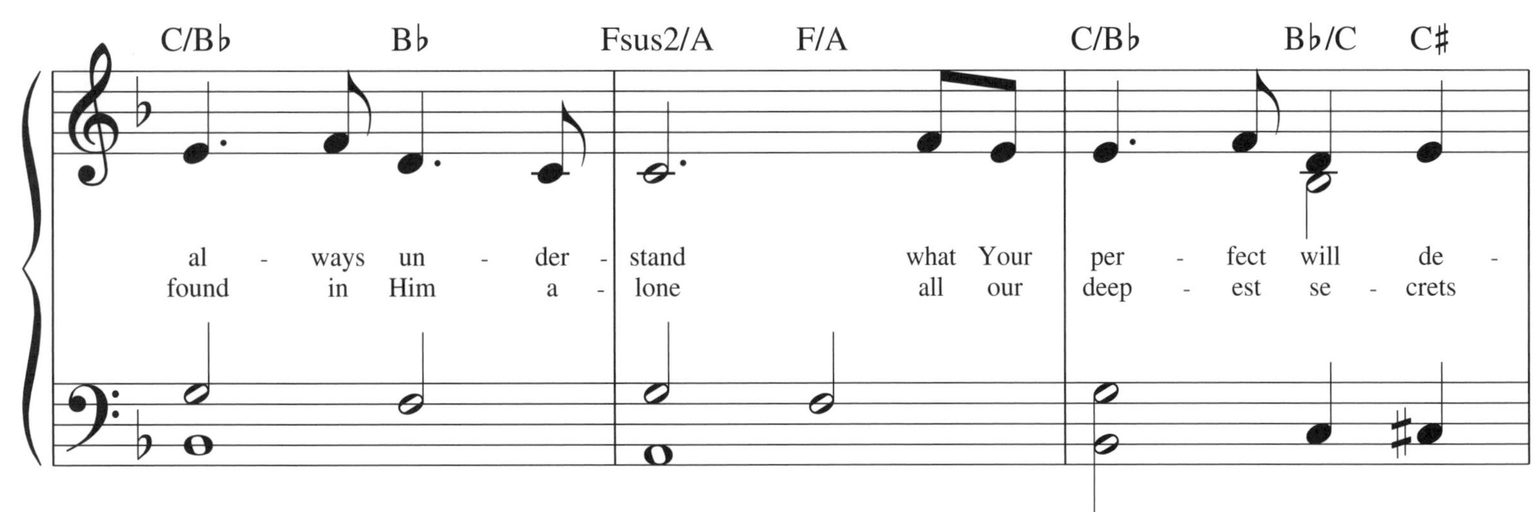
C/B♭
B♭
Fsus2/A
F/A
C/B♭
B♭/C
C♯
al - ways un - der - stand what Your per - fect will de -
found in Him a - lone all our deep - est se - crets

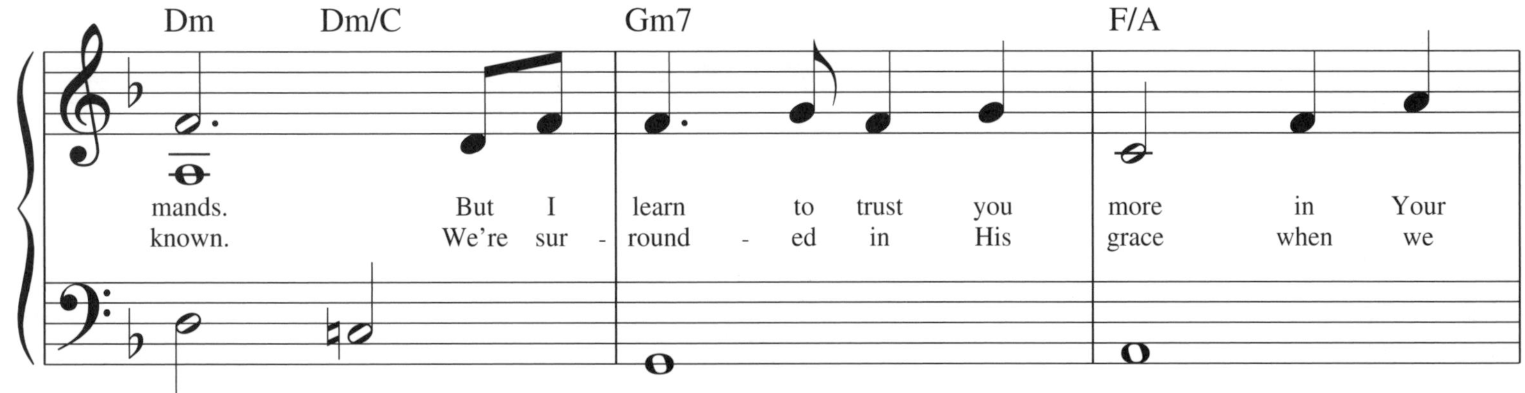
Dm
Dm/C
Gm7
F/A
mands. But I learn to trust you more in Your
known. We're sur - round - ed in His grace when we

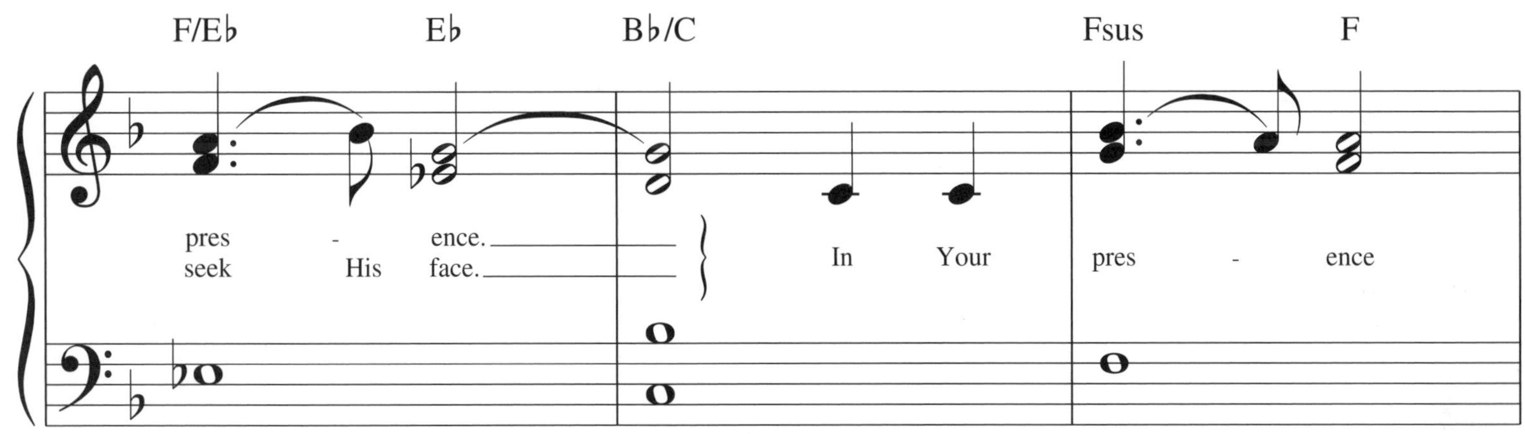
F/E♭
E♭
B♭/C
Fsus
F
pres - ence.
seek His face.
In Your pres - ence

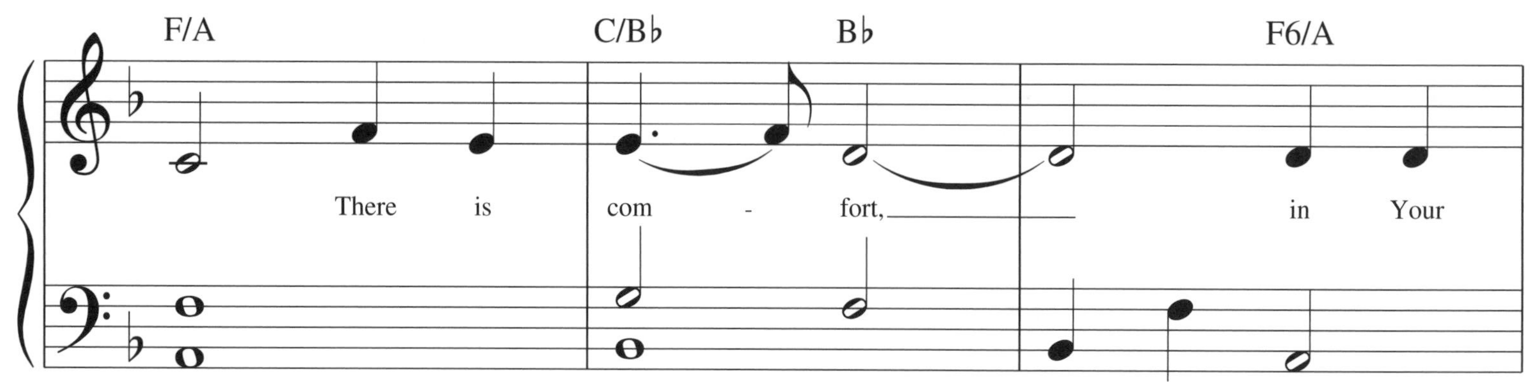
F/A
C/B♭
B♭
F6/A
There is com - fort, in Your

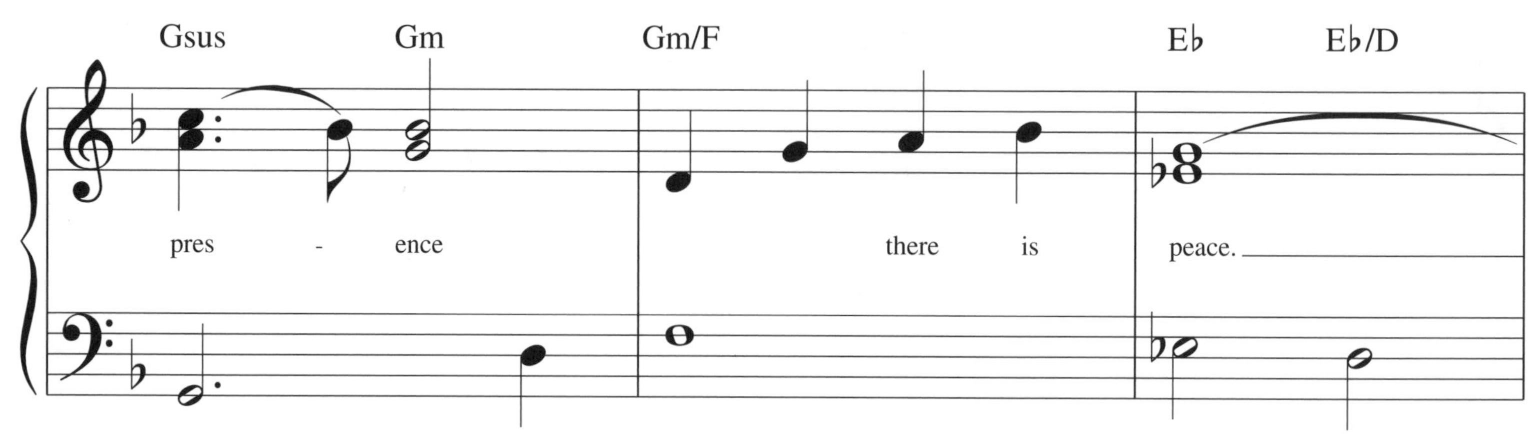
Gsus
Gm
Gm/F
E♭
E♭/D
pres - ence there is peace.

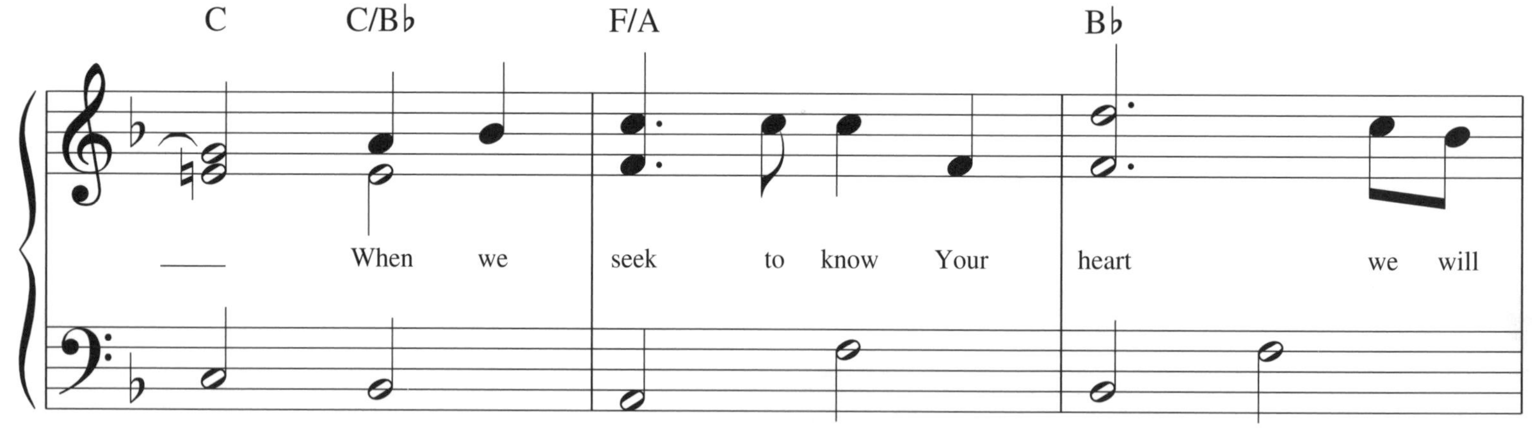
C
C/B♭
F/A
B♭
When we seek to know Your heart we will

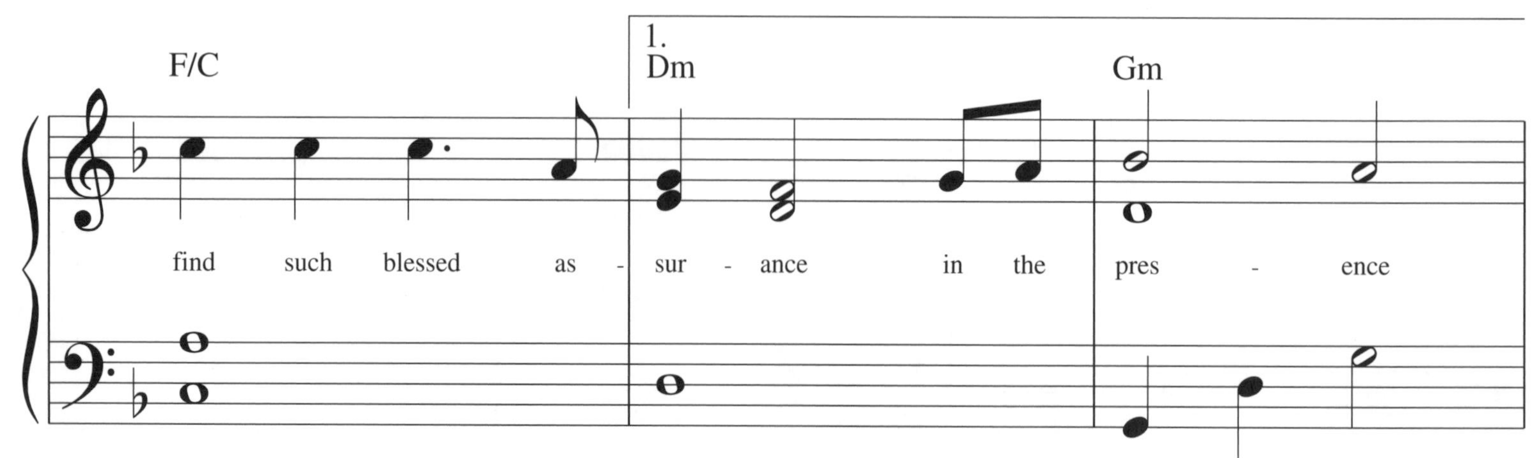
F/C
1.
Dm
Gm
find such blessed as - sur - ance in the pres - ence

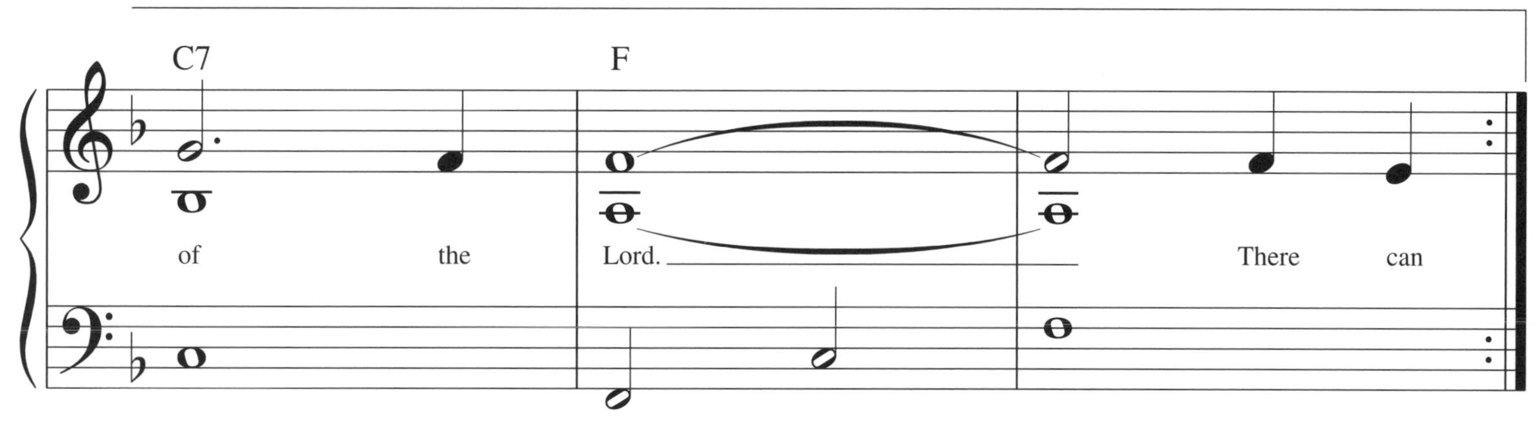
C7
F
of the Lord. There can

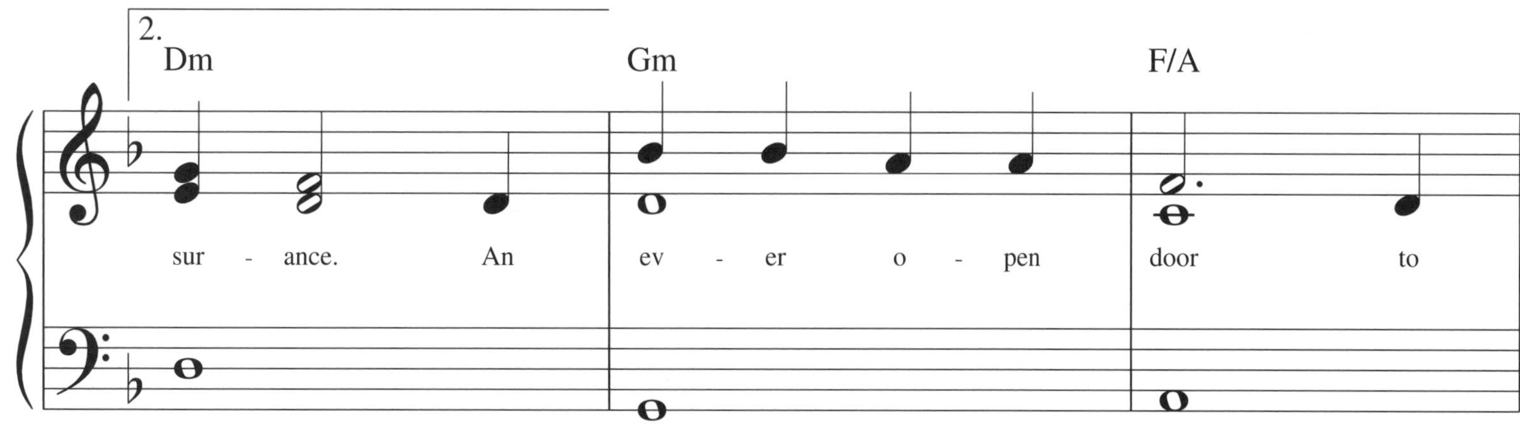
2.
Dm
Gm
F/A
sur - ance. An ev - er o - pen door to

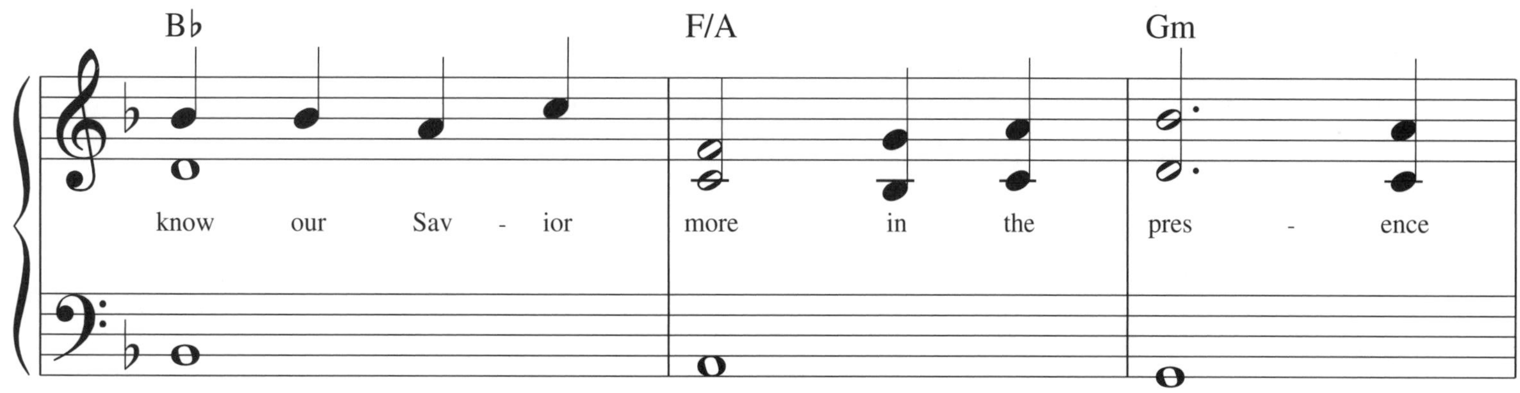
B♭
F/A
Gm
know our Sav - ior more in the pres - ence

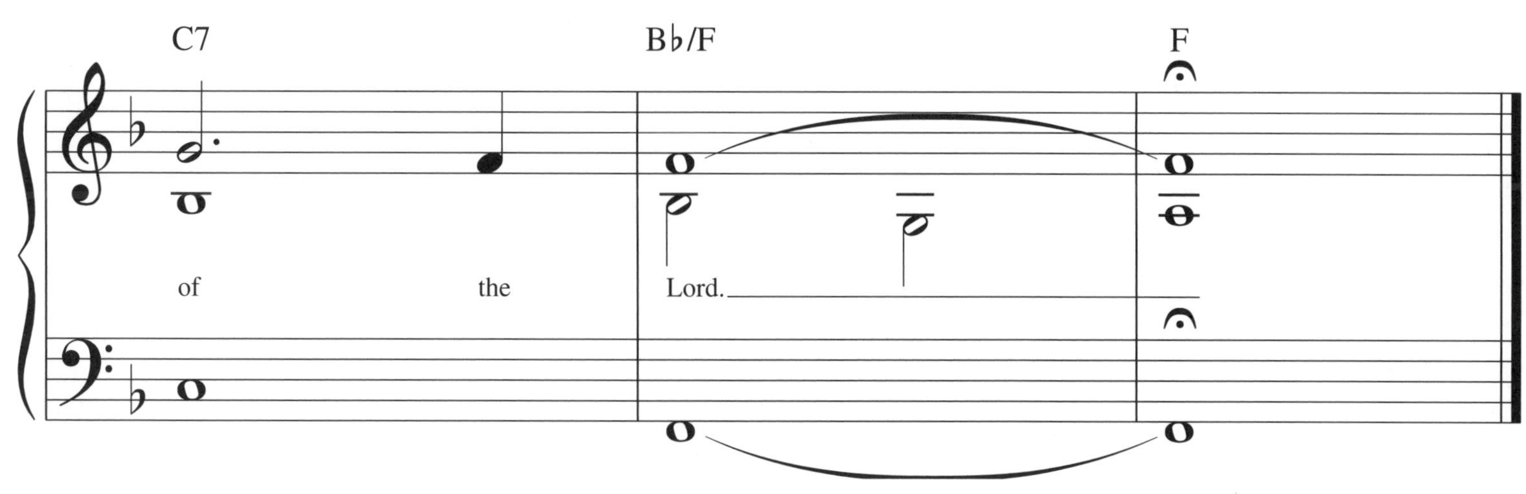
C7
B♭/F
F
of the Lord.

JESUS WILL STILL BE THERE

Words and Music by ROBERT STERLING
and JOHN MANDEVILLE

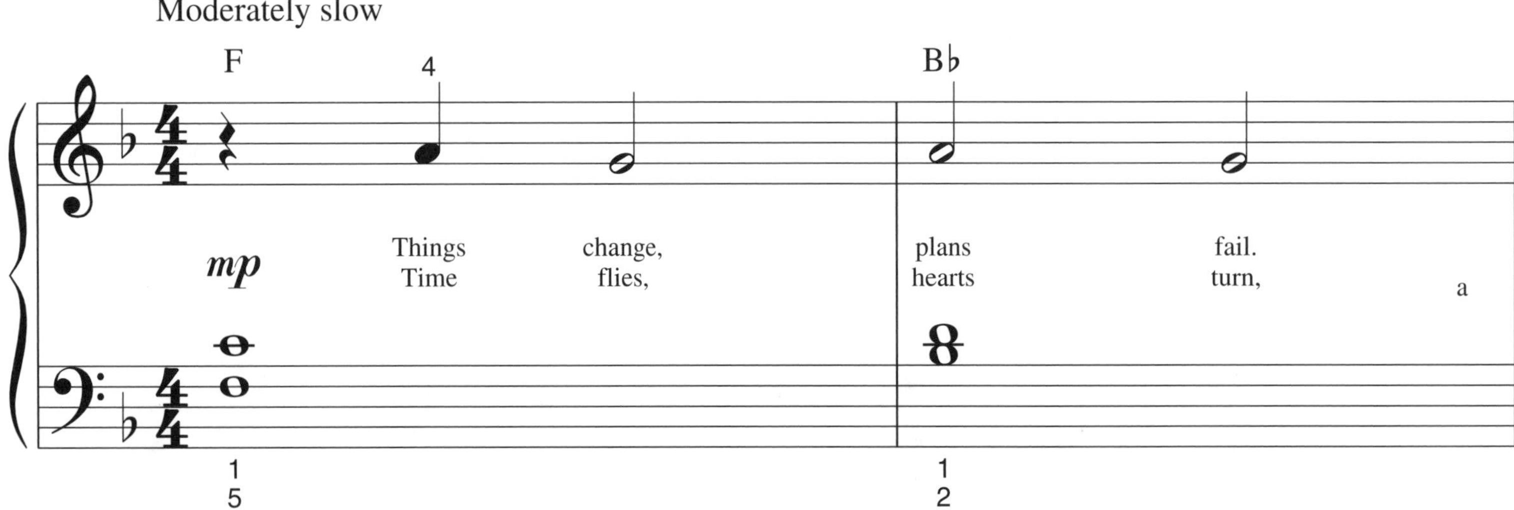

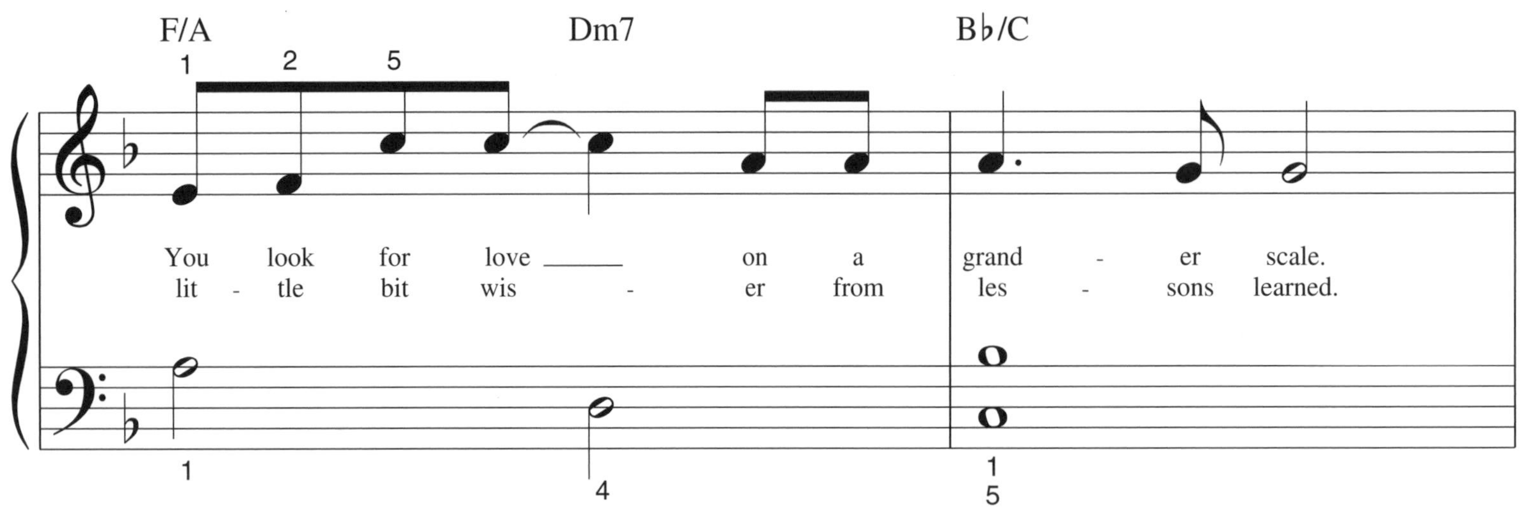

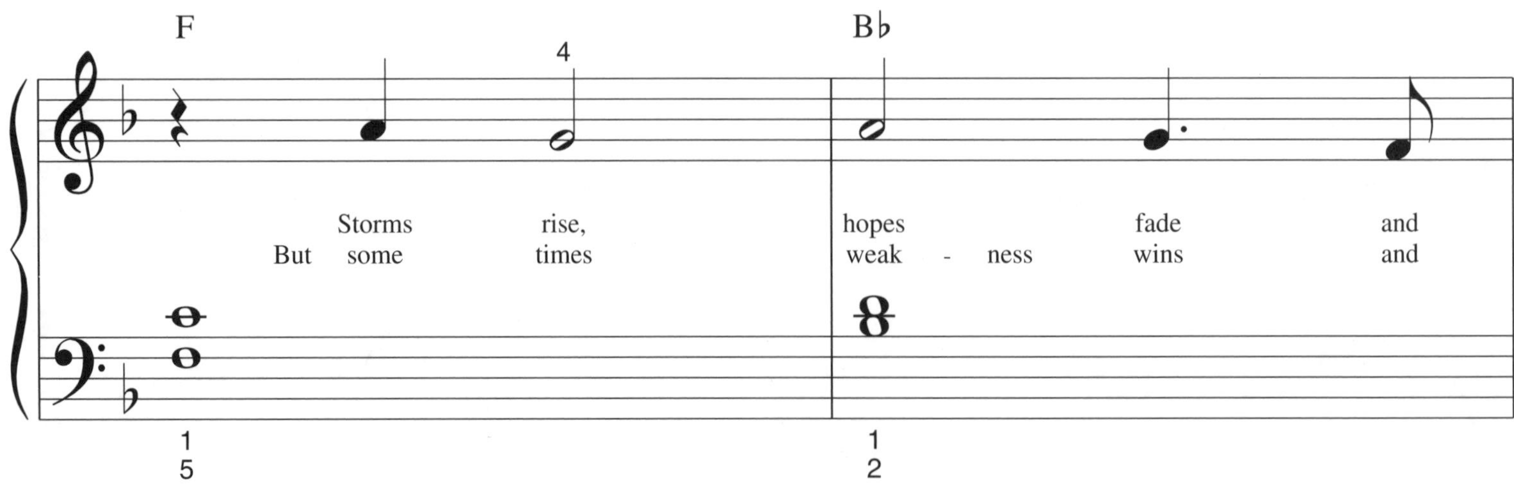

F/A Dm7 B♭/C Dm F/C
you place your bets on a - noth - er day. When the go - ing gets tough, when the
you lose your foot - hold once a - gain.
B♭ F/A Gm7 Gm/F C/E B♭/C
ride's too rough, when you're just not sure e - nough, Je - sus will
F C/E B♭/D C Gm Gm/F
still be there. His love will nev - er change. Sure as a
C B♭/C F C/E B♭/D C
stead - y rain, Je - sus will still be there. When no one else is

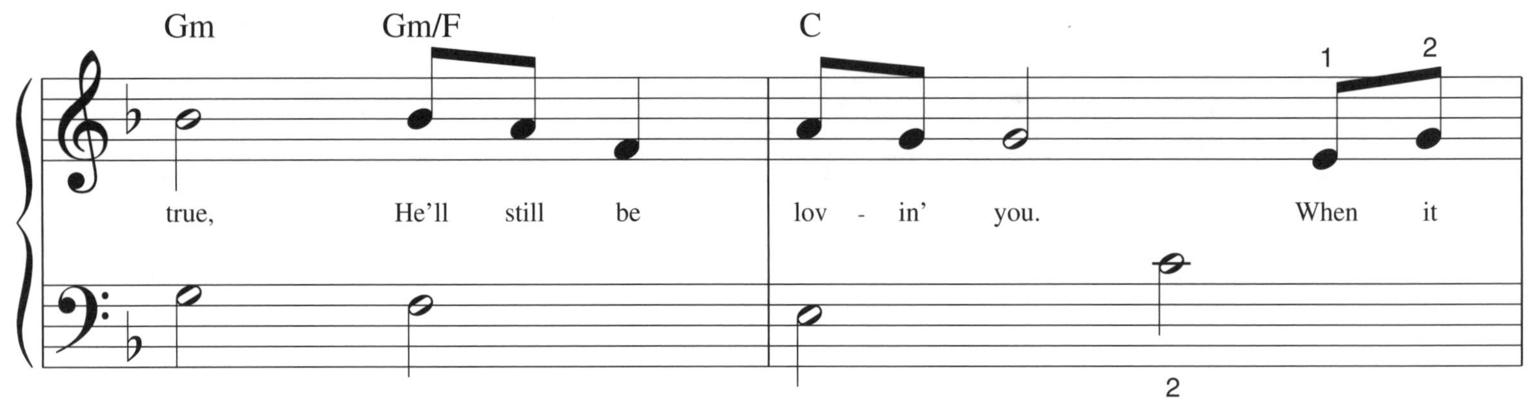
Gm
Gm/F
C
1
2
true, He'll still be lov - in' you. When it
2

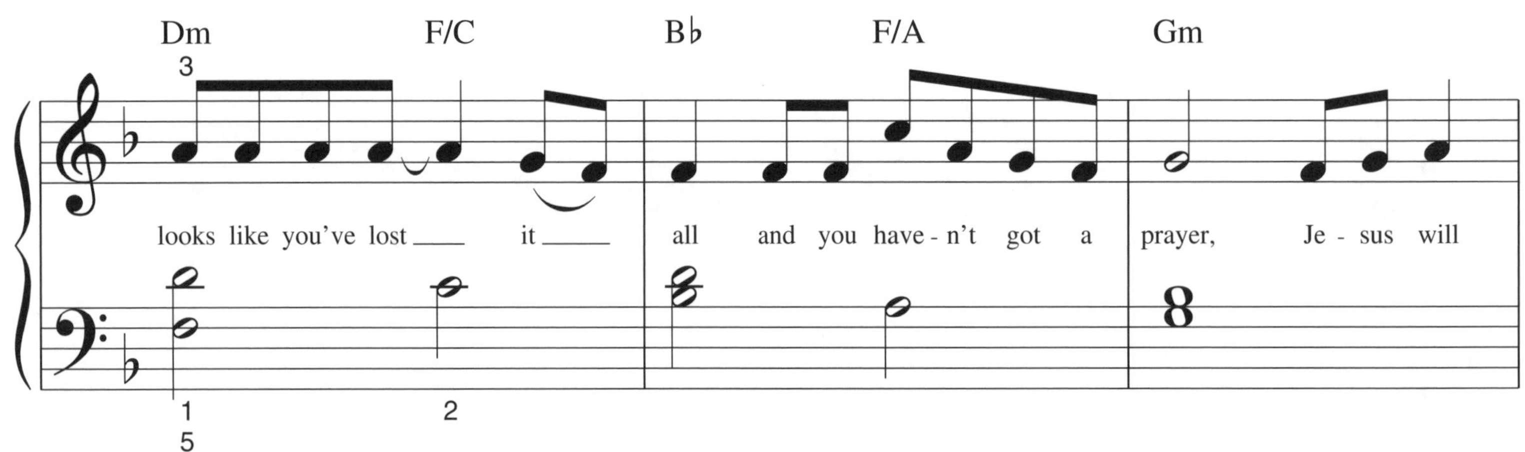
Dm
F/C
B♭
F/A
Gm
3
looks like you've lost ___ it ___ all and you have - n't got a prayer, Je - sus will
1
5
2

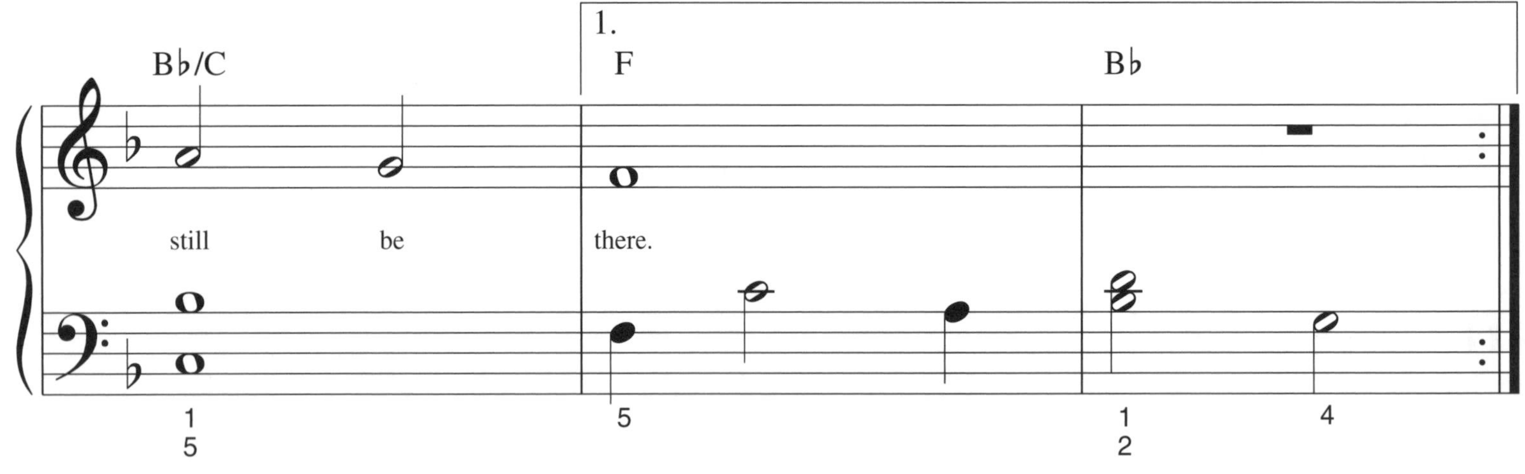
B♭/C
1.
F
B♭
still be there.
1
5
5
1
2
4

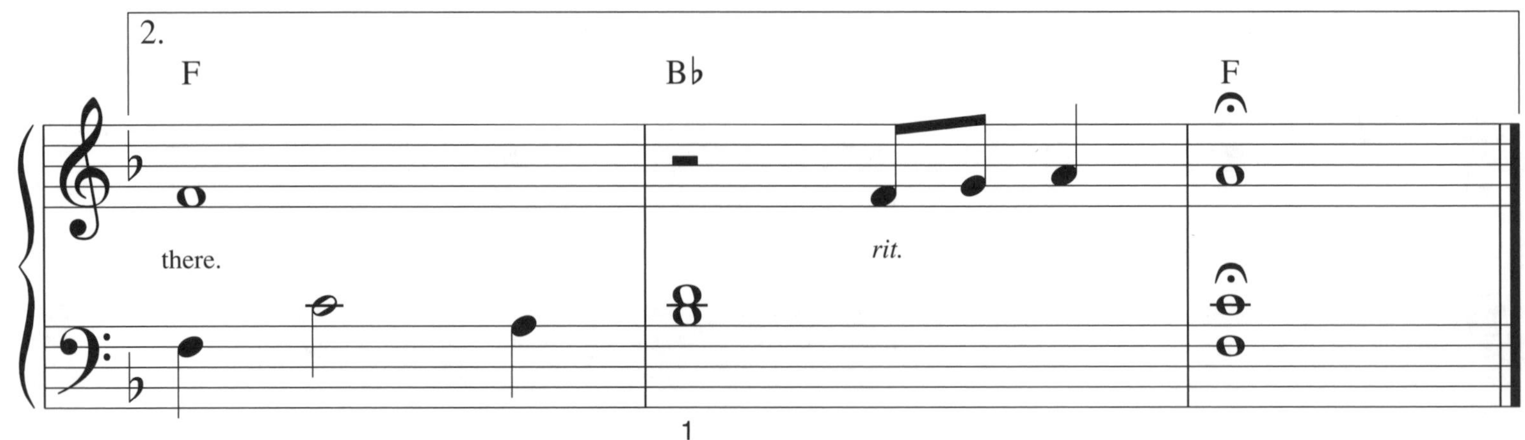
2.
F
B♭
F
there.
rit.
1
2

LET US PRAY

Words and Music by
STEVEN CURTIS CHAPMAN

58

C
Am
1
And in keep - ing with ___ con - ven - tion, I'll say
Let the Fa - ther hear ___ us say - ing what we

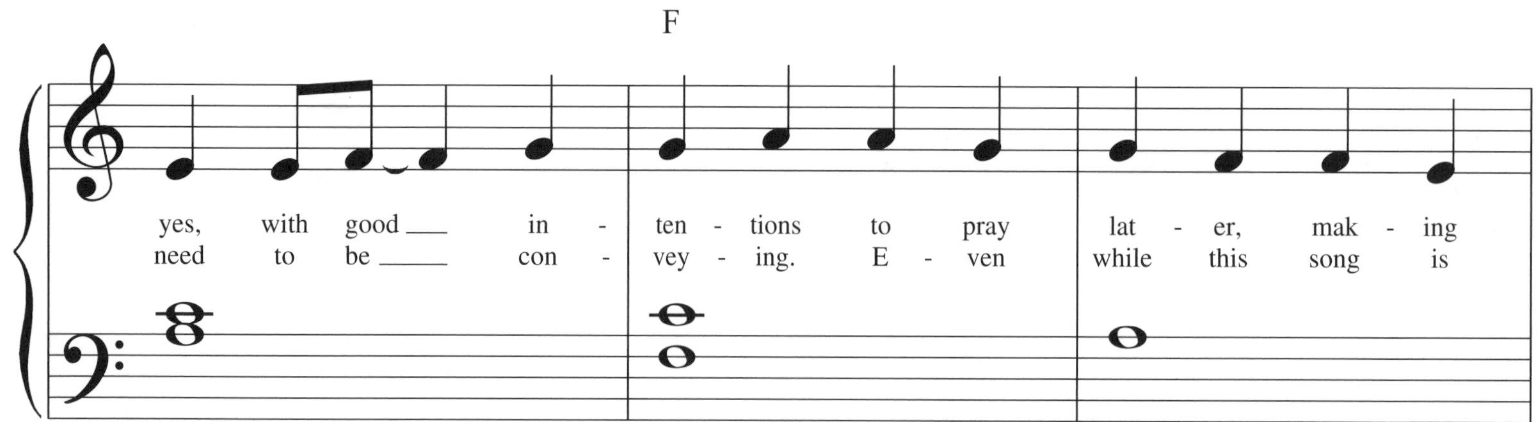
F
yes, with good ___ in - ten - tions to pray lat - er, mak - ing
need to be ___ con - vey - ing. E - ven while this song is

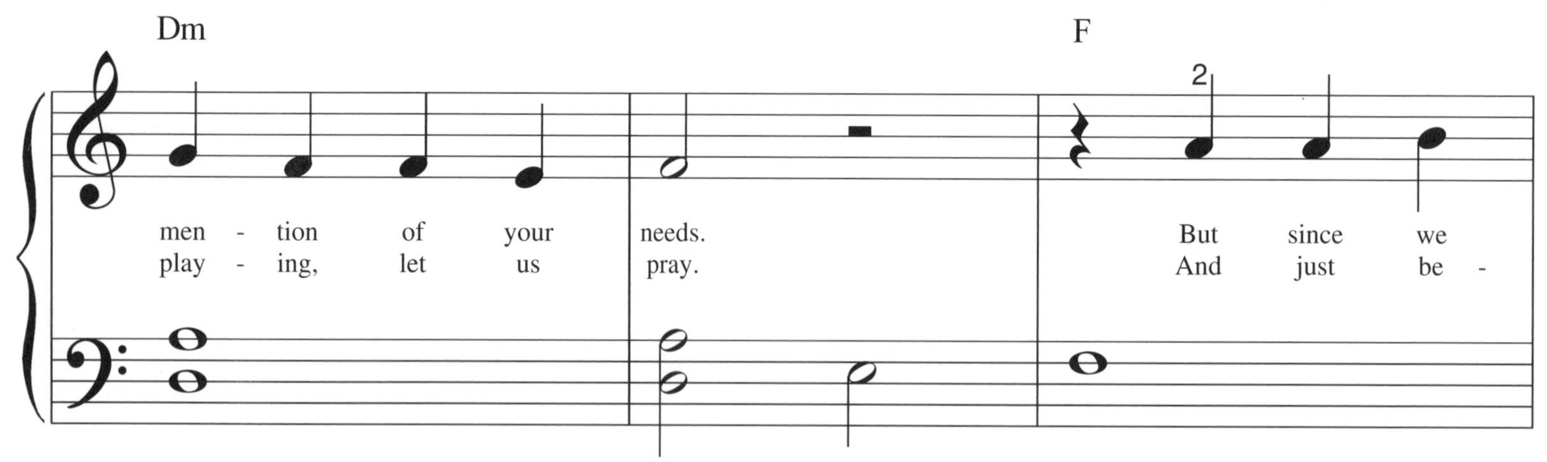
Dm
F
2
men - tion of your needs. But since we
play - ing, let us pray. And just be -

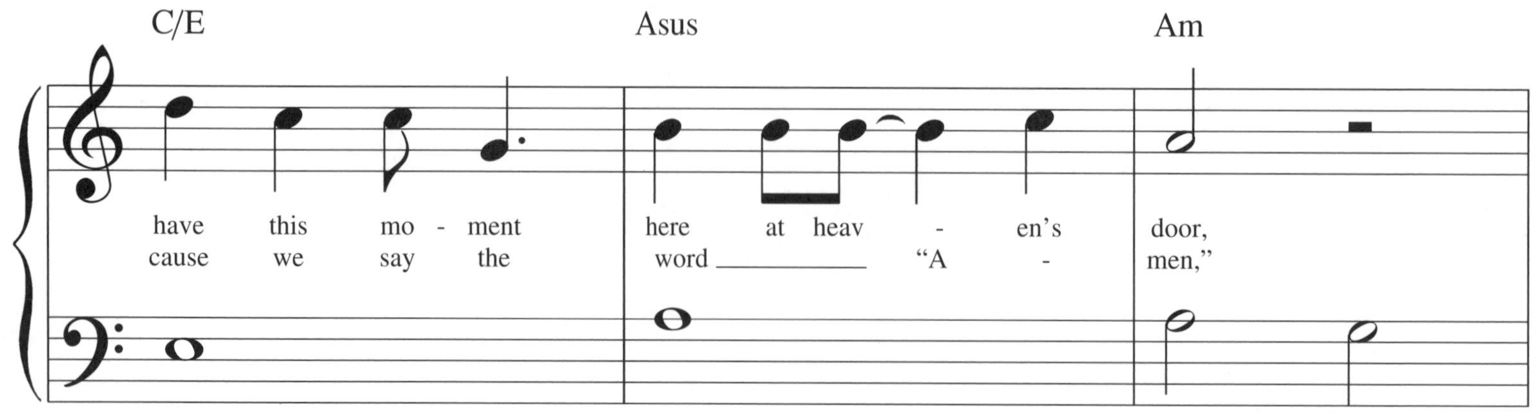
C/E
Asus
Am
have this mo - ment here at heav - en's door,
cause we say the word ___ "A - men,"

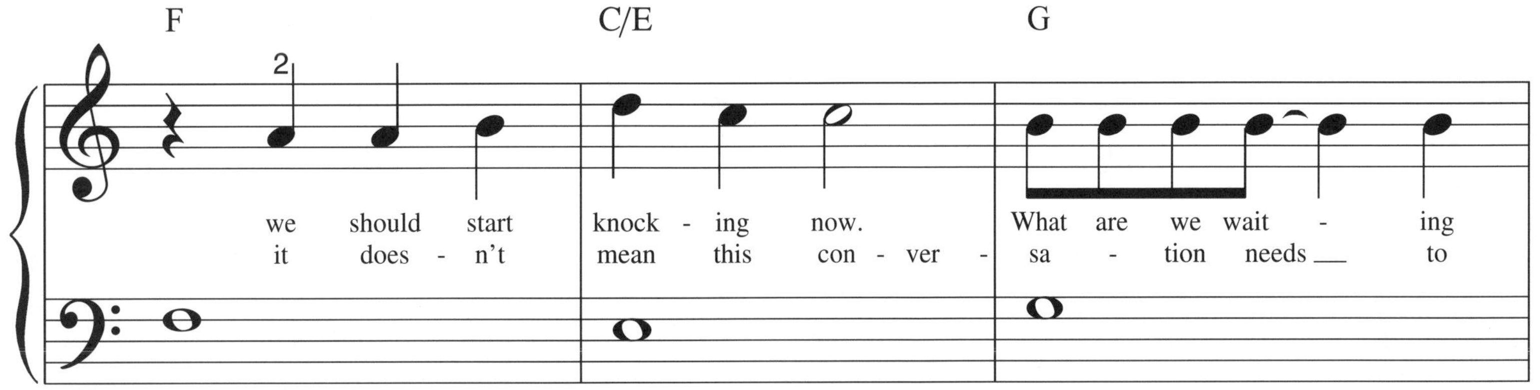
F
C/E
G
2
we should start knocking - ing now. What are we wait - ing
it does - n't mean this con - ver - sa - tion needs to

Am
F
C/E
3
for? end. Let us pray, let us pray, ev - 'ry -

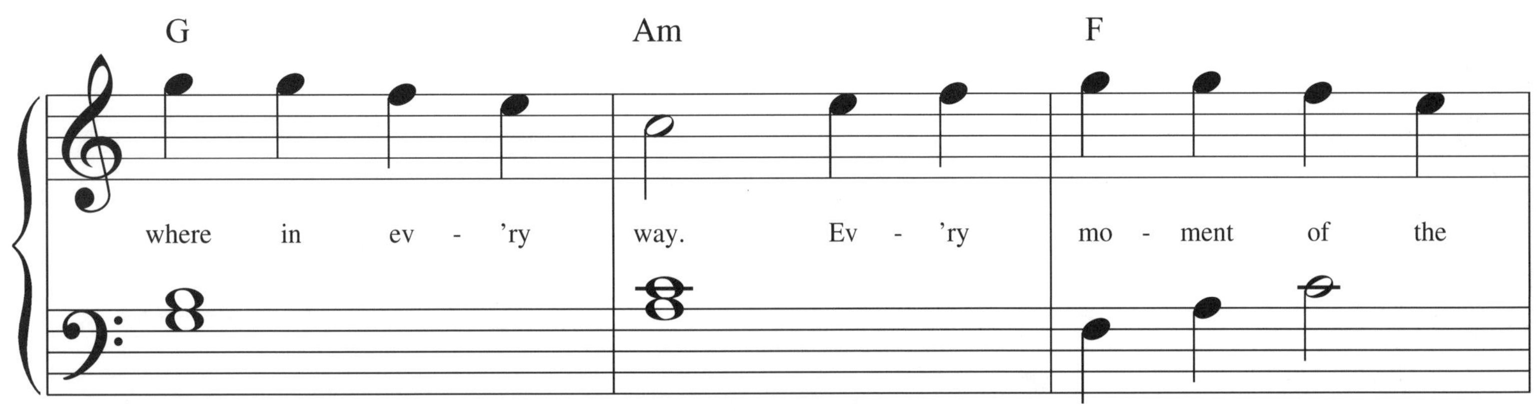
G
Am
F
where in ev - 'ry way. Ev - 'ry mo - ment of the

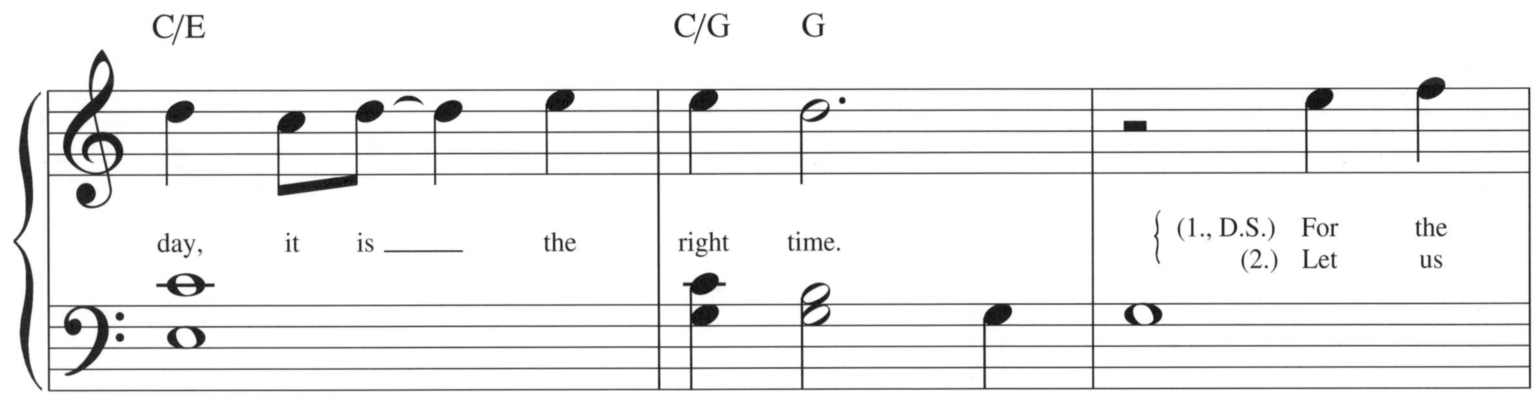
C/E
C/G
G
day, it is the right time.
(1., D.S.) For the
(2.) Let us

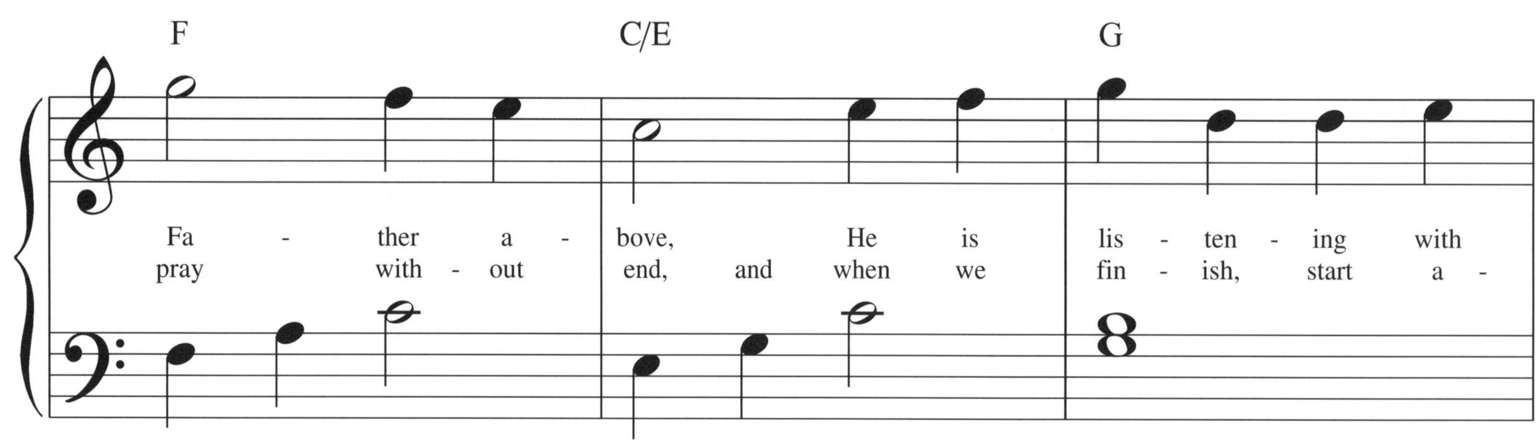
F
C/E
G
Fa - ther a - bove, He is lis - ten - ing with
pray with - out end, and when we fin - ish, start a -

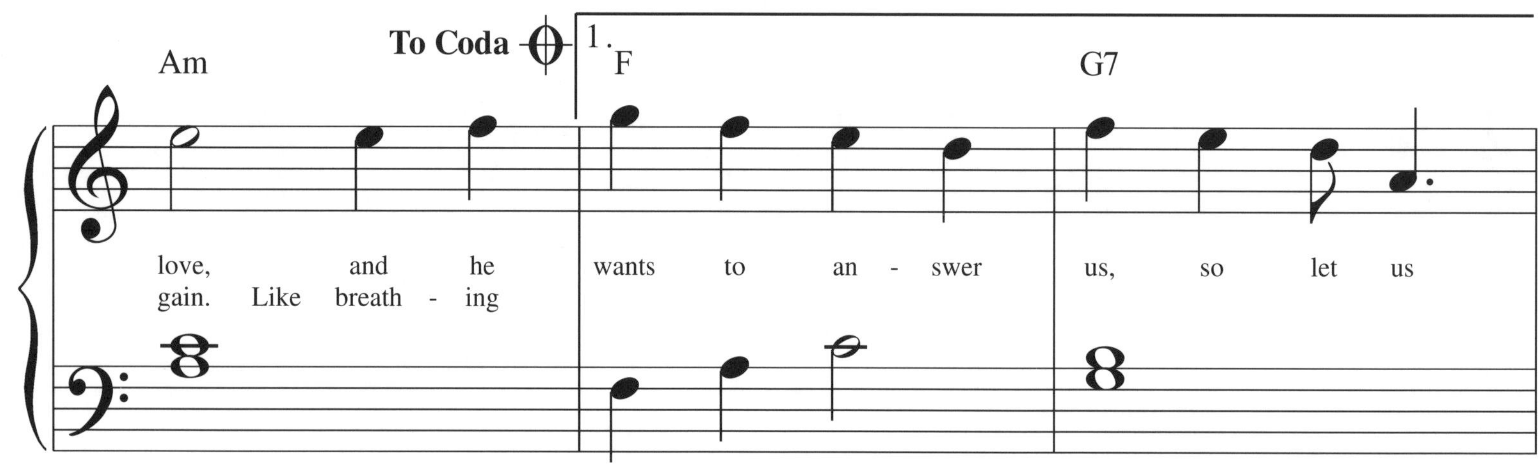
Am
To Coda
1.
F
G7
love, and he wants to an - swer us, so let us
gain. Like breath - ing

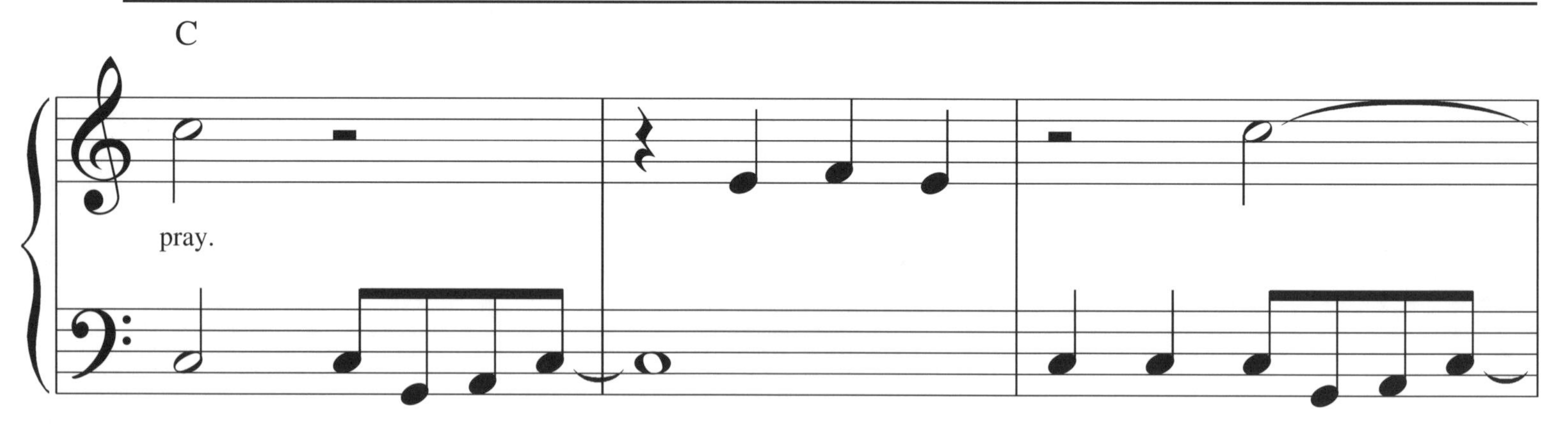
C
pray.

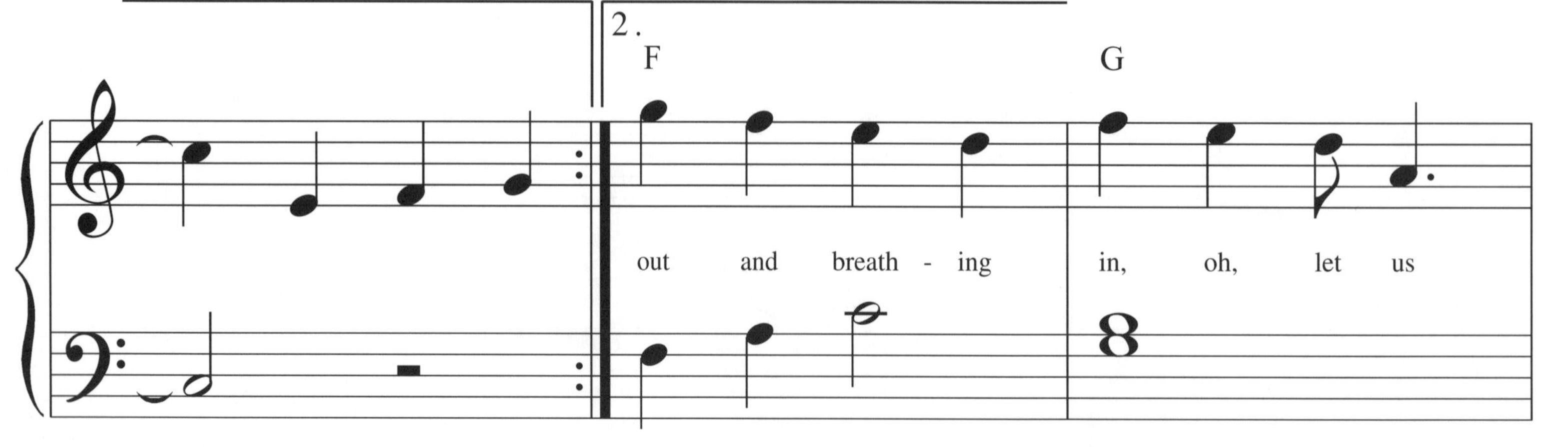
2.
F
G
out and breath - ing in, oh, let us

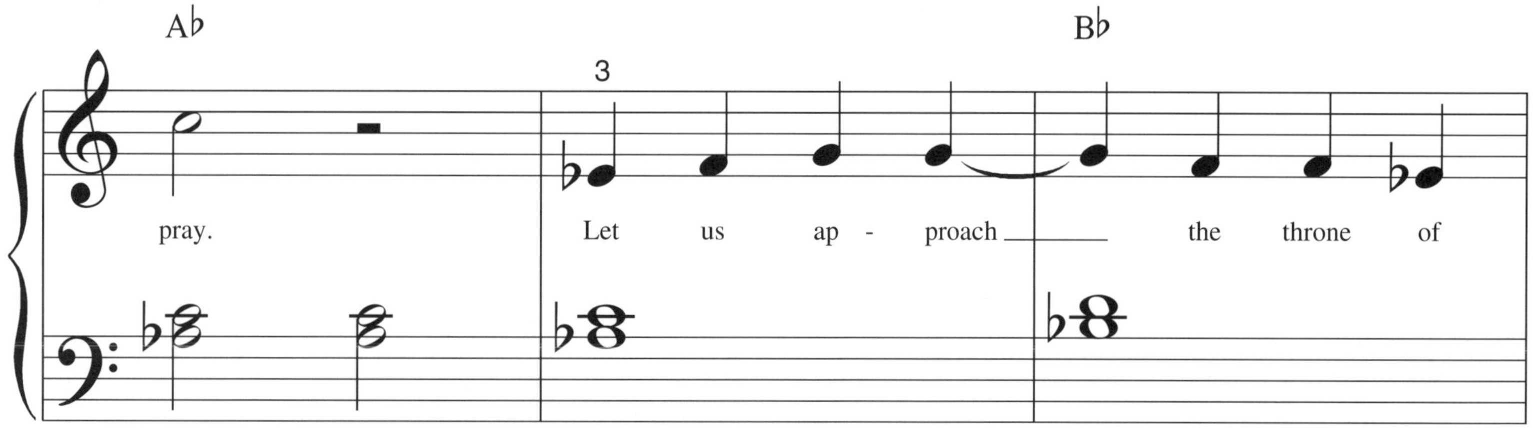
A♭
B♭
3
pray.
Let us ap - proach the throne of

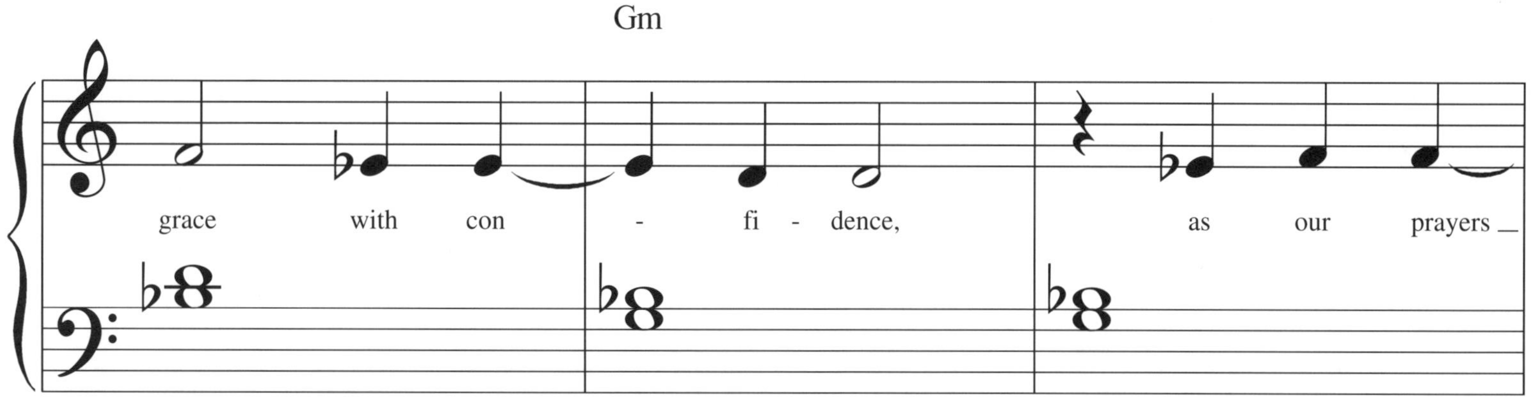
Gm
grace with con - fi - dence, as our prayers

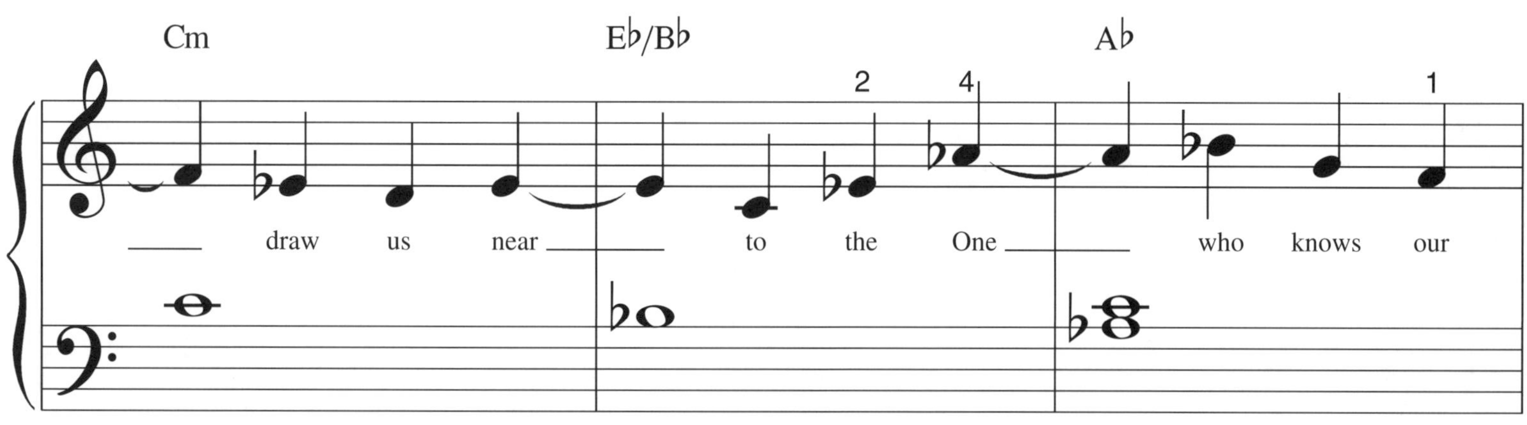
Cm
E♭/B♭
A♭
2
4
1
draw us near to the One who knows our

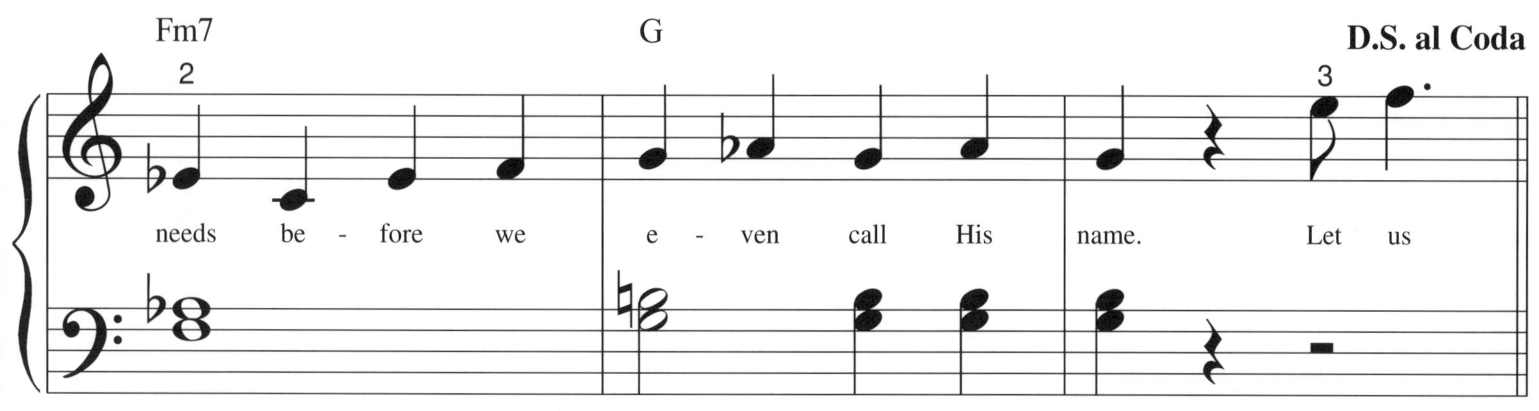
Fm7
G
D.S. al Coda
2
3
needs be - fore we e - ven call His name. Let us

CODA
F
G
F
4
wants to an - swer
us. Oh, let us
pray, let us

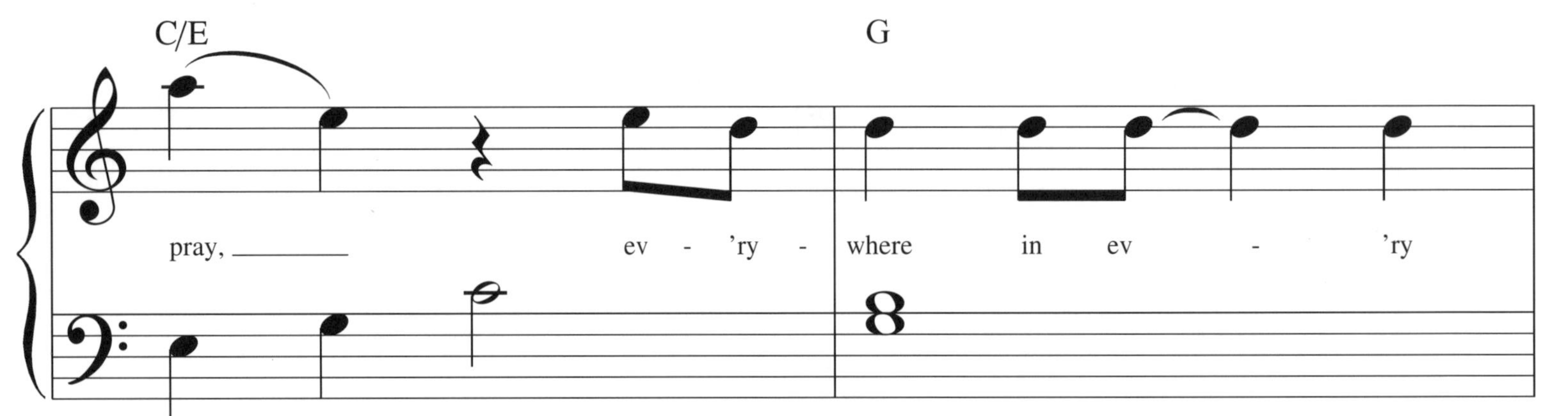
C/E
G
pray, ev - 'ry -
where in ev - 'ry

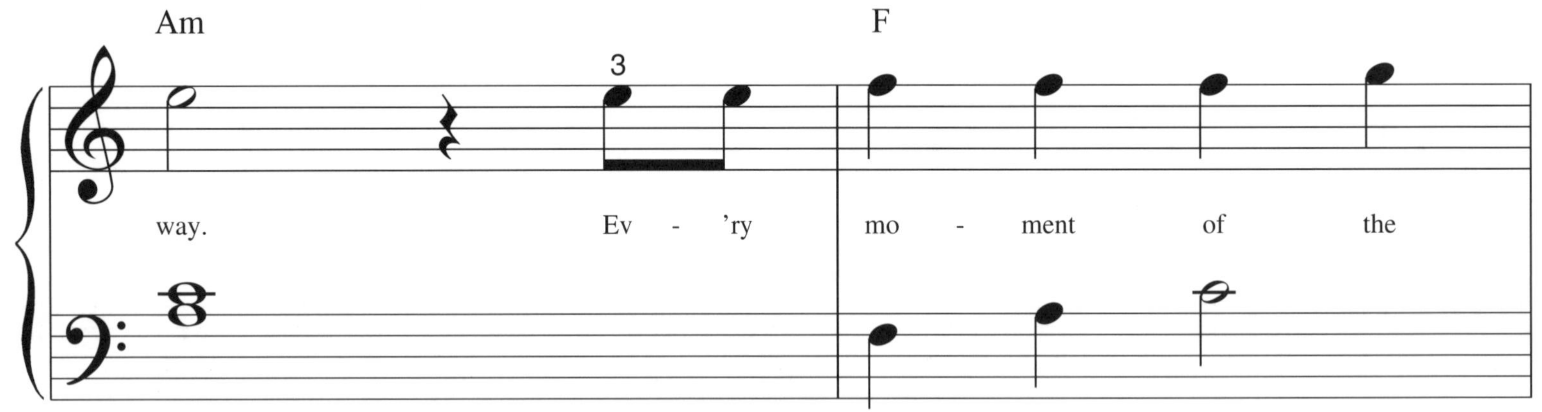
Am
F
3
way. Ev - 'ry
mo - ment of the

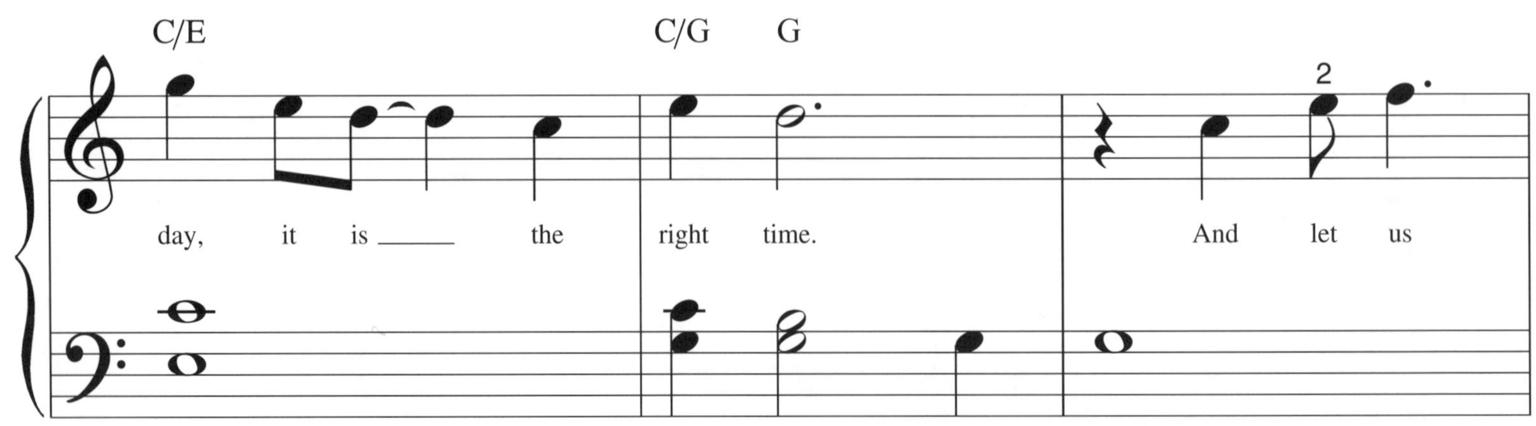
C/E
C/G G
2
day, it is the
right time.
And let us

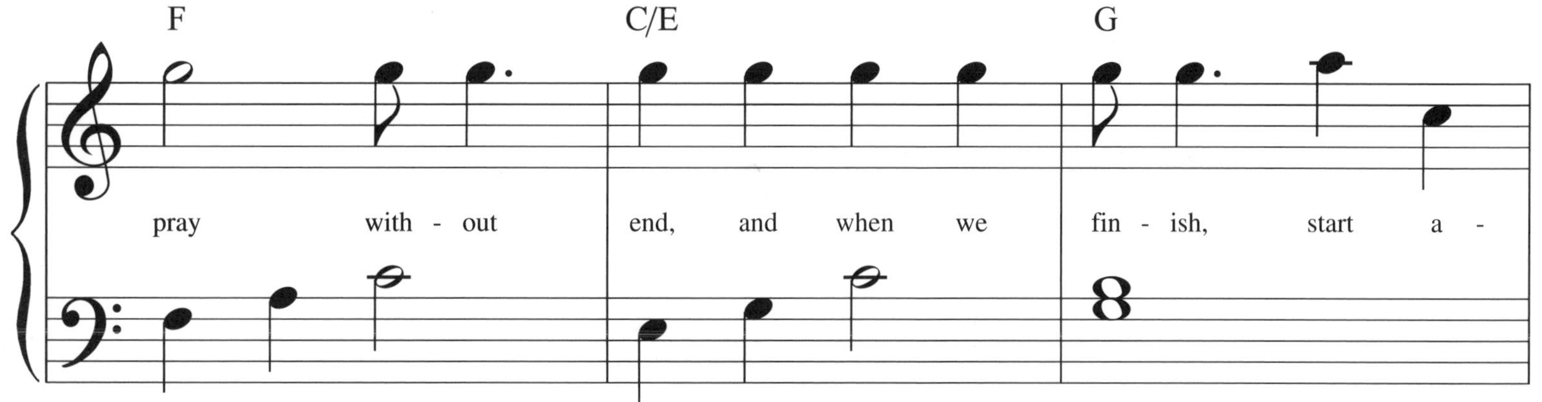
F
C/E
G
pray with - out
end, and when we
fin - ish, start a -

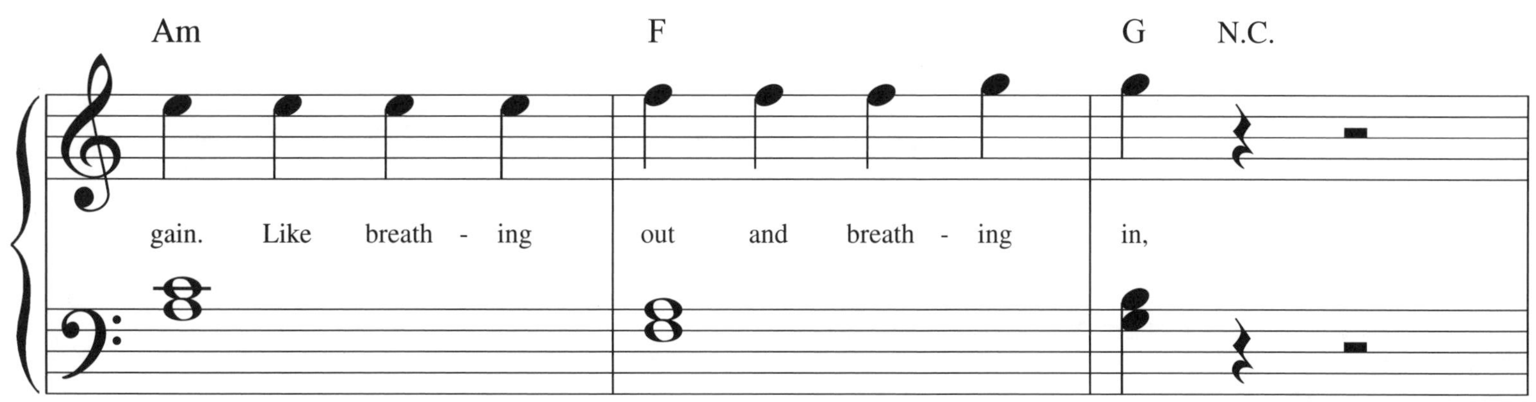
Am
F
G N.C.
gain. Like breath - ing
out and breath - ing
in,

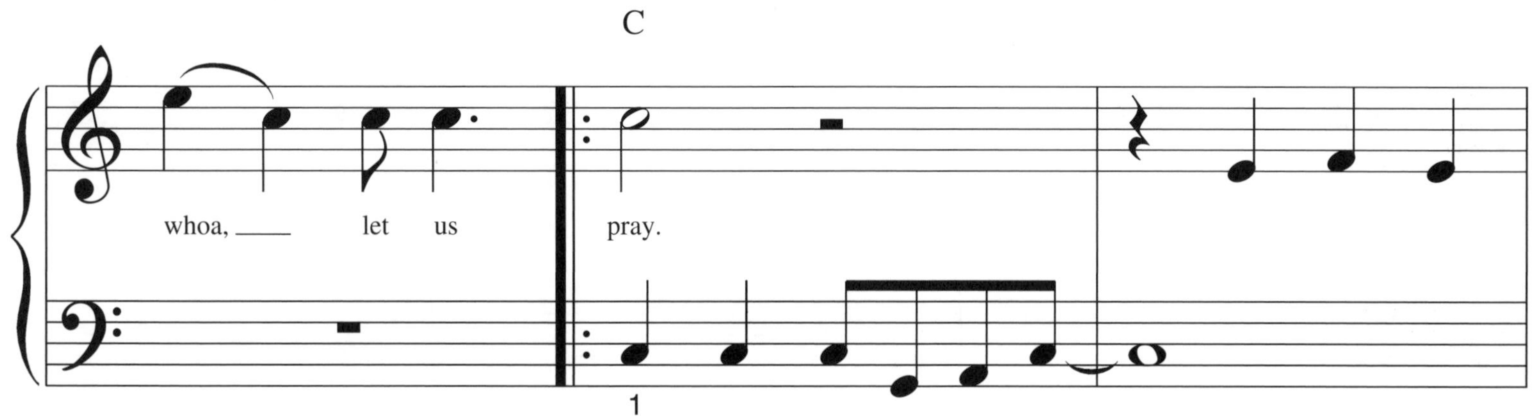
C
whoa, ___ let us
pray.
1

Oh, let us
pray,

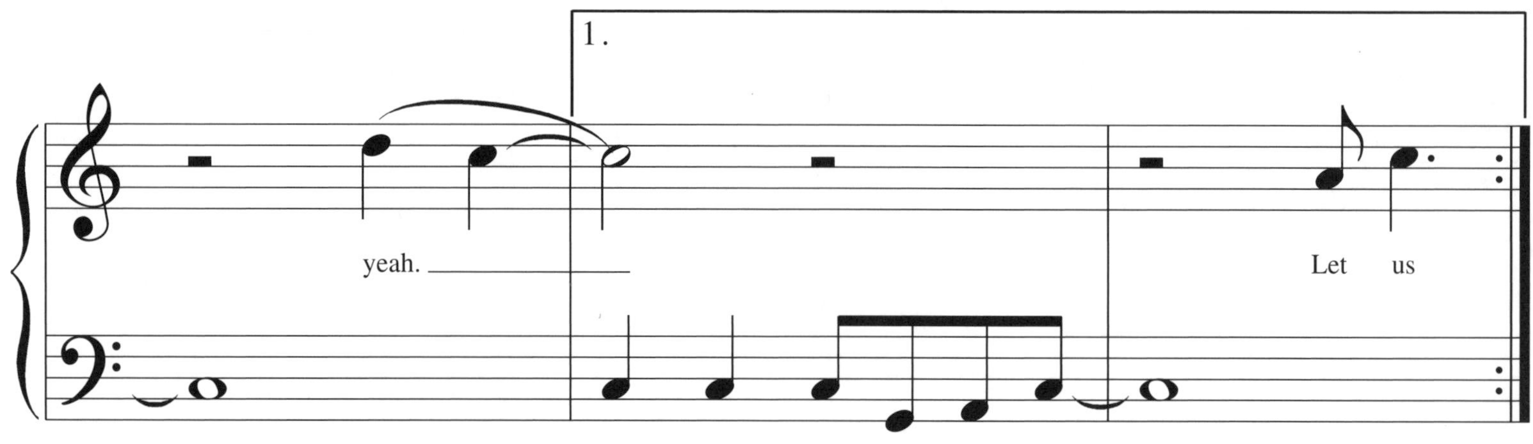
1.
yeah. ___
Let us

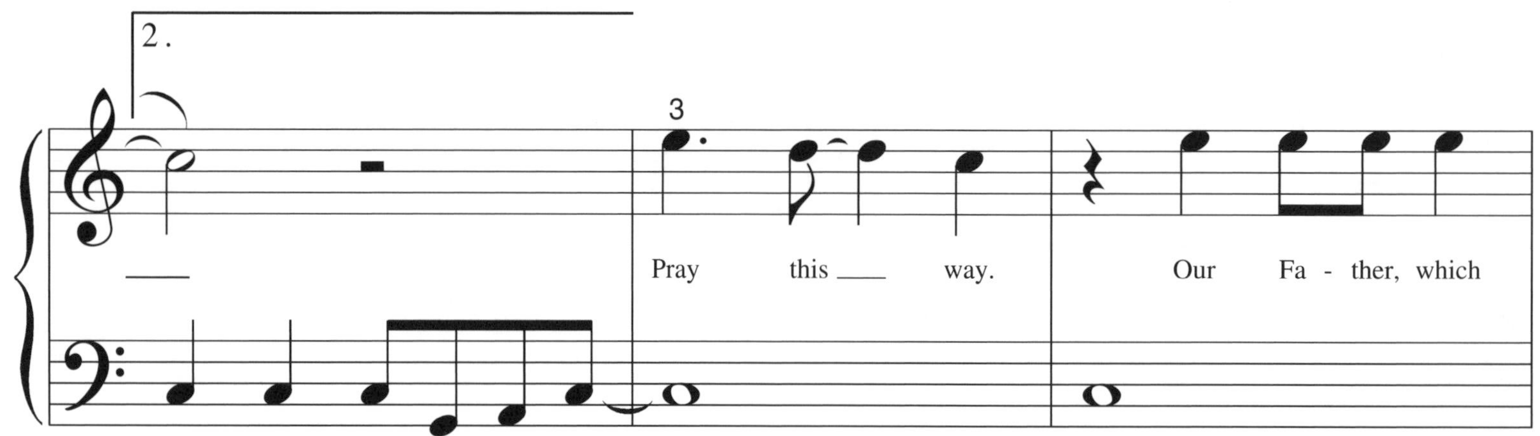
2.
3
Pray this ___ way.
Our Fa - ther, which

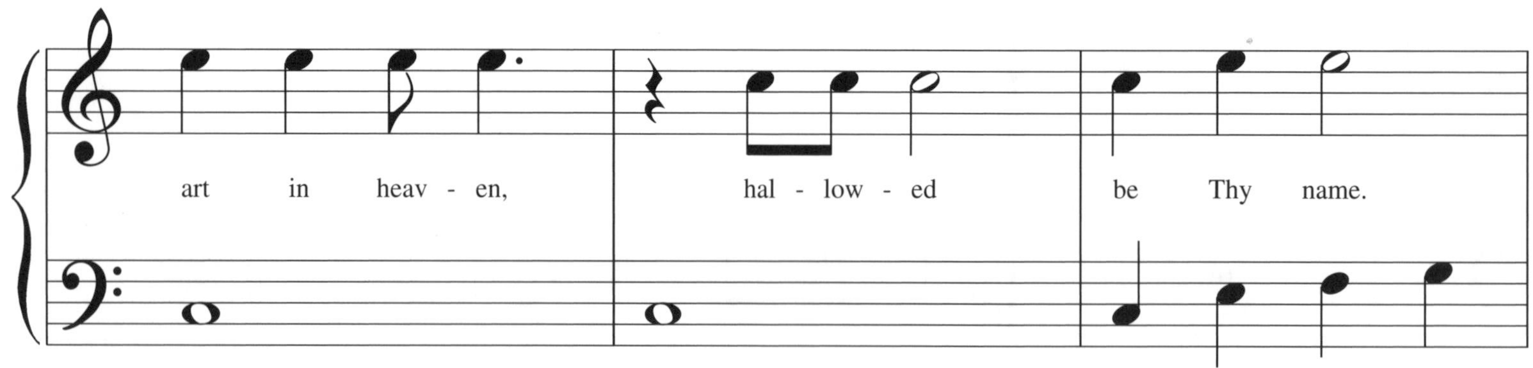
art in heav - en,
hal - low - ed
be Thy name.

Thy King - dom
come, Thy will ___ be

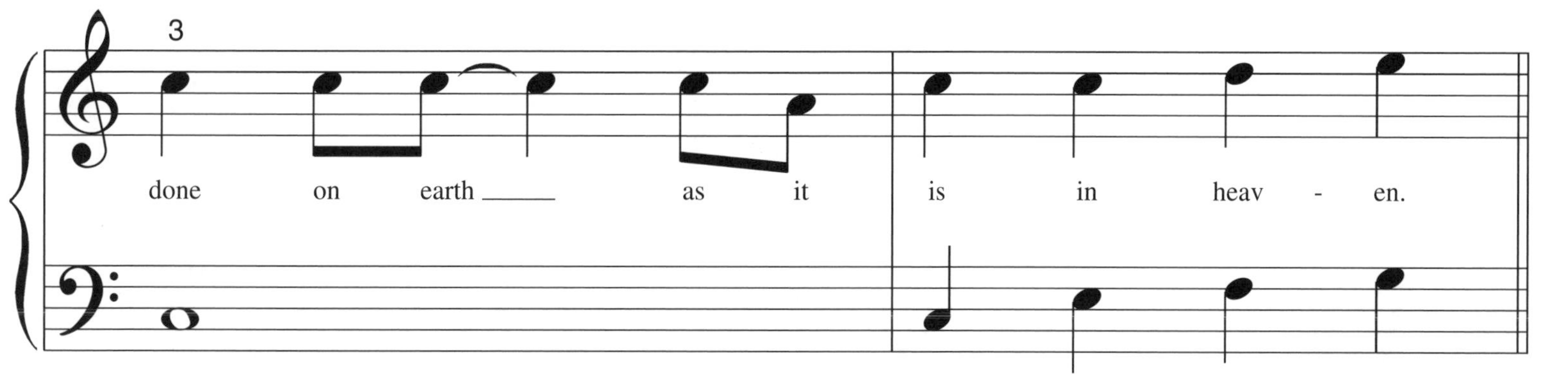
3
done on earth ___ as it is in heav - en.

C
Let us pray.
1

4
Let us pray, let us pray, oh, let us

pray, yeah. ___

JOY IN THE JOURNEY

Words and Music by
MICHAEL CARD

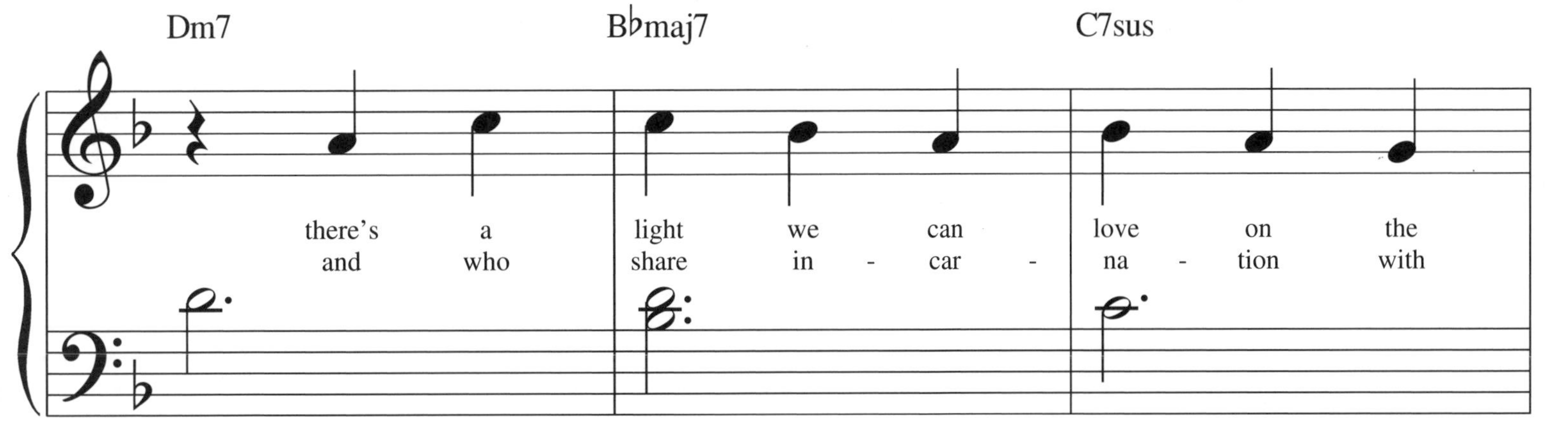
Dm7
B♭maj7
C7sus
there's a light we can love on the
and who share in - car - na - tion with

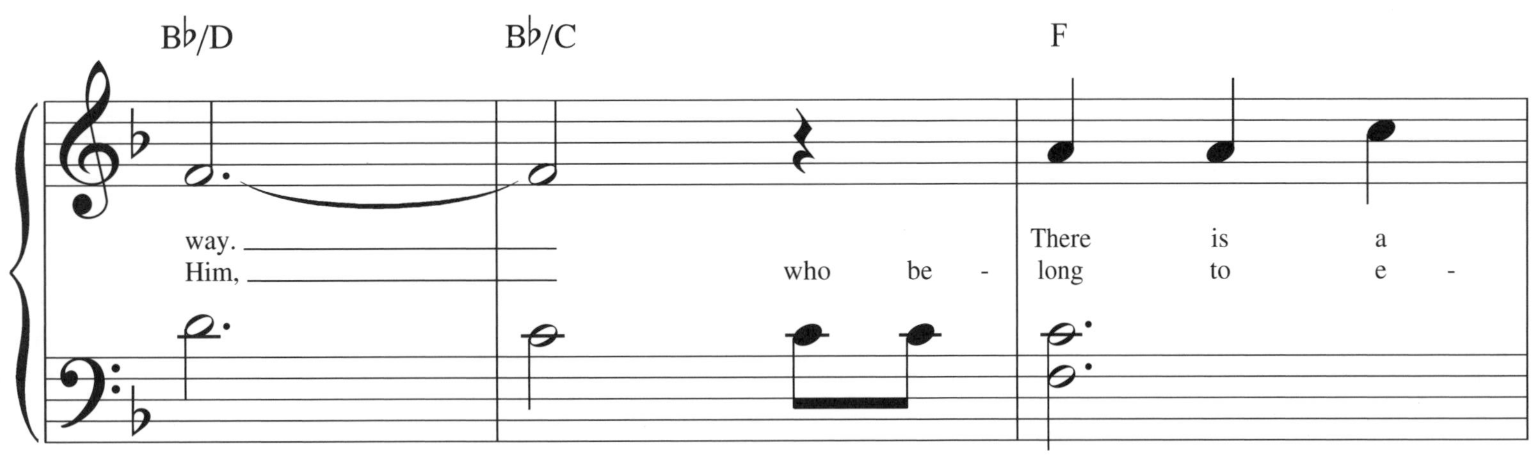
B♭/D
B♭/C
F
way.
Him, who be - long to e -
There is a

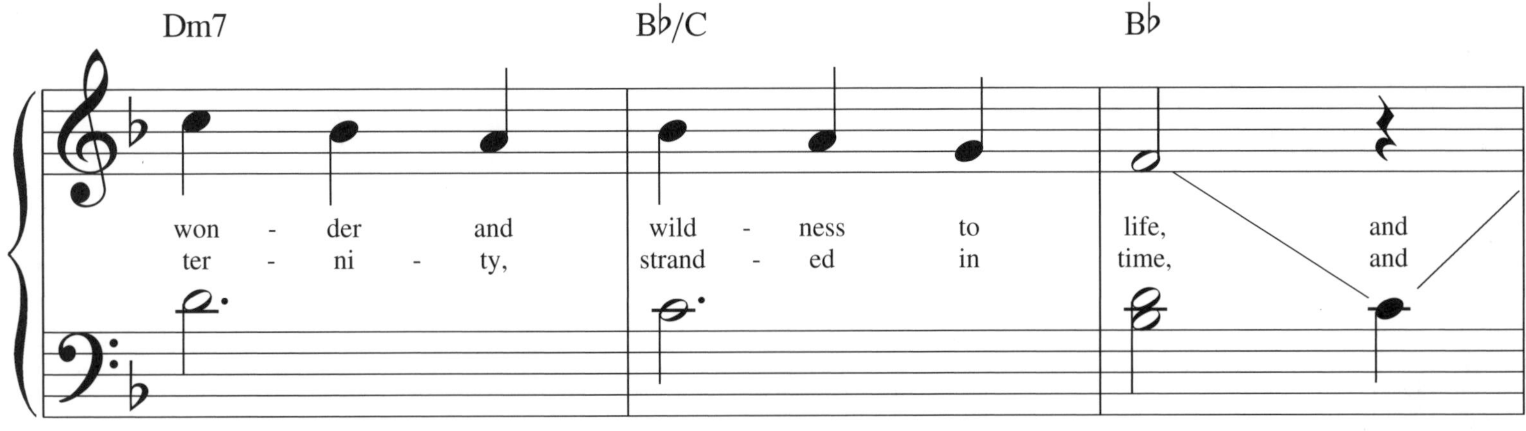
Dm7
B♭/C
B♭
won - der and wild - ness to life, and
ter - ni - ty, strand - ed in time, and

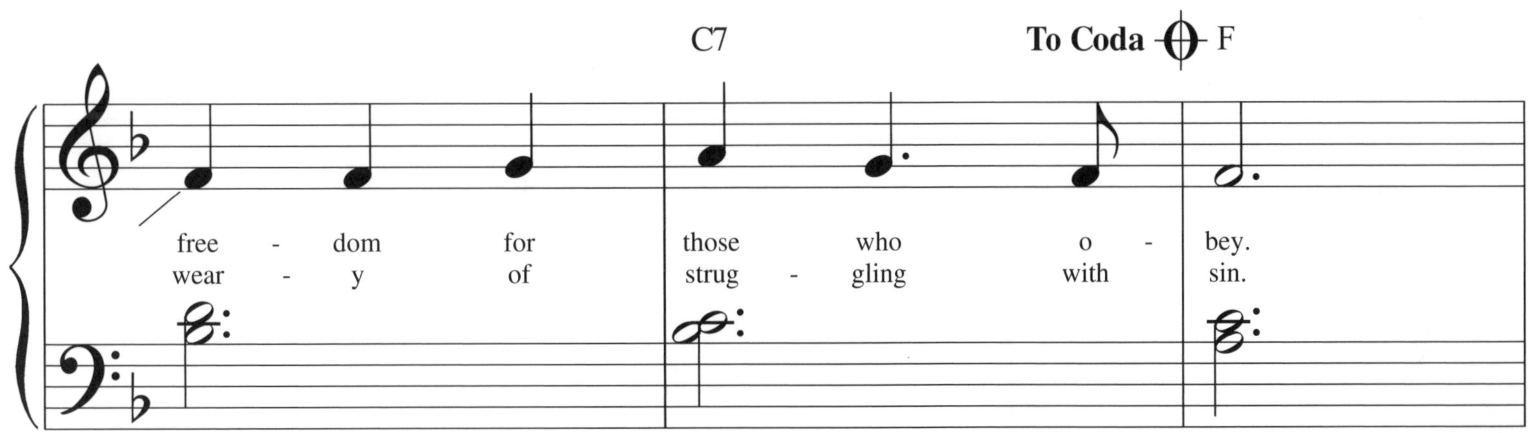
C7
To Coda
F
free - dom for those who o - bey.
wear - y of strug - gling with sin.

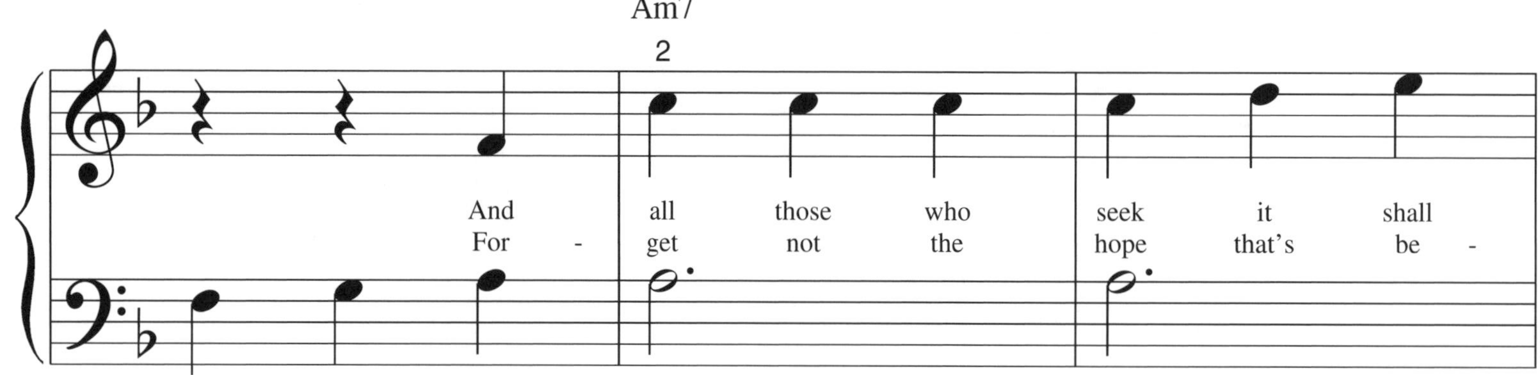
Am7
2
And all those who seek it shall
For - get not the hope that's be -

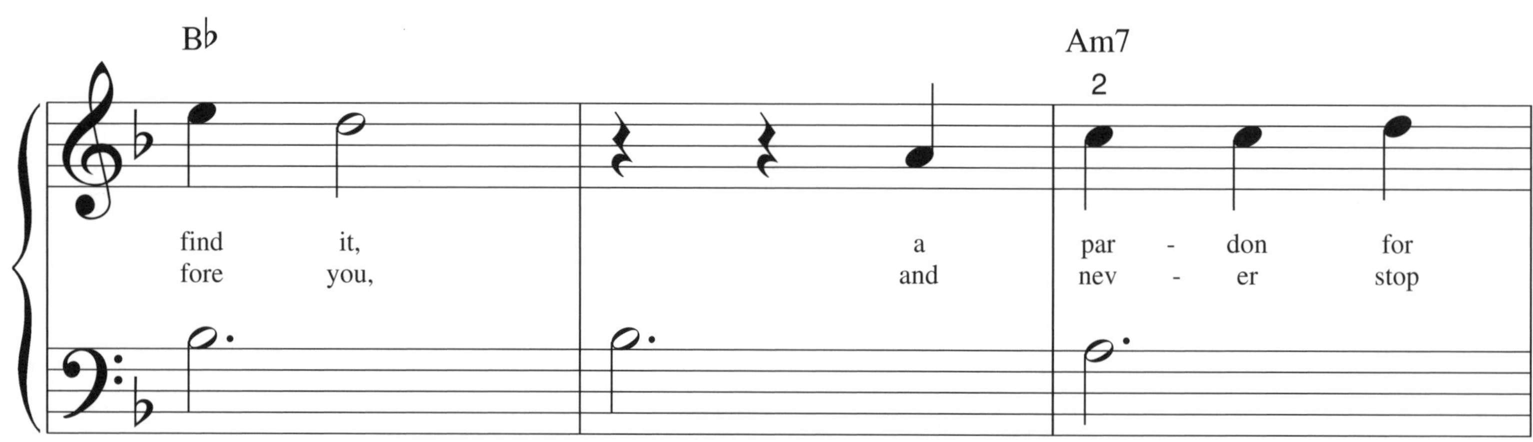
B♭
Am7
2
find it, a par - don for
fore you, and nev - er stop

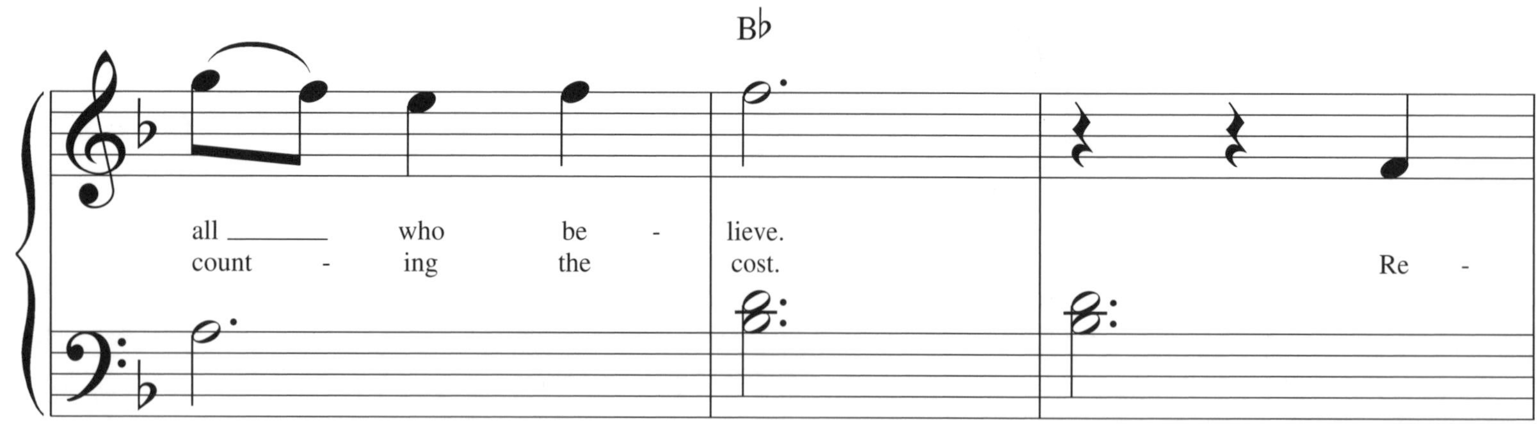
B♭
all who be - lieve.
count - ing the cost. Re -

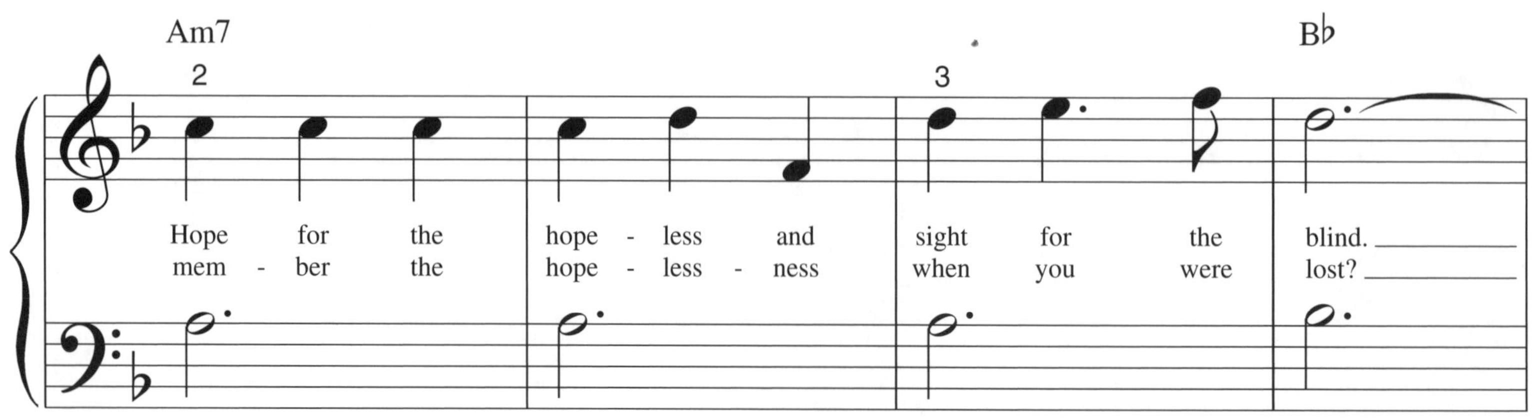
Am7
2
3
B♭
Hope for the hope - less and sight for the blind.
mem - ber the hope - less - ness when you were lost?

1.
2.
D.S. al Coda
5
5
CODA
F
B♭
C7
bey.
And
free - dom
for
those
who
o -
F
Dm7
F
Dm7
4
bey.
F
B♭maj7
C
B♭(add2)
1

LOVE IN ANY LANGUAGE

Words and Music by JOHN MAYS
and JON MOHR

Slowly (in 2)

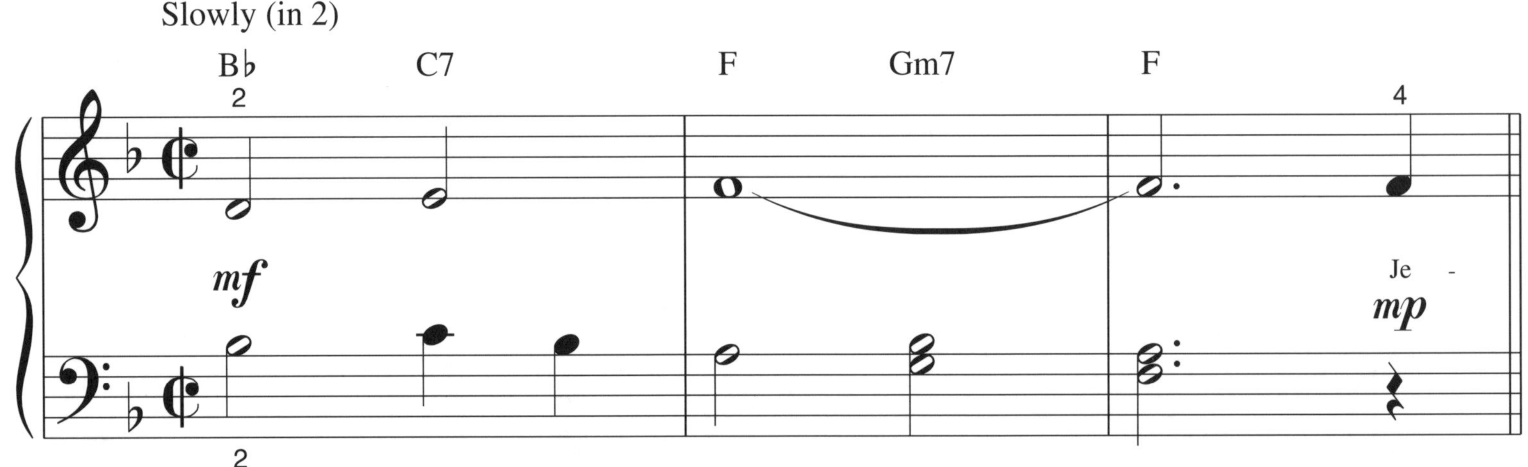

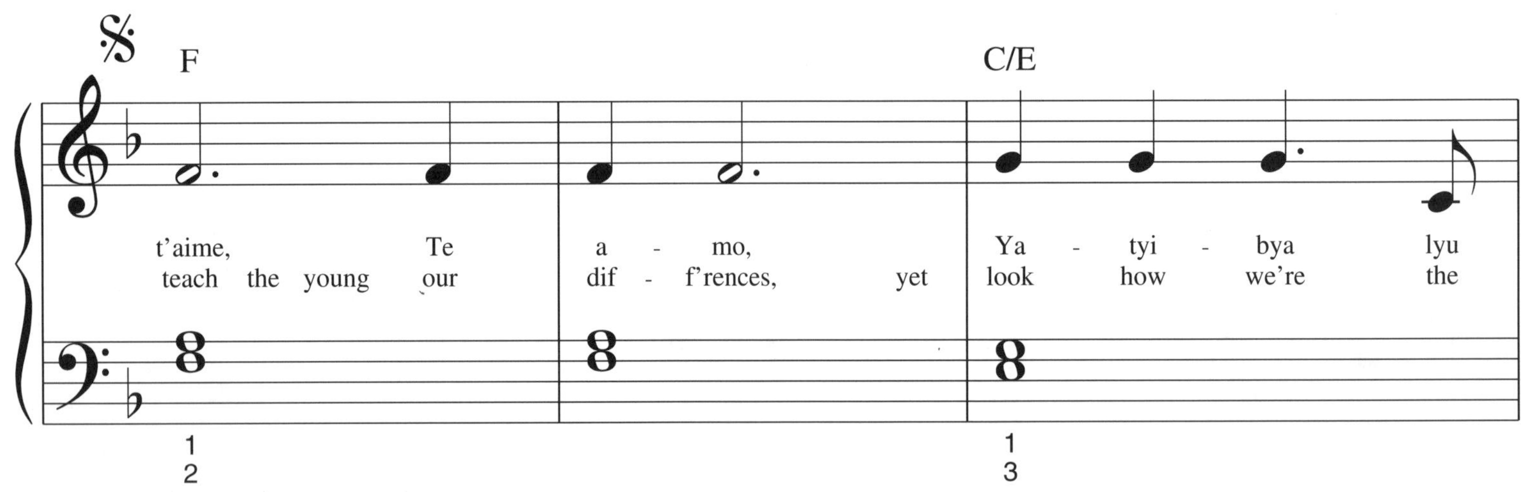

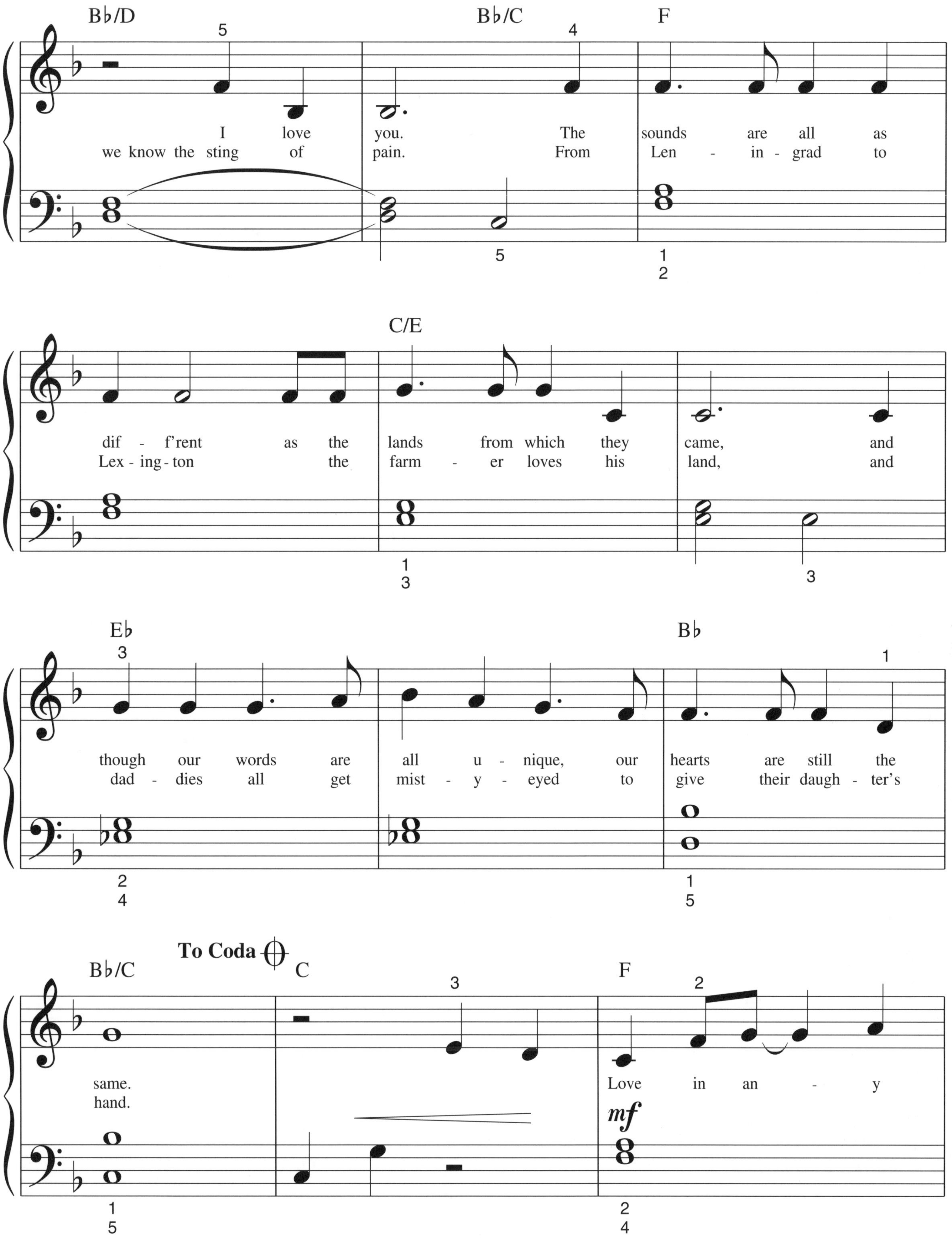

B♭/D B♭/C F

I love you. The sounds are all as
we know the sting of pain. From Len - in - grad to

C/E

dif - f'rent as the lands from which they came, and
Lex - ing - ton the farm - er loves his land, and

E♭ B♭

though our words are all u - nique, our hearts are still the
dad - dies all get mist - y - eyed to give their daugh - ter's

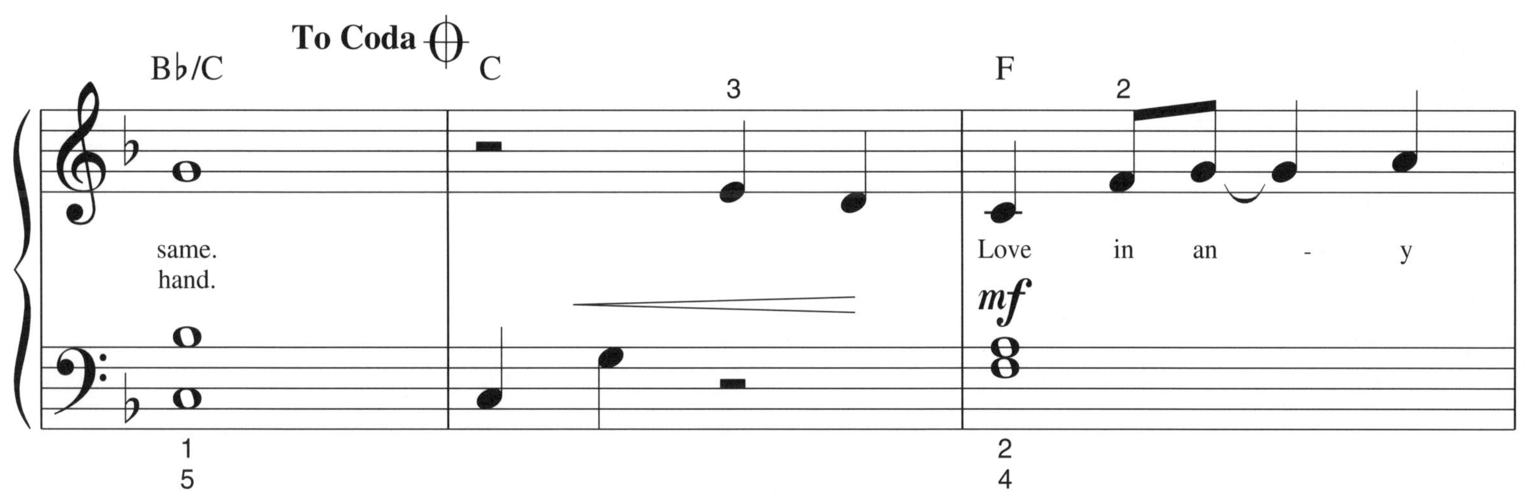

B♭
lan - guage, straight from the heart,
C
B♭
pulls us all to - geth - er, nev - er a -
Csus
C
F
part; And once we learn to speak it,
B♭
G
C
all the world will hear, love in an - y

B♭
C
F
lan - guage
flu - ent - ly spok - en
here.
D.S. al Coda
CODA
C
We
mp
Oh,
G
D/F♯
may - be when we
re - a - lize how
much there is to
mf
F
share, we'll
find too much in
com - mon to pre -

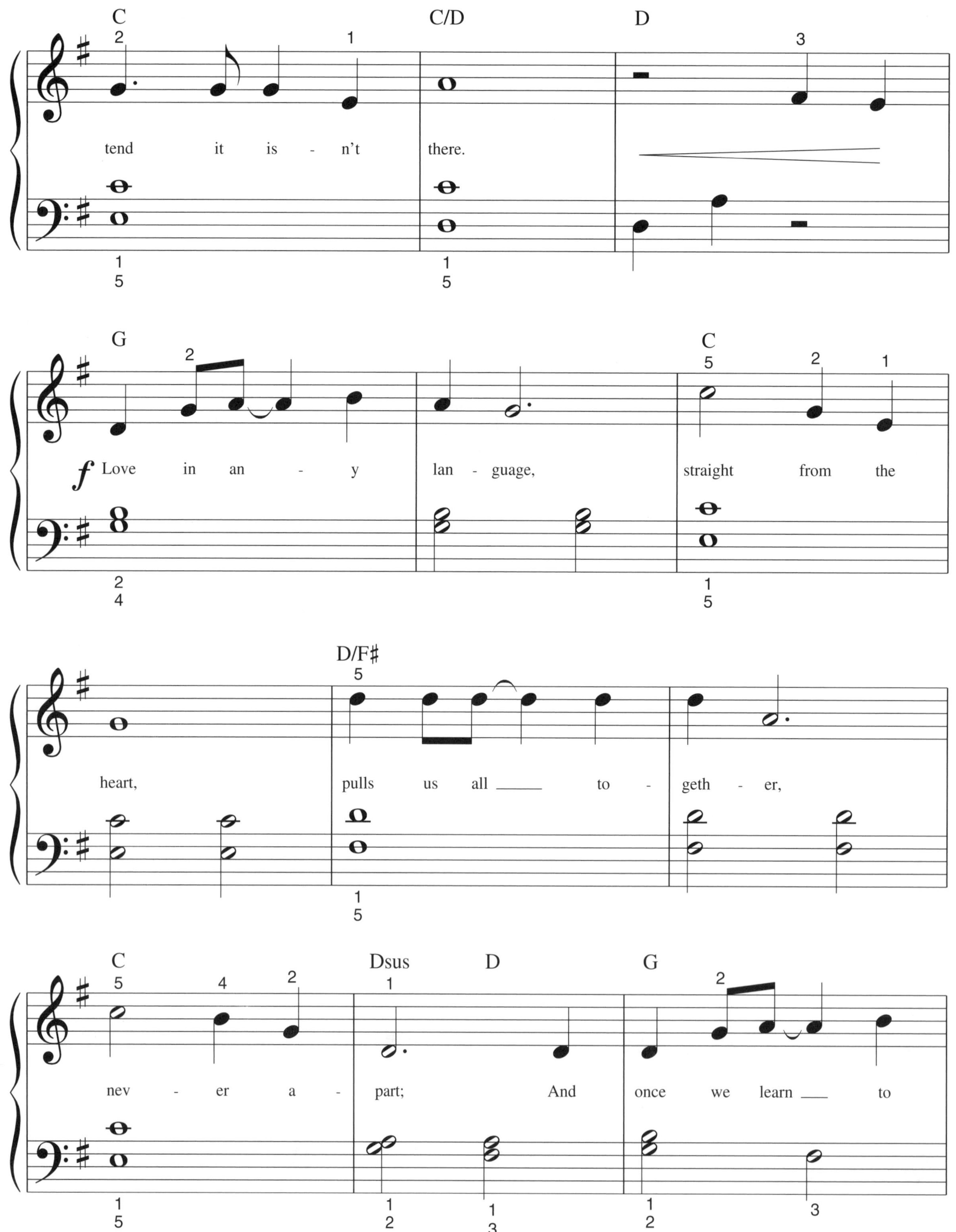
C
C/D
D
tend it is - n't there.
G
C
f Love in an - y lan - guage, straight from the
D/F#
heart, pulls us all ___ to - geth - er,
C
Dsus
D
G
nev - er a - part; And once we learn ___ to

C
A
5
1
speak it, all the world ___ will hear,
1
4
1
2
3
D/F#
C
D
5
3
1
love in an - y lan - guage flu - ent - ly spo - ken
4
3
5

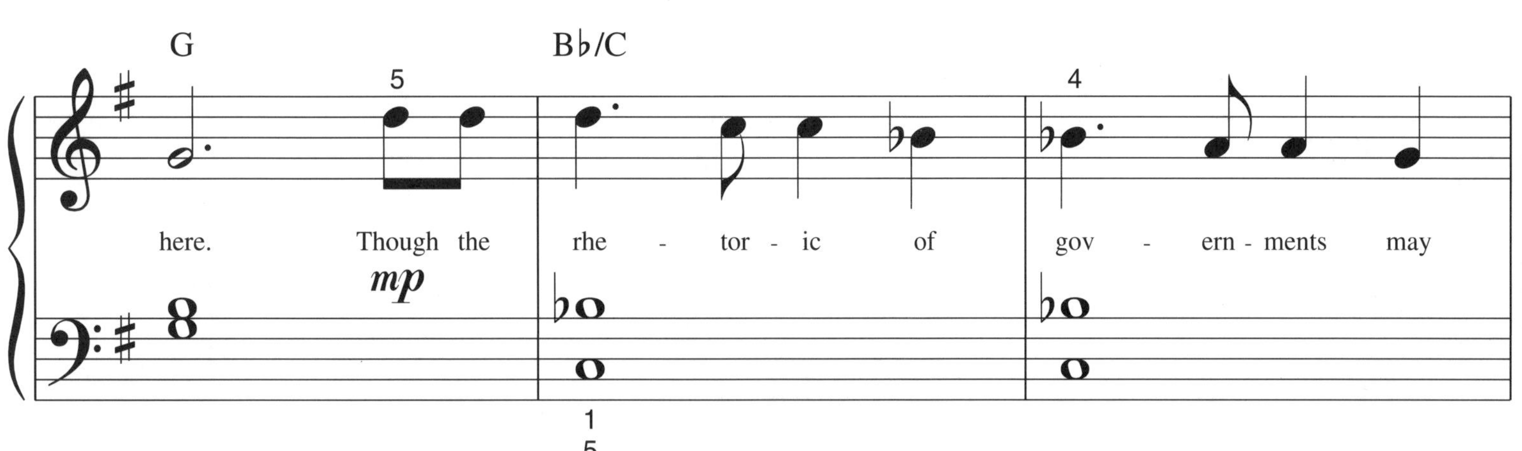
G
B♭/C
5
4
here. Though the rhe - tor - ic of gov - ern - ments may
mp
1
5

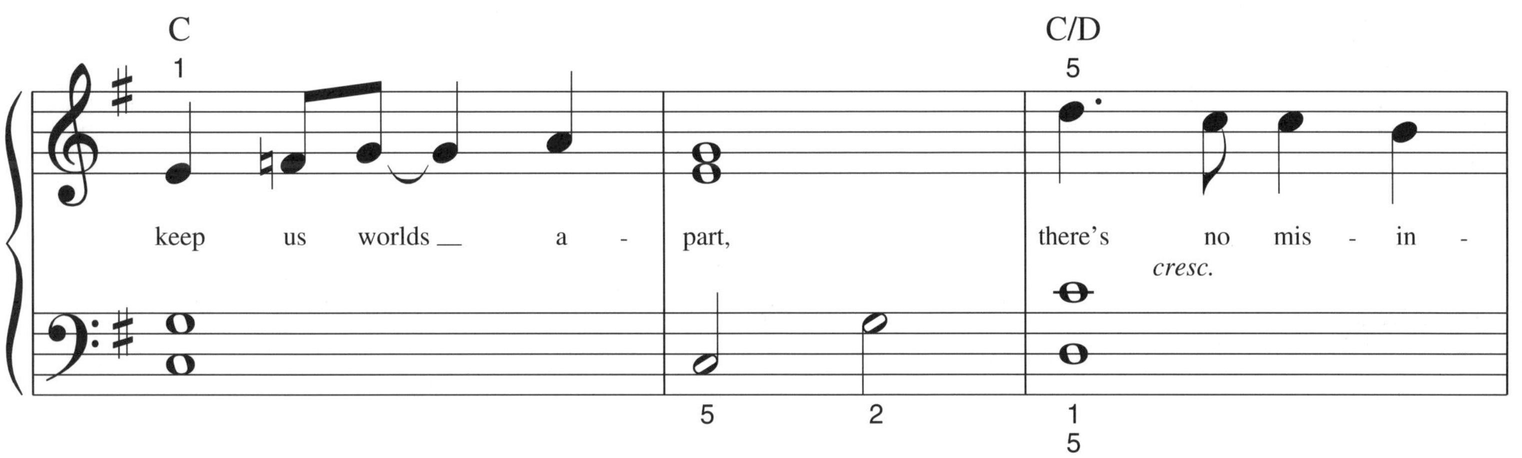
C
C/D
1
5
keep us worlds ___ a - part, there's no mis - in -
cresc.
5
2
1
5

Am
Bm
C
ter - pret - ing the
lan - guage
of the
D
heart.
G
Love in an - y
f
8
lan - guage,
C
straight from the
heart,
D
pulls us all
to -
geth - er,

C
Dsus
D
G
nev - er a - part; And once we learn to
speak it, all the world will hear,
A
D/F♯
love in an - y lan - guage flu - ent - ly
spo - ken here!

PEOPLE NEED THE LORD

Words and Music by PHILL McHUGH
and GREG NELSON

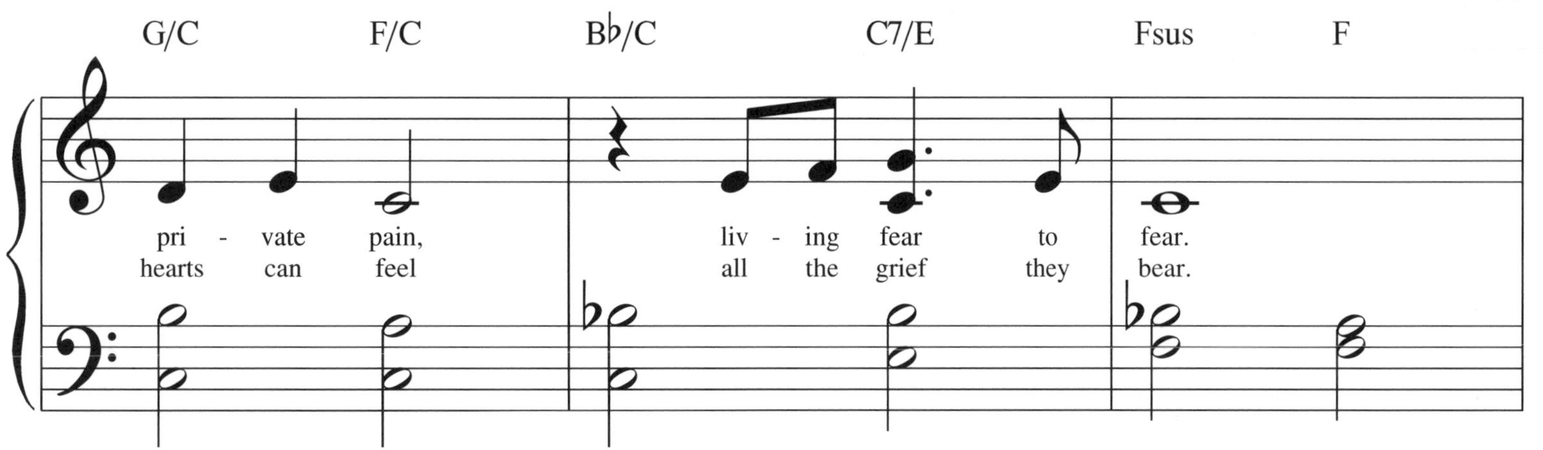
G/C F/C B♭/C C7/E Fsus F
pri - vate pain, liv - ing fear to fear.
hearts can feel all the grief they bear.

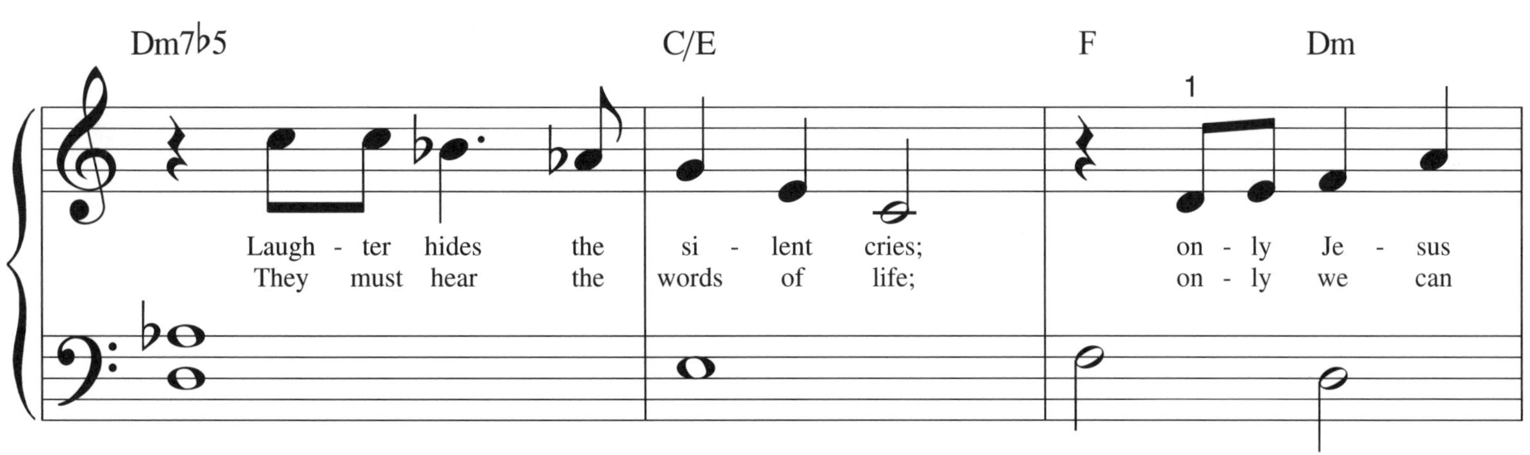
Dm7♭5 C/E F Dm
1
Laugh - ter hides the si - lent cries; on - ly Je - sus
They must hear the words of life; on - ly we can

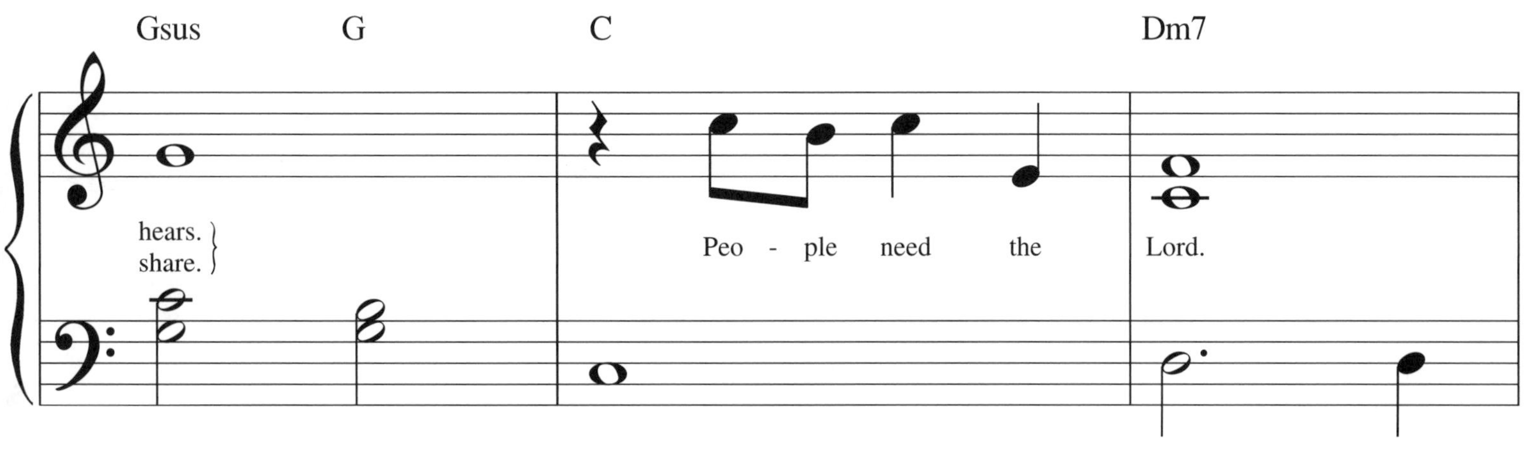
Gsus G C Dm7
hears.
share.
Peo - ple need the Lord.

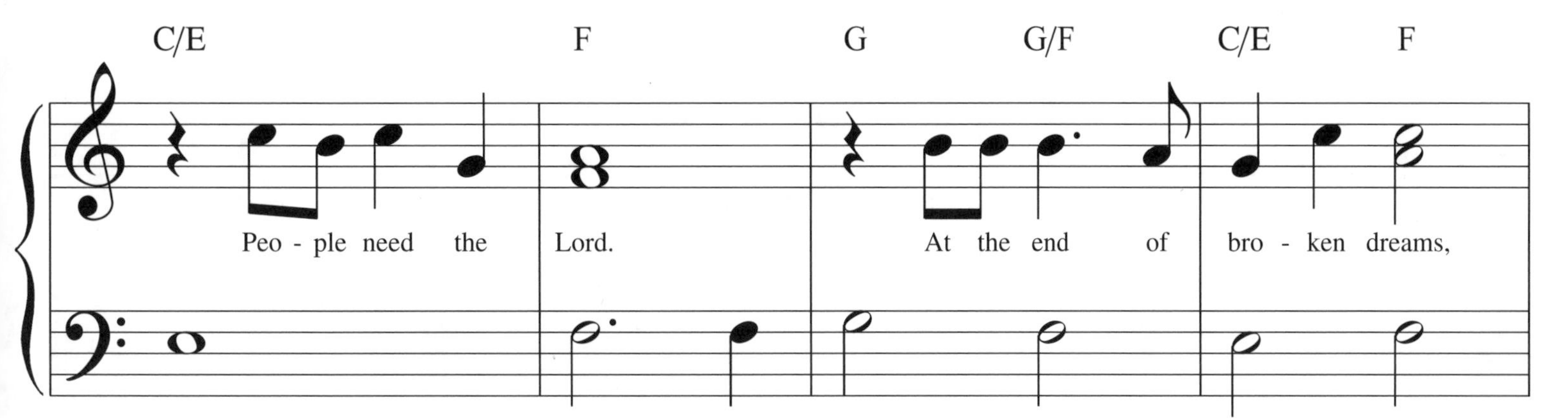
C/E F G G/F C/E F
Peo - ple need the Lord. At the end of bro - ken dreams,

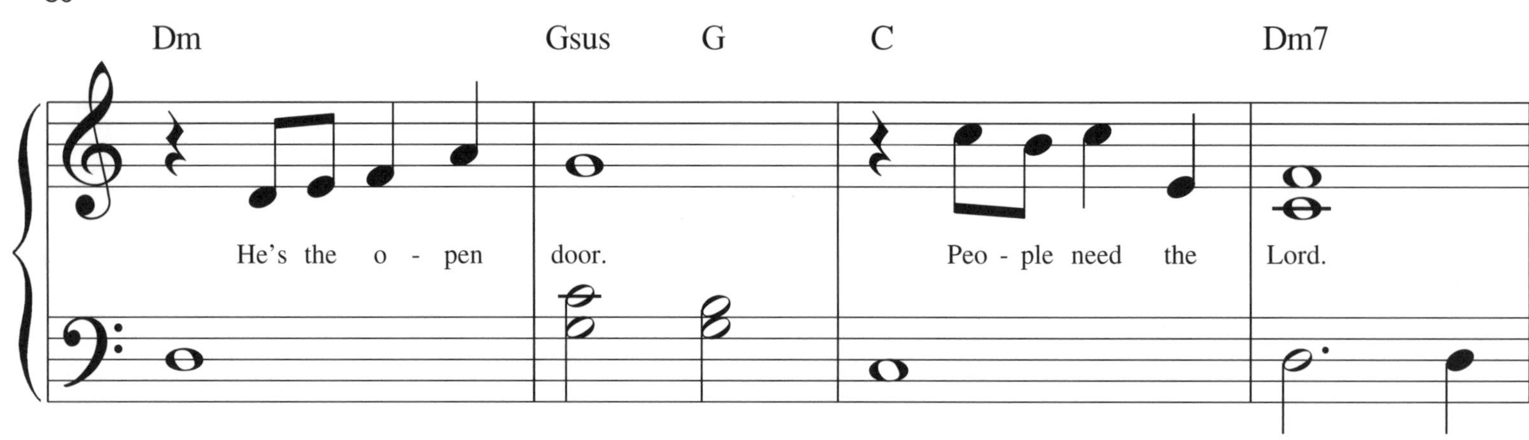
Dm
Gsus
G
C
Dm7
He's the o - pen
door.
Peo - ple need the
Lord.

C/E
F
G
G/F
Peo - ple need the
Lord.
When will we

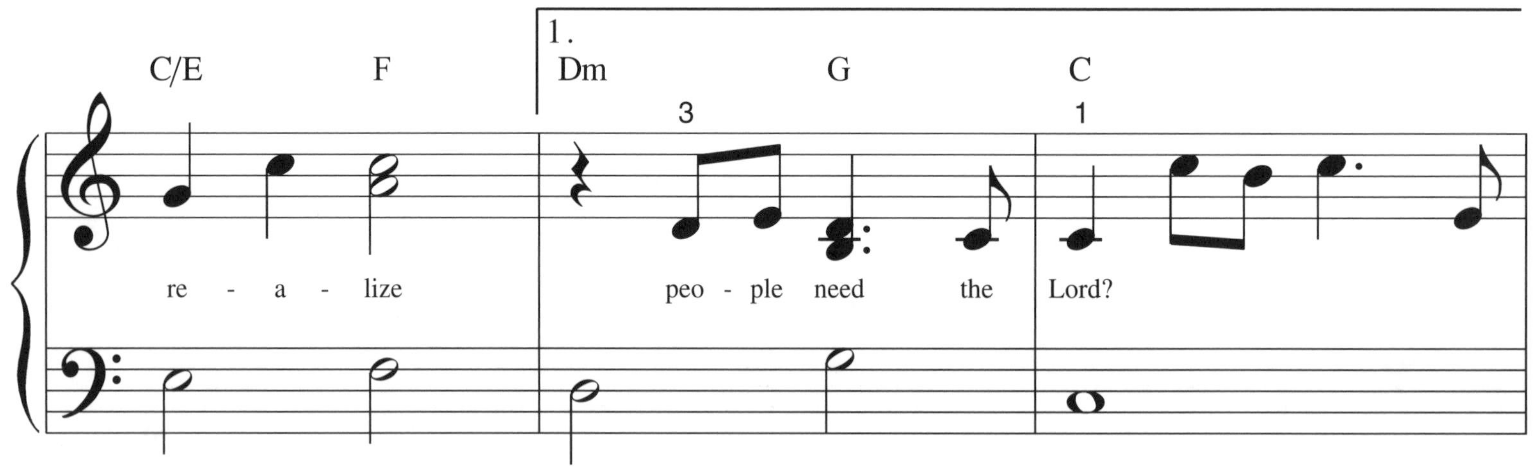
C/E
F
1.
Dm
G
C
3
1
re - a - lize
peo - ple need the
Lord?

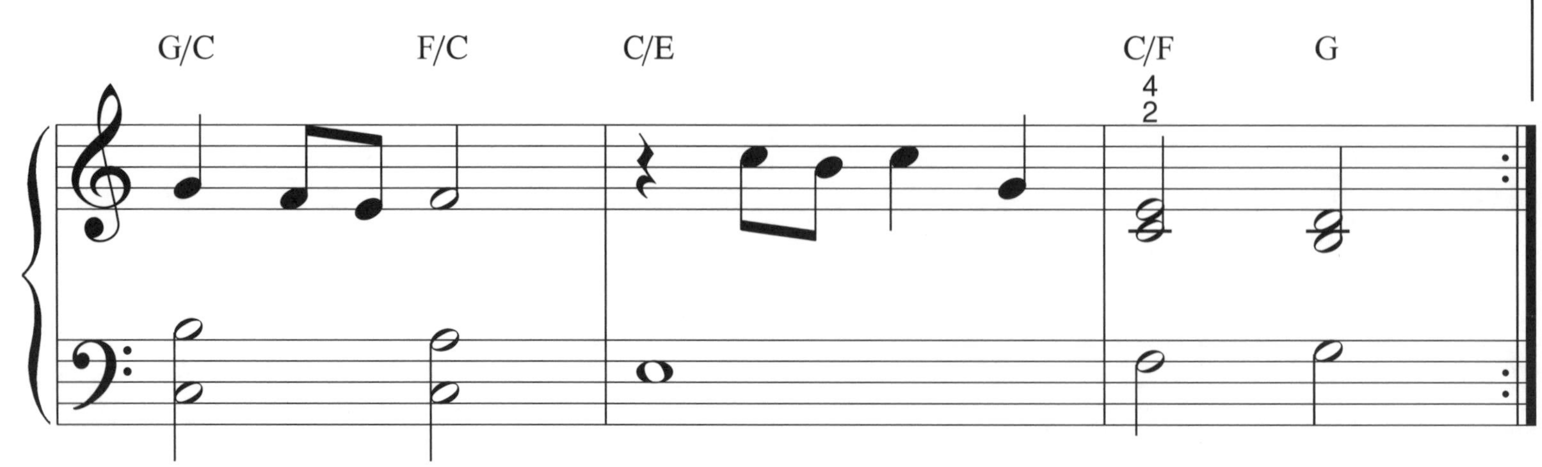
G/C
F/C
C/E
C/F
G
4
2

2.
G/D
G/F
C/E
F
Dm
that we must give our lives, for peo - ple
G7
Am
D7
need the Lord.
Dm
G7
C
Peo - ple need the Lord.
G/C
F/C
C/E
C/F
G
C
4
2

PLACE IN THIS WORLD

Words by WAYNE KIRKPATRICK and AMY GRANT
Music by MICHAEL W. SMITH

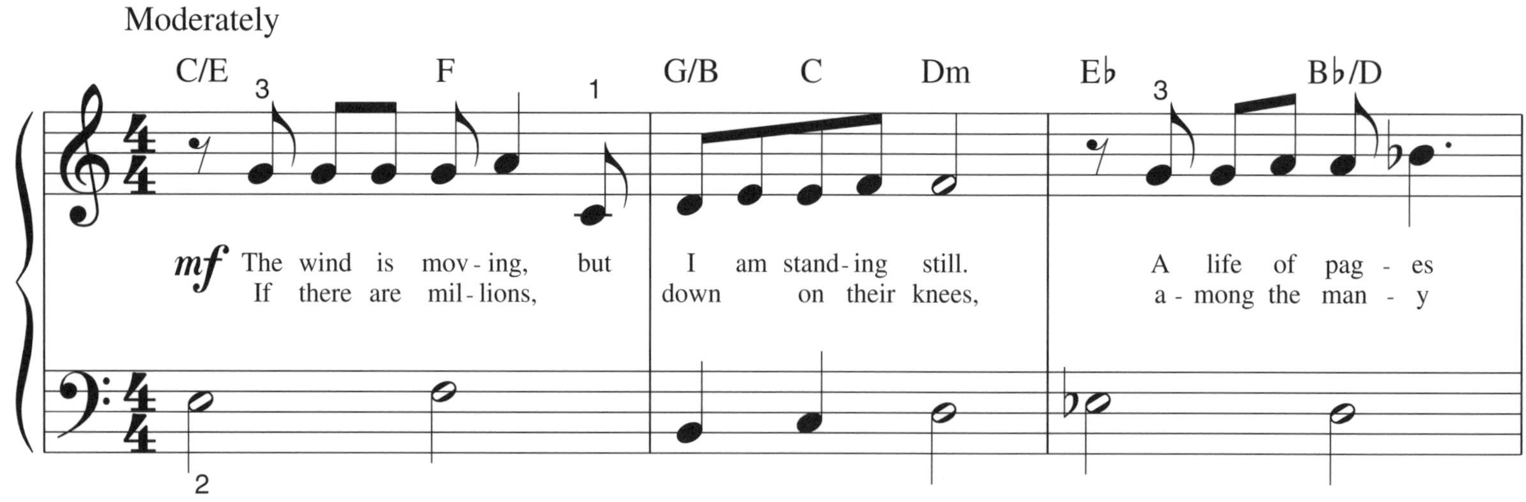

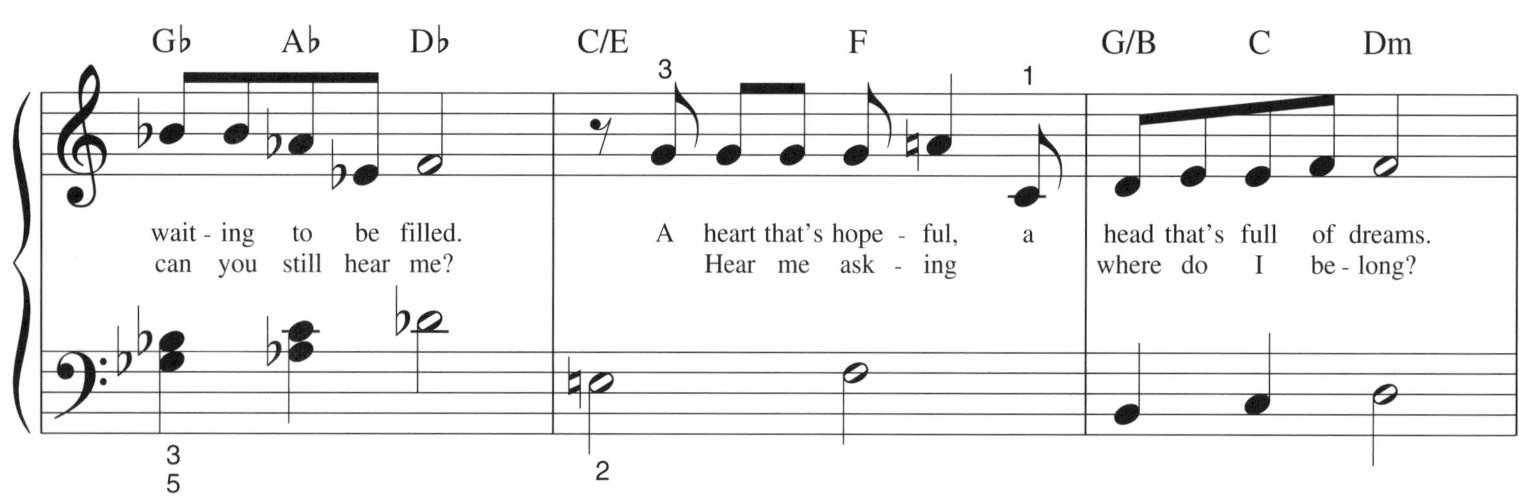

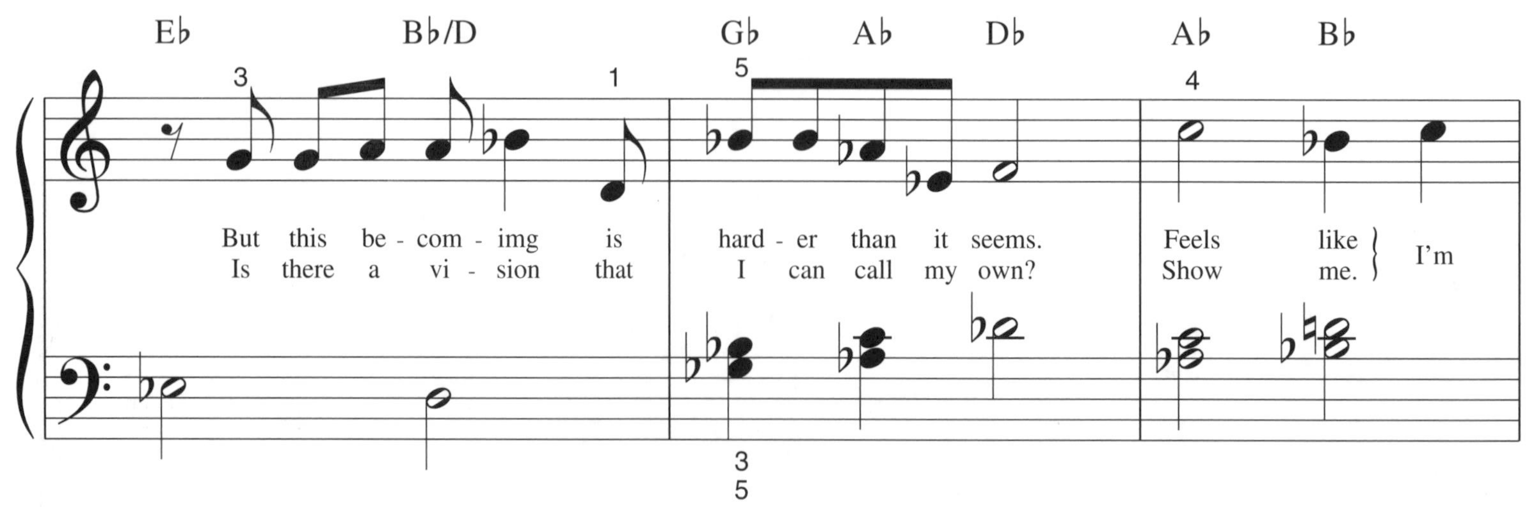

C
G/B
F/A
C/G
look - ing for a rea - son,
roam - ing through the night to find my
C/E
F
B♭
G
C
G/B
place in this world. My
place in this world.
Not a lot to lean on. I
F/A
C/G
C/E
F
B♭
G
need Your light to help me find my
place in this world. My
place in this world.
1.
C
F
G/B
C
Dm
2.
C

SHINE ON US

Words and Music by MICHAEL W. SMITH
and DEBBIE SMITH

C
us.
us.
Lord,
Lord,
F/C
C
Em/G
let Your light,
let Your grace,
light of Your
grace from Your
F
G/B
C
face
hand
shine on
fall on
us,
us,
4
F
G/B
that
we
may be

C
F
G/B
saved,
that
we
may
have
C
C/E
F
E/G♯
life
to
find
our
way
in
the
dark
-
est
2
Am
C/G
F
C/G
2
night.
Let
Your
light
shine
Let
Your
grace
fall
G7sus
1.
C
F/C
on
on
us.

2.
C
2 3
F
4
us.
Lord, ___
5

B♭/F F Am/C
___ let Your love, love ___ with no

B♭ C/E F
end come ___ o - ver us.
come ___ o - ver us,

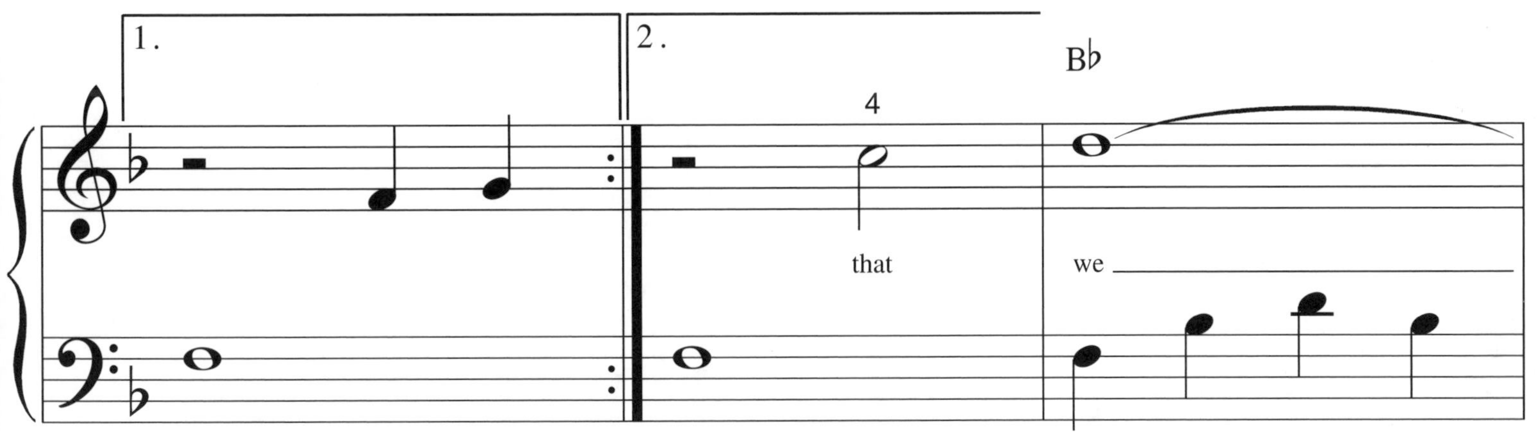

C/E
F
may
be
saved,
that

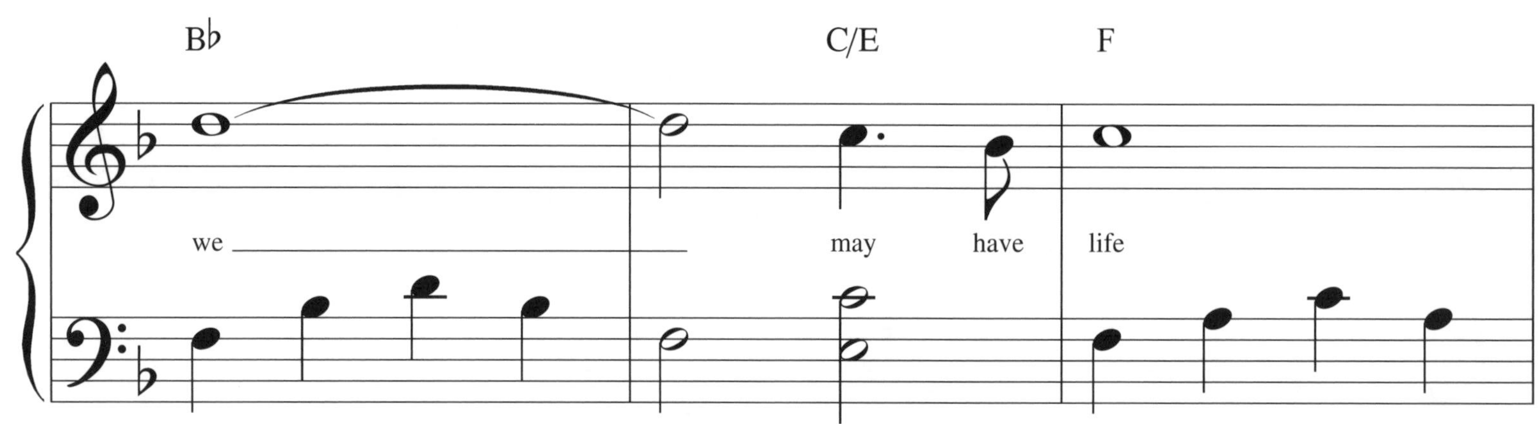
B♭
C/E
F
we
may
have
life

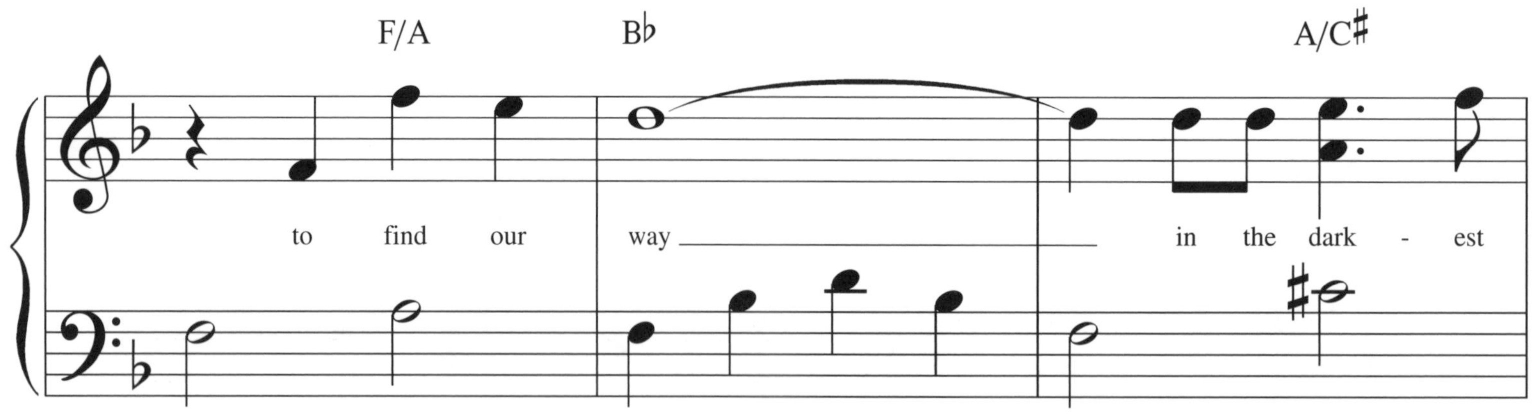
F/A
B♭
A/C♯
to
find
our
way
in
the
dark
-
est

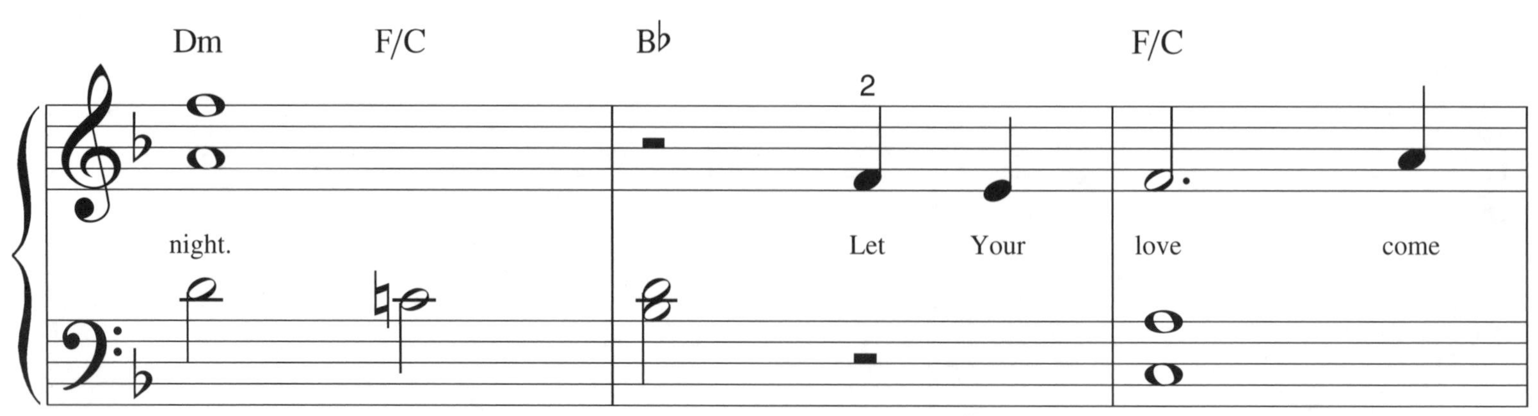
Dm
F/C
B♭
F/C
2
night.
Let
Your
love
come

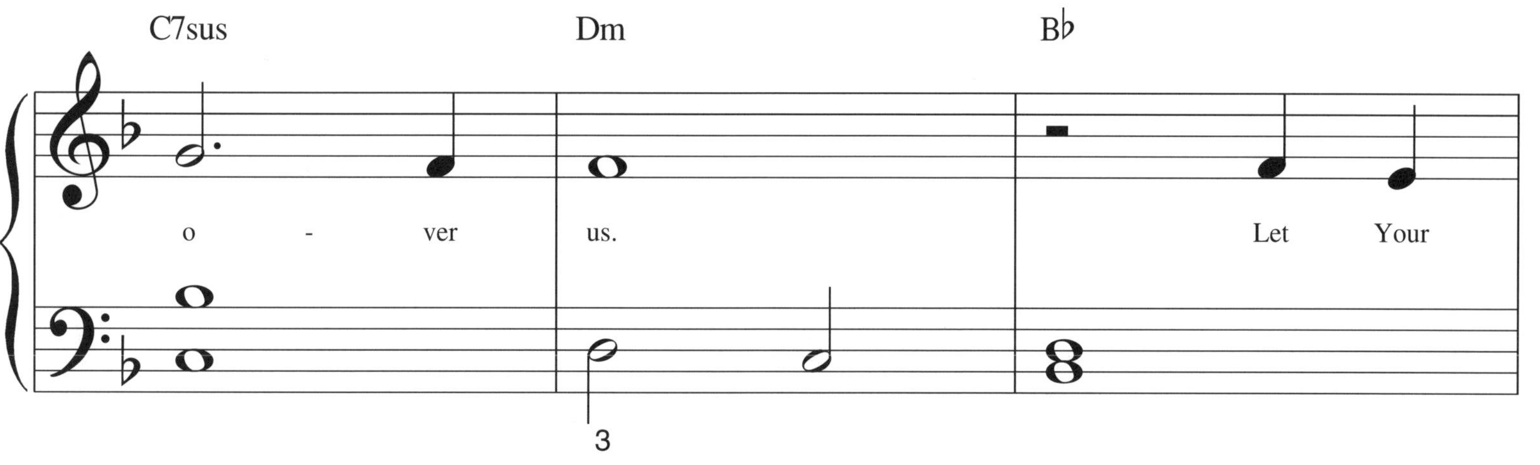
C7sus
Dm
B♭
o - ver us. Let Your
3

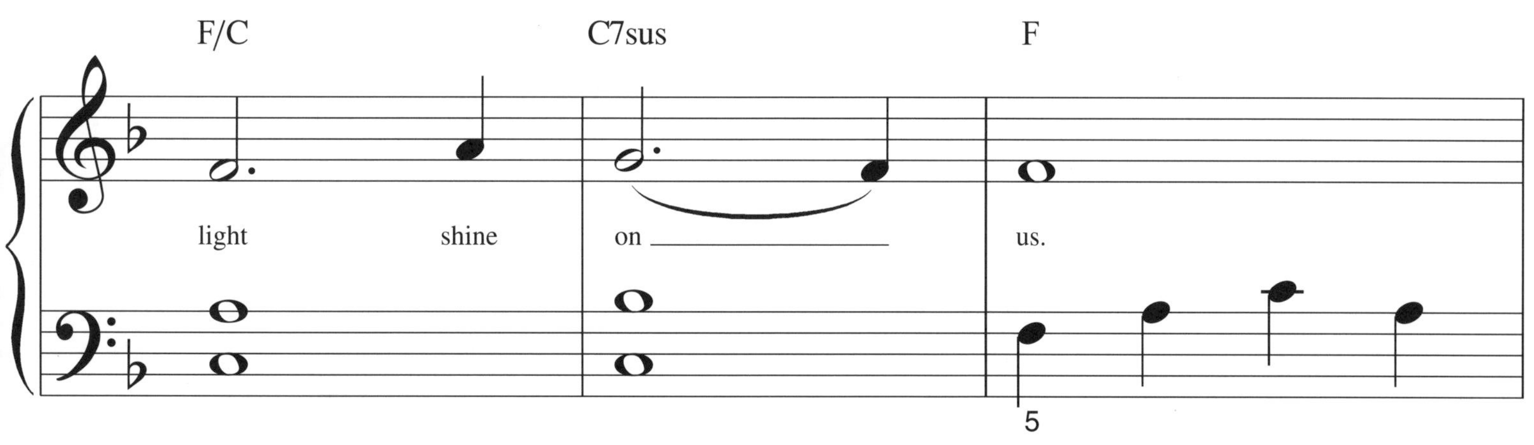
F/C
C7sus
F
light shine on us.
5

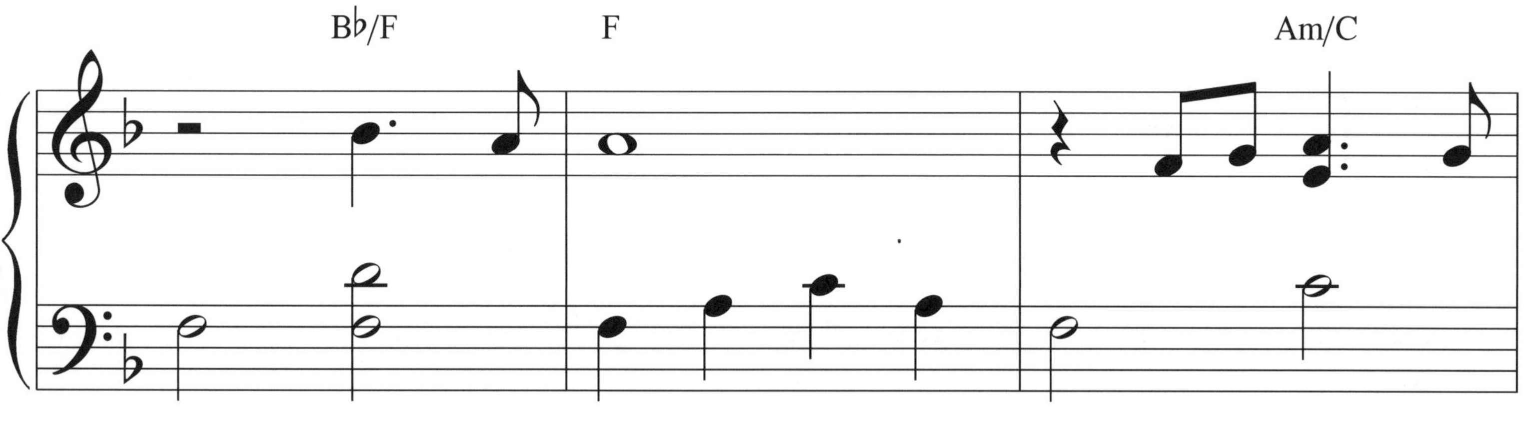
B♭/F
F
Am/C

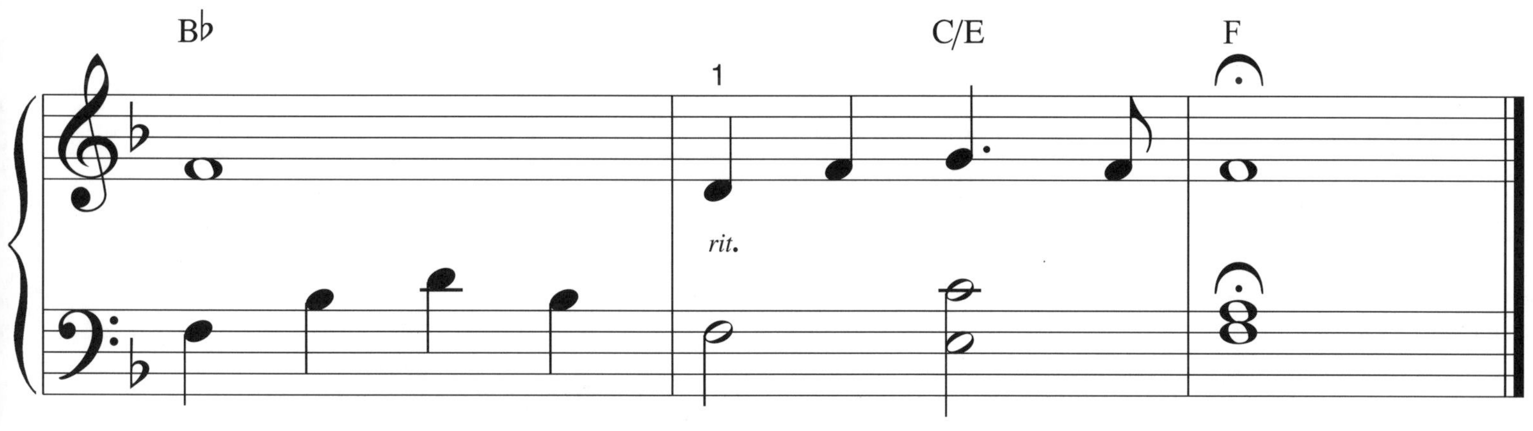
B♭
C/E
F
1
rit.

THY WORD

Words and Music by MICHAEL W. SMITH
and AMY GRANT

Firmly

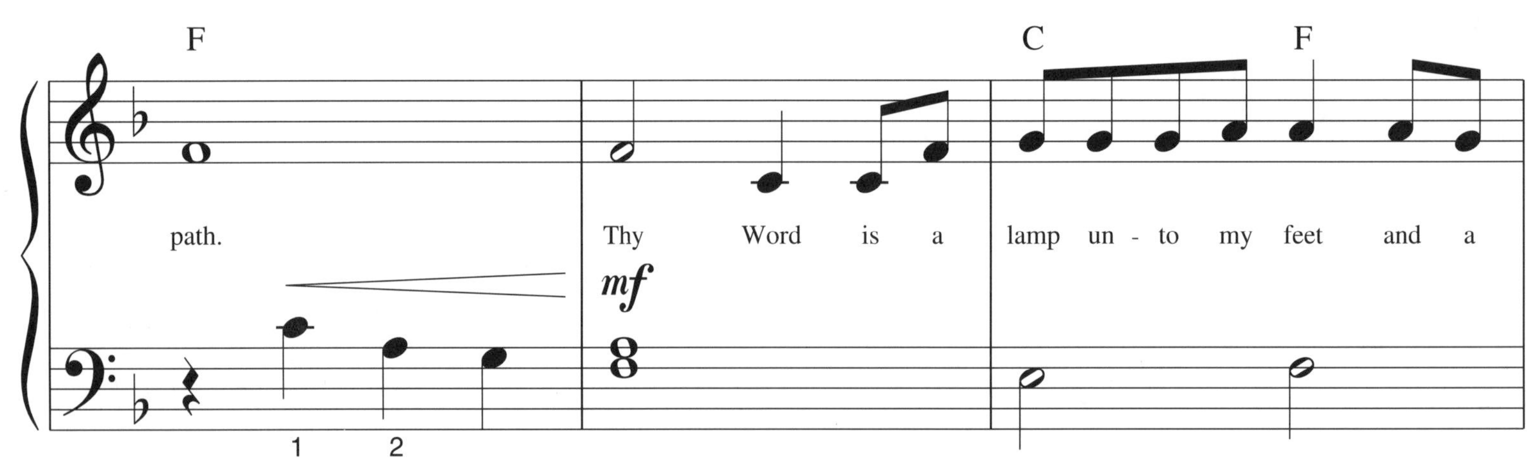

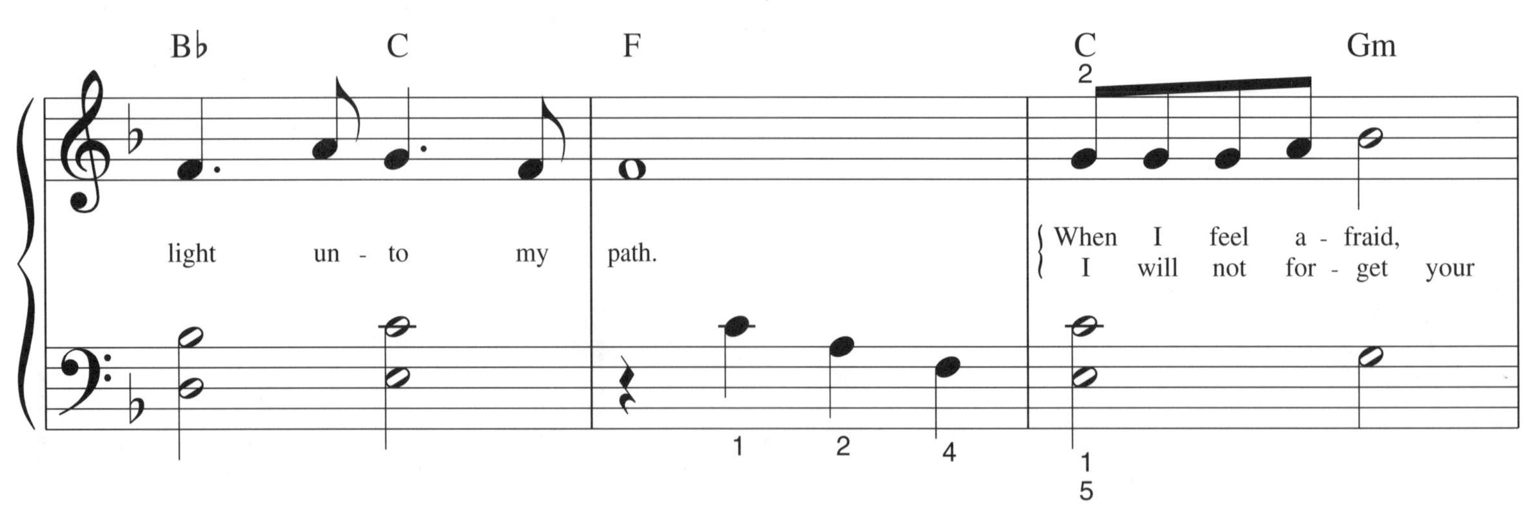

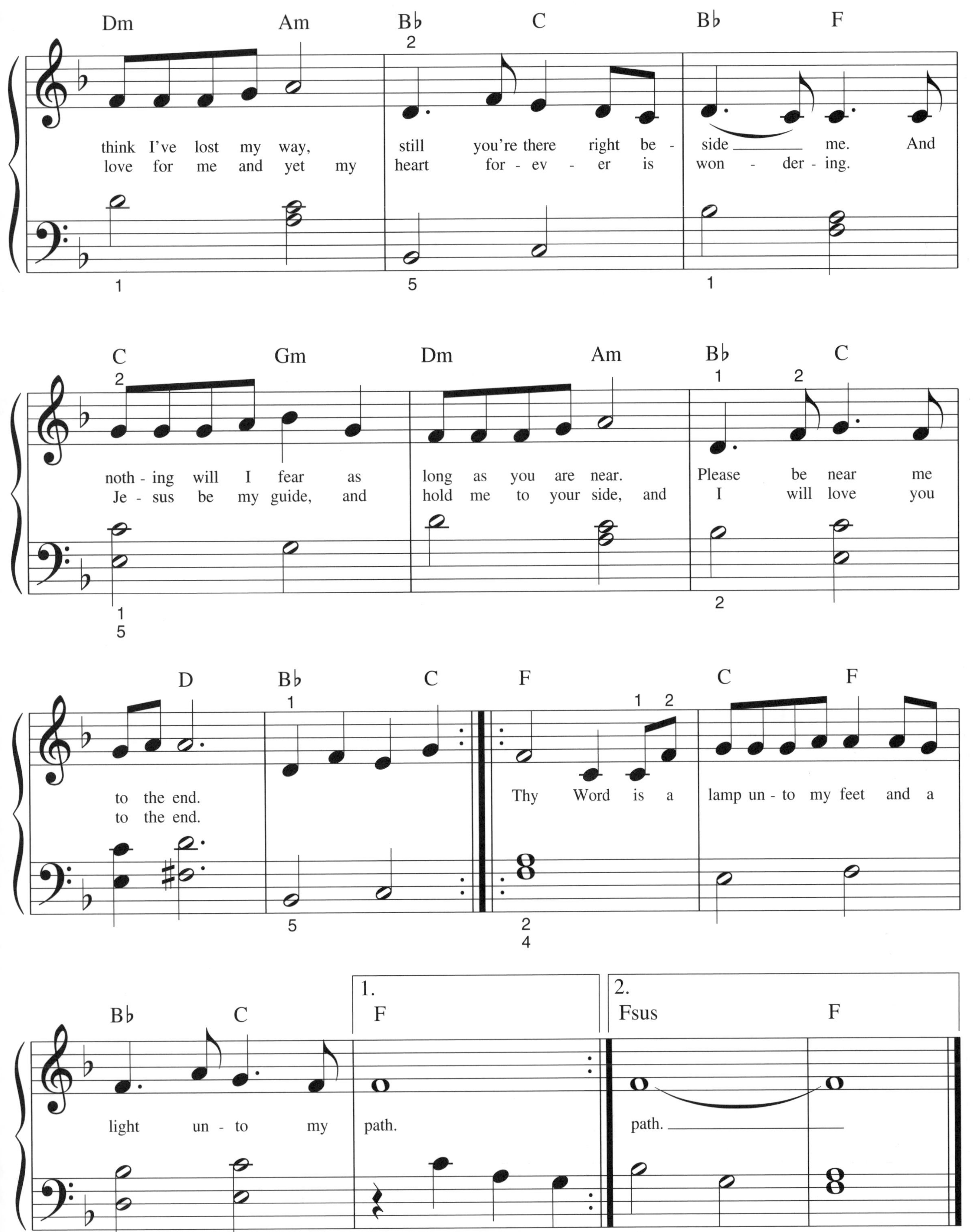
Dm Am B♭ C B♭ F
think I've lost my way, still you're there right be - side me. And
love for me and yet my heart for - ev - er is won - der - ing.
C Gm Dm Am B♭ C
noth - ing will I fear as long as you are near. Please be near me
Je - sus be my guide, and hold me to your side, and I will love you
D B♭ C F C F
to the end. Thy Word is a lamp un - to my feet and a
to the end.
B♭ C 1. F 2. Fsus F
light un - to my path. path.

THE WARRIOR IS A CHILD

Words and Music by
TWILA PARIS

Moderately

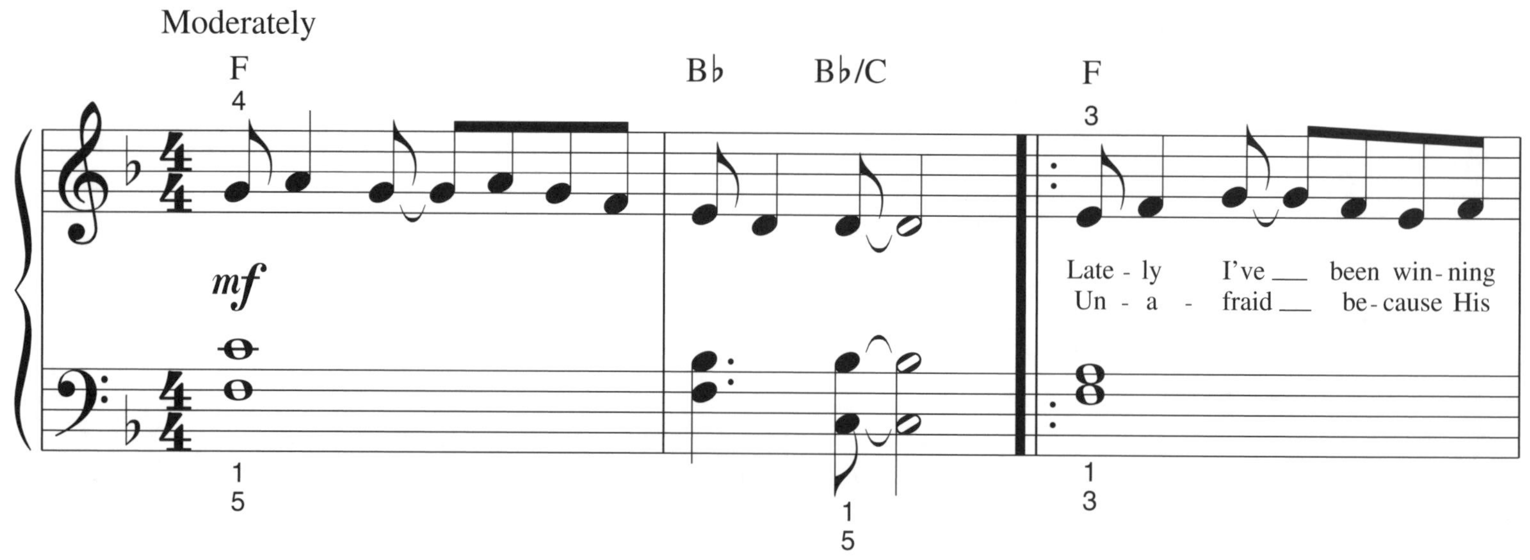

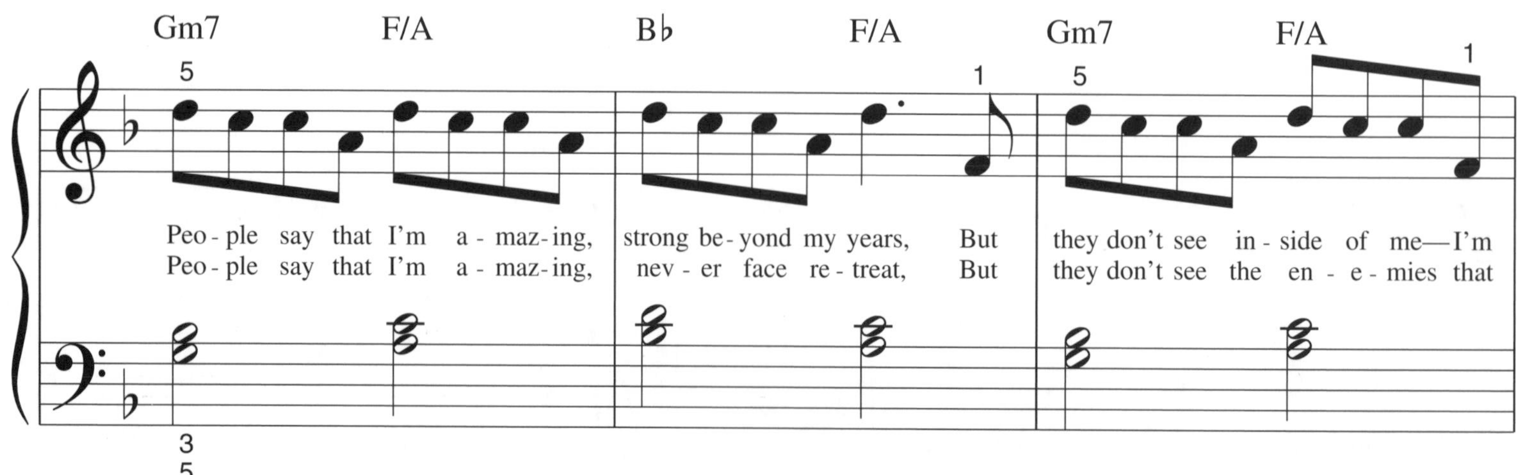

B♭ B♭/C F F/A B♭ C
hid - ing all the tears. They don't know that I go run - ning home when I fall down, They don't
lay me at His feet.
F F/A B♭ C Dm Dm/C
know who picks me up when no one is a - round; I drop my sword and cry for just a
(look up for a
B♭ F/A Gm7 F/A B♭ B♭/C
while, 'Cause deep in - side this ar - mor the war - rior is a
smile,)
1. F B♭ B♭/C
child.
2. F
child.

OH LORD, YOU'RE BEAUTIFUL

Words and Music by
KEITH GREEN

Slowly

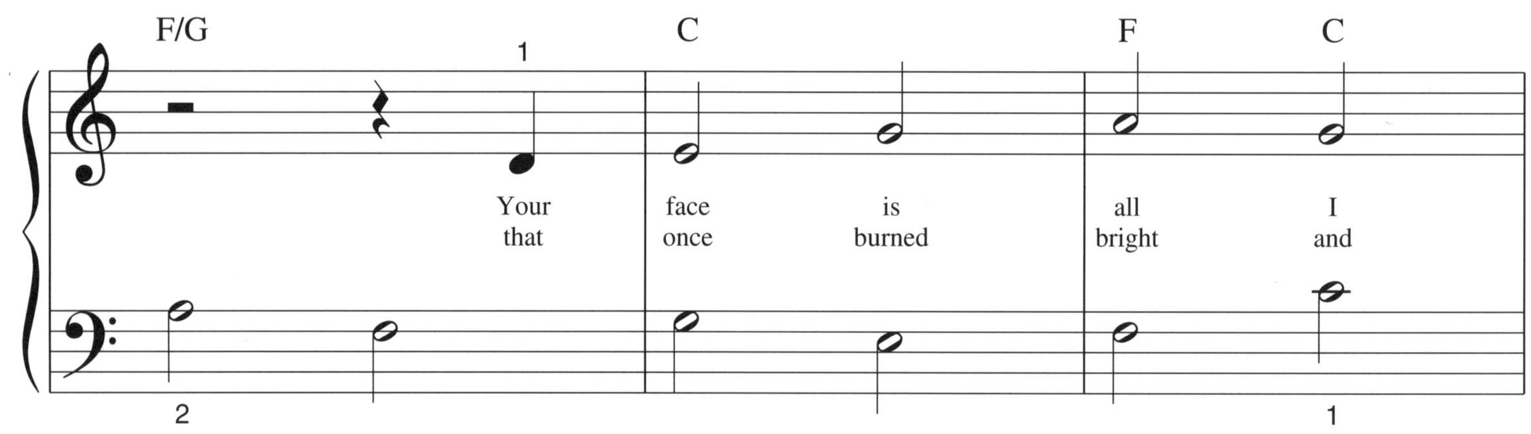

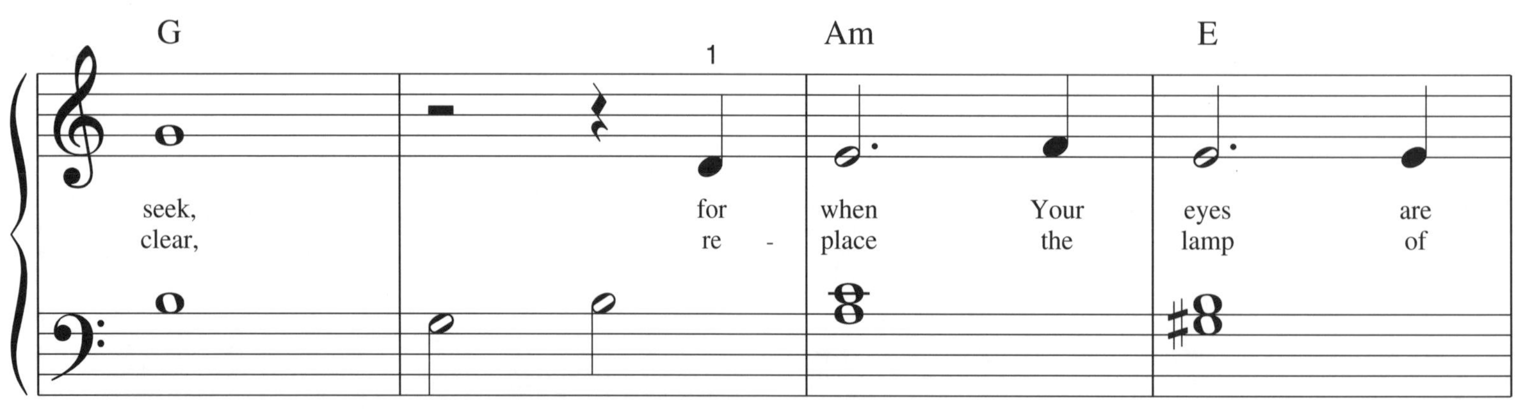

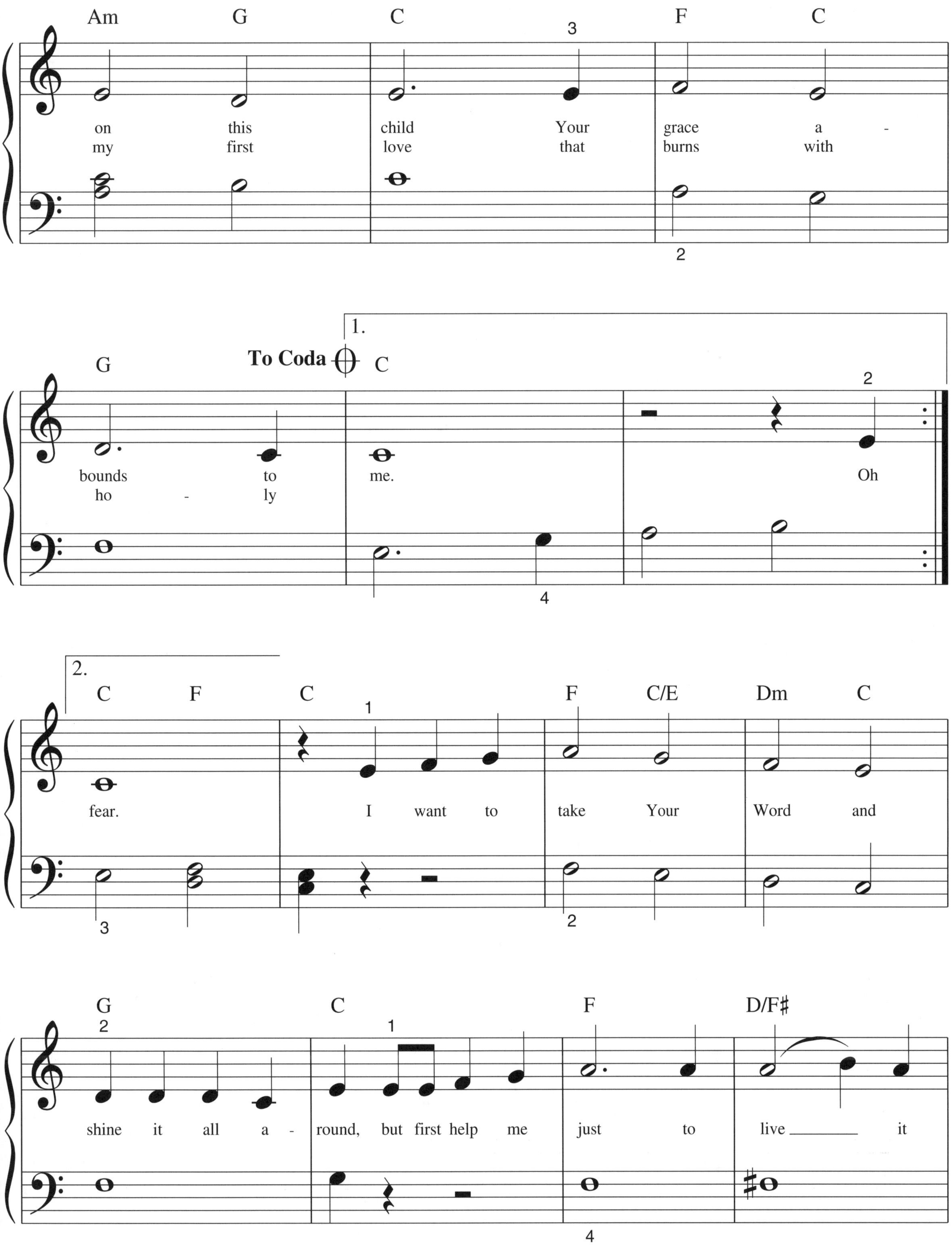

Am G C F C

3

on this child Your grace a -
my first love that burns with

2

1.

G To Coda C

2

bounds to me. Oh
ho - ly

4

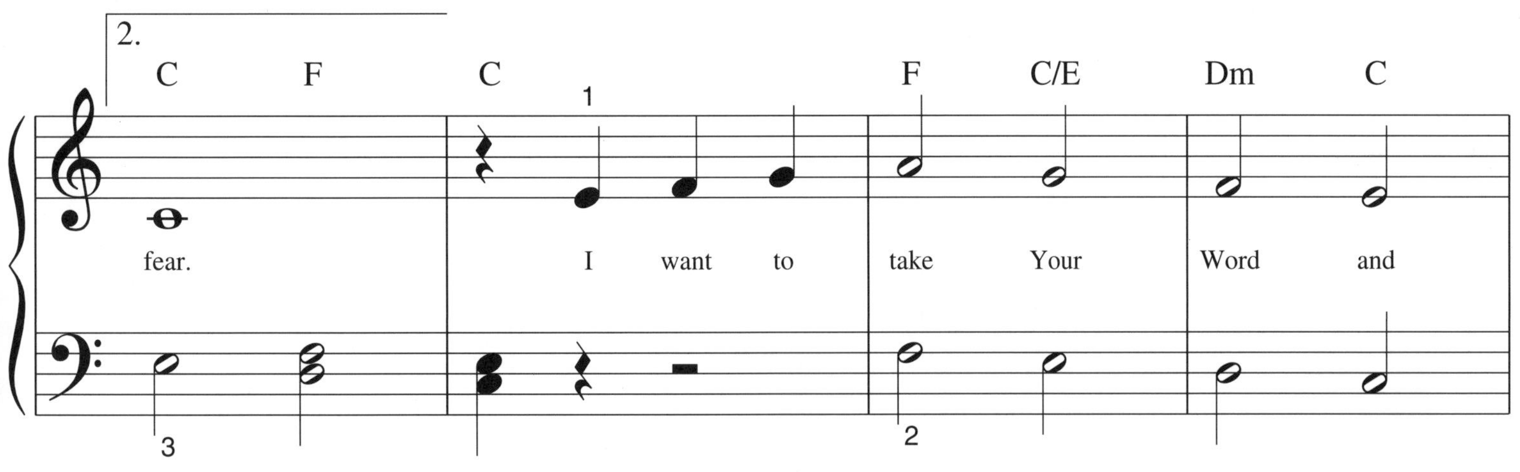

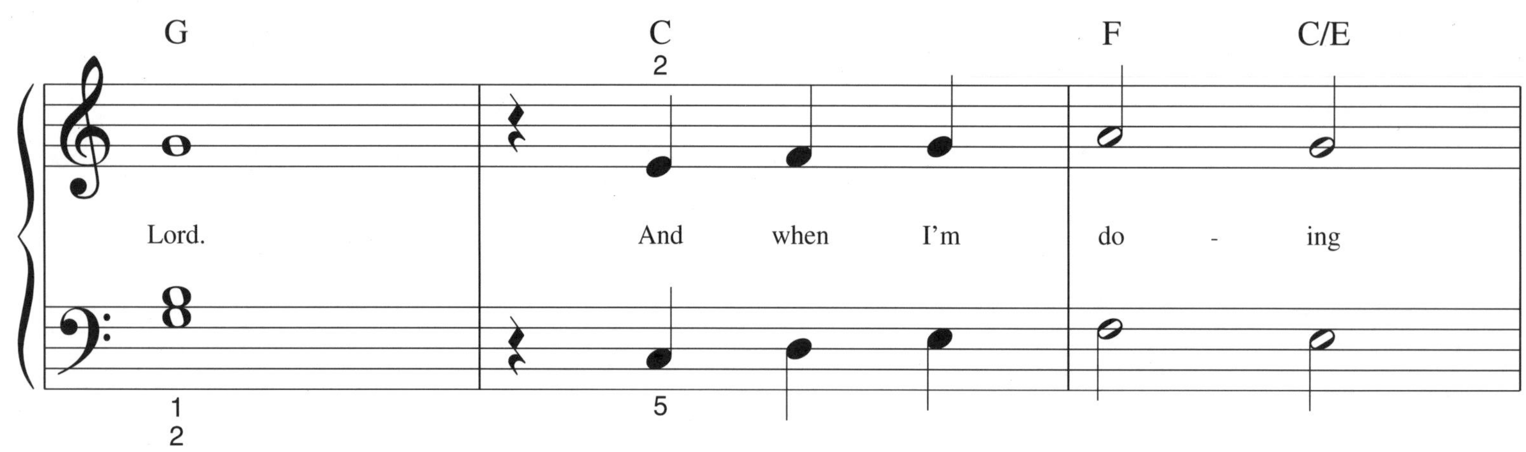
G
C
F
C/E
Lord.
And when I'm
do - ing

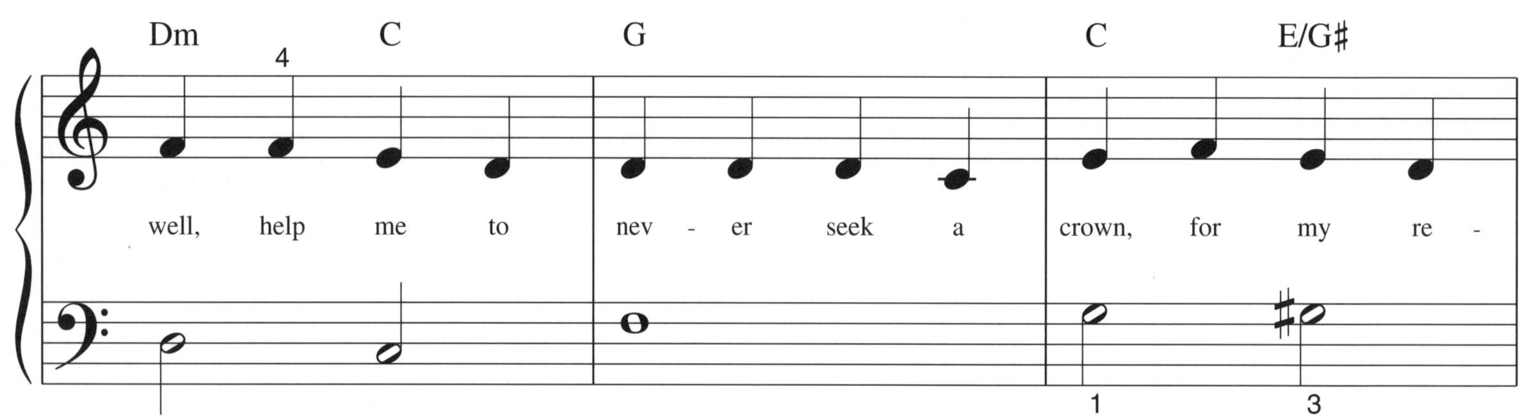
Dm
C
G
C
E/G♯
well, help me to
nev - er seek a
crown, for my re -

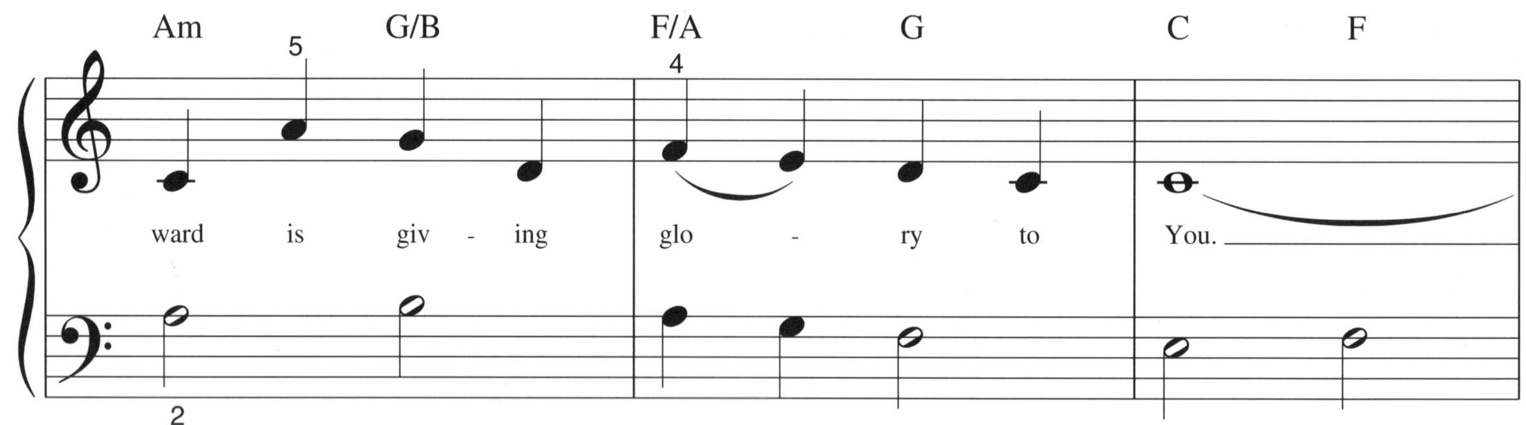
Am
G/B
F/A
G
C
F
ward is giv - ing
glo - ry to
You.

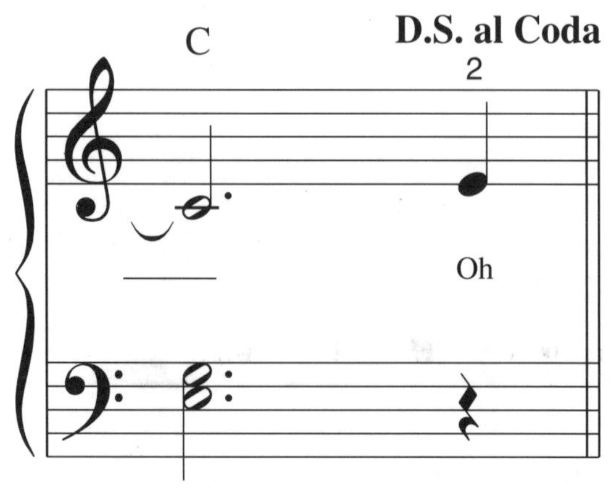
C
D.S. al Coda
Oh

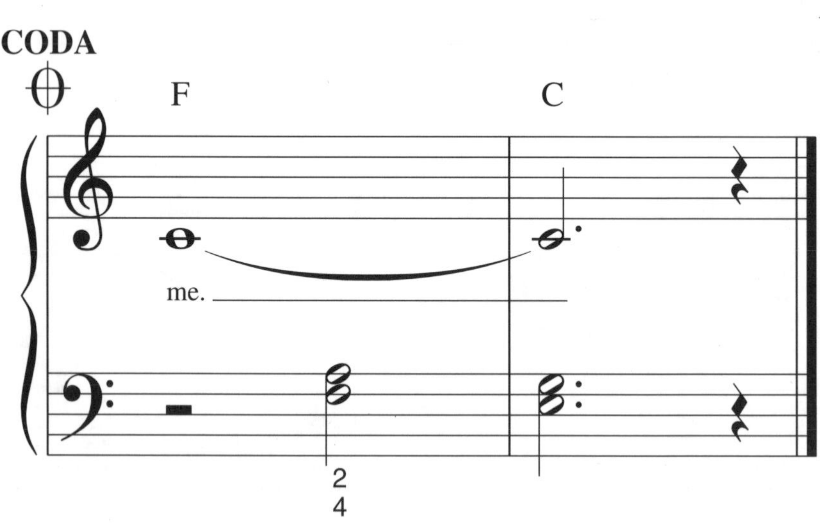
CODA
F
C
me.